# Indigenous-Settler Relations in Australia and the World

Volume 6

**Series Editors**

Sarah Maddison, School of Social and Political Sciences, University of Melbourne, Melbourne, Australia

Sana Nakata, University of Melbourne, Melbourne, Australia

Julia Hurst, University of Melbourne, Parkville, Australia

**Editorial Board**

Miriam Jorgensen, Native Nations Institute, University of Arizona, Tucson, USA

Sheryl Lightfoot, Department of Political Science, University of British Columbia, Vancouver, Canada

Morgan Brigg, University of Queensland, St. Lucia, Australia

Yin Paradies, Deakin University, Burwood, Australia

Jeff Denis, McMaster University, Hamilton, Canada

Bronwyn Fredericks, University of Queensland, St. Lucia, Australia

Libby Porter, RMIT University, Melbourne, Australia

The series, Indigenous-Settler Relations in Australia and the World, brings together scholars interested in examining contemporary Indigenous affairs through questions of relationality. This is a unique approach that represents a deliberate move away from both settler-colonial studies, which examines historical and present impacts of settler states upon Indigenous peoples, and from postcolonial and decolonial scholarship, which is predominantly interested in how Indigenous peoples speak back to the settler state. Closely connected to, but with meaningful contrast to these approaches, the Indigenous-Settler Relations series focuses sharply upon questions about what informs, shapes and gives social, legal and political life to relations between Indigenous peoples and non-Indigenous peoples, both in Australia and globally.

This is an important and timely endeavour. In Australia, relations between Aboriginal and Torres Strait Islander peoples and the state are at an impasse. In the wake of the government's rejection of the Uluru Statement in 2017 there is no shared view on how Indigenous-settler relationships might be 'reset', or even if this is possible. The contemporary Indigenous affairs policy domain is characterised by confusion, frustration and disappointment that, despite a seemingly endless succession of policy regimes, efforts to 'close the gap' between Aboriginal and Torres Strait Islander peoples and other Australians have not resulted in progress.

It is into this contested space that the Indigenous-Settler Relations series seeks to intervene with new, agenda-setting research. The series editors are based in a research unit in the Faculty of Arts at the University of Melbourne—the Indigenous Settler Relations Collaboration. The series will build on the work of the Collaboration in bringing together scholars and practitioners from around Australia, and around the world—particularly other Anglophone settler colonial societies such as Canada, the United States and New Zealand—whose work is concerned with Indigenous-settler relations across a range of disciplines. The multi-faceted approach to Indigenous-Settler Relations that defines the series seeks to capture how the question of relationality is already being asked by scholars across disciplines including political science, history, sociology, law, media, and cultural studies.

Readers of this series will look to it for fresh perspectives and new ideas about how to transform Indigenous-settler relations in Australia and elsewhere. They will learn from the leading lights in an emerging field who will connect their rich, multi-disciplinary scholarship to urgent social and political questions at the heart of Indigenous-Settler relations.

Genevieve Grieves · Amy Spiers
Editors

# Art and Memorialisation

Truth-Telling Through Creative Practice in Settler Colonial Australia

*Editors*
Genevieve Grieves
GARUWA
Garramilla/Darwin, Australia

Amy Spiers
RMIT University
Naarm/Melbourne, Australia

ISSN 2524-5767          ISSN 2524-5775 (electronic)
Indigenous-Settler Relations in Australia and the World
ISBN 978-981-97-6288-0          ISBN 978-981-97-6289-7 (eBook)
https://doi.org/10.1007/978-981-97-6289-7

© The Editor(s) (if applicable) and The Author(s), under exclusive license to Springer Nature
Singapore Pte Ltd. 2024

This work is subject to copyright. All rights are solely and exclusively licensed by the Publisher, whether
the whole or part of the material is concerned, specifically the rights of translation, reprinting, reuse
of illustrations, recitation, broadcasting, reproduction on microfilms or in any other physical way, and
transmission or information storage and retrieval, electronic adaptation, computer software, or by similar
or dissimilar methodology now known or hereafter developed.
The use of general descriptive names, registered names, trademarks, service marks, etc. in this publication
does not imply, even in the absence of a specific statement, that such names are exempt from the relevant
protective laws and regulations and therefore free for general use.
The publisher, the authors and the editors are safe to assume that the advice and information in this book
are believed to be true and accurate at the date of publication. Neither the publisher nor the authors or
the editors give a warranty, expressed or implied, with respect to the material contained herein or for any
errors or omissions that may have been made. The publisher remains neutral with regard to jurisdictional
claims in published maps and institutional affiliations.

This Springer imprint is published by the registered company Springer Nature Singapore Pte Ltd.
The registered company address is: 152 Beach Road, #21-01/04 Gateway East, Singapore 189721,
Singapore

If disposing of this product, please recycle the paper.

# Acknowledgements

We respectfully acknowledge all First Peoples across this continent known as 'Australia', and their strength, resilience and enduring connection to Country and culture. We pay deep respect to all Ancestors and Elders, past and present. Sovereignty was never ceded.

This book was developed on the unceded lands of the Wurundjeri Woi Wurrung and Boon Wurrung/Bunurong peoples in Naarm (Melbourne) and the Larrakia peoples in Garramilla (Darwin).

The conception, development and realisation of this book spans more than five years. It began in 2018 with an invitation from Sana Nakata and Sarah Maddison of University of Melbourne's former Indigenous Settler Relations Collaboration (ISRC), now Australian Centre, to co-edit a volume of essays on art and memorialisation for the book series *Indigenous-Settler Relations in Australia and the World*. The book, however, has beginnings that extend even further to Genevieve's earlier research into First Peoples artists who resist colonial denial and memorialise the violence of invasion and perseverance of the survivors, including the exhibition she curated, *The Violence of Denial*, at Arts House, Naarm (Melbourne) for Yirramboi festival in 2017. That important exhibition and accompanying talks program showcased many of the artists who are also featured in this book—Dianne Jones, Vicki Couzens, Julie Gough and r e a—and the book is indebted to Genevieve's prior groundwork, relationships with artists and significant research into First Peoples' creative challenges to settler colonial Australia's memorial culture that both powerfully intervenes on distorted histories and regenerates First Peoples' culture and community. Additionally, Amy's creative research into public commemorative art and counter-monuments to difficult histories, as well as non-Indigenous artists' ancillary contributions to truth-telling about Australia's colonial past, has also informed this collection.

The editors thank Sana Nakata and Sarah Maddison for their invitation and encouragement to undertake this project and for their assistance in generating this collection of essays, as well as The Australian Centre which provided support to both of us as we developed this collection. We also thank the publishers and editors at Springer for their patience and commitment to this project.

We also thank all the creatives and researchers who contributed to the 3-day online symposium the editors convened, and that preceded and informed this book: *Counter-Monuments: Indigenous Settler Relations in Australian Contemporary Art and Memorial Practices* that was hosted by Australian Centre for Contemporary Art (ACCA), from 17 to 19 March 2021. We extend deep thanks to the presenters who generously shared their ideas and practices: Paola Balla, Lilly Brown, Fiona Foley, Kate Golding, Julie Gough, Dianne Jones, Djon Mundine OAM, Odette Kelada, Clare Land, Carol Que, Joel Sherwood Spring and Unbound Collective (Ali Gumillya Baker, Simone Ulalka Tur, Faye Rosas Blanch and Natalie Harkin). Thanks also to our presenting partners ACCA, ISRC and Contemporary Art and Social Transformation (CAST) research group at RMIT University. We are also grateful for the assistance from the Australian Government through the Australia Council, its arts funding and advisory body.

We are thankful as well to all the creatives who allowed us to reproduce their artworks and creative writing in this collection: Vicki Couzens, Julie Gough, r e a, Dianne Jones, Fiona Foley, Jason Wing, Kristen Lyttle, Kate Golding, Robbie Thorpe and Charmaine Papertalk Green. We are very grateful also to Tristen Harwood who provided editorial assistance on some early draft chapters for this book.

We extend our deepest thanks to the writers who persisted and contributed to this collection, despite navigating a range of professional, personal and societal pressures that were only further complicated and compounded by the global COVID-19 pandemic and accompanying lockdowns and restrictions of 2020 and 2021. We are deeply grateful that the writers in this collection overcame countless demands on their time to entrust and share with us their considerable knowledge and expertise in truth-telling Australia's past through creative practice. We are proud to share their important writing and thinking with the world.

# About This Book

## Cultural Sensitivity Warning

First Peoples readers are advised this book may contain images, names and descriptions of deceased persons, as well as their artwork.

Readers are warned that some of the content in this book may be upsetting as it contains descriptions of historical colonial violence and ongoing trauma. The book also includes culturally sensitive words, terms or descriptions that may be considered inappropriate and cause offence as well as distress. Such material does not present the views of the editors or authors. While such content may not reflect current respectful and culturally safe understanding, it is provided to give a social or historical context.

All care has been taken to ensure this book is accurate and current at the time of writing. We apologise for any inadvertent errors, oversights or omissions.

The editors also wish to acknowledge that this is by no means a definitive book on the subject of artists who counter the culture of denial embedded in settler colonial Australia's memorial landscape, or a comprehensive survey of all the artists tirelessly engaged in this bold memory-work. It is the editors' hope that countless more books are produced to address this rich and under-written subject, of which this book is just one contribution.

## Notes on Language and Terminology

The authors use their preferred terms throughout their chapters, however, below is context to some of the key words and phrases used across the book.

The term 'First Peoples' and 'First Nations' are used as general terms to discuss Aboriginal and Torres Strait Islander people over the alternatives as they are often preferred by the communities in which we live. While the word 'Aboriginal' is still used by many people, it is also considered by others as a generic term that does not reflect First Peoples' sovereignty or diversity. 'Indigenous', a term also used at times in this book, is equally generic but does connect mainland peoples to Torres Strait Islanders, and the struggles and experience with Indigenous people overseas. 'Koorie' or 'Koori' is a term also used and employed by many First Peoples in Victoria and New South Wales to describe themselves and their culture. Additionally, 'Blak', a term first coined by Kuku and Erub/Mer artist Destiny Deacon, is employed in the book to refer to the distinct experience of First Nations people in settler colonial Australia, and to differentiate it from the racialised experiences of other communities of colour. 'Mob' is a colloquial term largely used by First Peoples to refer to a group or collective of people, frequently in relation to First Peoples and Country (for example, 'Gunditjmara mob').

The 'Southeast' is a cultural space in which First Peoples share ancient cultural connections and frameworks encompassing law, language, kinship and more recently, historical and contemporary experiences of colonisation, having been invaded early in the Australian nation's history. This region encompasses areas that are known today as Victoria, New South Wales, parts of South Australia and in some contexts Tasmania.

Many words related to First Peoples are capitalised out of respect for their cultural significance. 'Country', for example, is capitalised to denote the importance this element has to First Peoples. It is a concept beyond land and one that encompasses spirit, people, belonging and identity.

While 'Frontier Wars' and 'frontier conflict' are commonly used phrases to refer to violent contact, conflicts and massacres, and First Peoples' acts of resistance, that have occurred since the arrival of British invaders in 1788, some First Peoples have a preference for terms that foreground their perspective of the conflict, such as 'Homeland Wars' or 'homeland conflict'. As Taunwurrung Elder, storyteller and cultural leader, Uncle Larry Walsh, has explained: we need to call it 'homeland violence' as the idea of a 'frontier' isn't ours.

Where possible the editors and authors give precedence to First Peoples' names for places discussed followed by the colonial place name in brackets. For example, the Boon Wurrung/Bunurong and Wurundjeri Woi Wurrung term, 'Naarm' or 'Narrm', is increasingly used to refer to the city known as 'Melbourne', and as such, in the book appears as 'Naarm (Melbourne)'. We acknowledge the city region is also referred to as Birrarung-ga.

The editors and authors also try to refer to First Peoples individuals or groups via their preferred Country name (or language group, Nation or other collective name). For example, the Wurundjeri people can also be identified as part of the Woi Wurrung language group, as well as the Kulin Nation, an alliance of five First Peoples groups of south central Victoria: the Taungurung, Wurundjeri, Wadawurrung, Boon Wurrung/ Bunurong and Dja Dja Wurrung peoples.

This book refers to 'truth-telling' about the past, a process or activity that First Peoples have repeatedly called for in settler colonial Australia to address colonial atrocities, such as genocides and massacres, frequently silenced or denied in settler social memory and nation-building histories. 'Truth-telling' seeks a collective confrontation with colonisers' violence and disregard of First Peoples' Country, law and sovereignty through national and state-based truth and justice commissions and localised, community-based processes. First Peoples assert truth-telling is a crucial step towards healing that will transform race relations between First Nations and settler communities, develop a shared understanding of the past and inform initiatives of justice and redress such as Treaties (Commonwealth of Australia, 2017; Appleby & Davis, 2018; Yoorrook Justice Commission, 2022).

This book also refers to 'settler colonial Australia', to acknowledge that the nation known as 'Australia' is deeply settler colonial, and to this day, a colonising society. As Patrick Wolfe has observed, in places like Australia settlers never left, they came to stay, and as such colonisation is ongoing: 'a structure, not an event' (2006, p. 388). We also use the term 'settler' to acknowledge, and implicate, non-Indigenous people living in Australia within this ongoing structure and the history of its violence. Eve Tuck and K. Wayne Yang have observed how this *structure* operates:

> In order for the settlers to make a place their home, they must destroy and disappear the Indigenous peoples that live there … For the settlers, Indigenous peoples are in the way and, in the destruction of Indigenous peoples, Indigenous communities, and over time and through law and policy, Indigenous peoples' claims to land under settler regimes, land is recast as property and as a resource. Indigenous peoples must be erased, must be made into ghosts. (2012, p. 6)

Settler colonialism in Australia continues to be active in disappearing and destroying First Peoples. To resist this erasure, our book contends, First Peoples employ creative and cultural practices to defiantly reinscribe public memory with First Nations' sovereign presence, to disclose the true history and intent of the settler colonial Australian nation, and to celebrate the endurance of the world's oldest continuing culture.

## References

Appleby, G. & Davis, M. (2018). The Uluru Statement and the Promises of Truth. *Australian Historical Studies* 49(4), 501–509.

Commonwealth of Australia. (2017). Final Report of the Referendum Council 30 June 2017. Referendum Council. https://www.referendumcouncil.org.au/sites/default/files/report_attachments/Referendum_Council_Final_Report.pdf. Accessed 30 April 2024.

Tuck, E. & Yang, K. W. (2012). Decolonization is not a metaphor. *Decolonization:Indigeneity, Education & Society*, 1(1), 1–40.

Wolfe, P. (2006). Settler colonialism and the elimination of the native. *Journal of Genocide Research*, 8(4), 387–409.

Yoorrook Justice Commission. (2022). Yoorrook with Purpose: Interim Report June 2022. https://yoorrookjusticecommission.org.au/wp-content/uploads/2022/06/Yoorrook-Justice-Commission-Interim-Report.pdf. Accessed 30 April 2024.

# Contents

**1 Introduction: Artists confronting the violence of denial in Australia** .................................................... 1
Genevieve Grieves and Amy Spiers

**Part I  The Violence of Denial**

**2 The Violence of Denial: Genevieve Grieves in conversation with Vicki Couzens and Julie Gough** .......................... 23
Genevieve Grieves, Vicki Couzens, and Julie Gough

**3 The Violence of Denial: Genevieve Grieves in Conversation with Dianne Jones and r e a** .................................. 43
Genevieve Grieves, Dianne Jones, and r e a

**4 The Violence of Denial: Genevieve Grieves in Conversation with Tony Birch** .............................................. 61
Genevieve Grieves and Tony Birch

**Part II  Truth-Telling with Creative Practice in Settler Colonial Australia**

**5 The Wind Has Not Yet Answered!** ............................ 79
Charmaine Papertalk Green

**6 Remembering Those Who Have Gone Before** ................... 83
Fiona Foley

**7 Mass Exposure: Memory Laundering, Racial Literacy and the Art of Truth-Telling** .................................. 101
Odette Kelada and Dianne Jones

**8 This Full Agency, This Decolonised Spirit: Talking Blak to Cooks' Cottage** ............................................ 123
Paola Balla, Kate Golding, and Clare Land

xi

**9 What Should the City of Melbourne Do with the Inaccurate and Offensive John Batman Memorial Obelisk?** .................. 149
Amy Spiers

**10 Exposure Therapy: Spectacles, Monuments and the Question of Care** ...................................................... 173
Arlie Alizzi and Neika Lehman

# Editors and Contributors

## About the Editors

**Genevieve Grieves** is a Worimi woman from Southeast Australia currently based in Garramilla (Darwin). She is an award-winning artist, curator and content creator committed to sharing First Peoples' histories and cultures and interrogating colonising frameworks and practices. Her recent projects include *The Violence of Denial* exhibition (2017) as part of the Yirramboi Festival; *Barangaroo Ngangamay* (2016), a place-based Augmented Reality app that shares and celebrates the living cultures of Sydney Aboriginal women, and she was the lead curator of the internationally celebrated permanent exhibition, *First Peoples* (2013), at the Melbourne Museum. She is a passionate advocate of decolonising and community-engaged practice and teaches these methodologies in university, institutional and community contexts. Her current role is co-founder and creative director of GARUWA, a First Nations storytelling agency.

**Amy Spiers** is an artist and researcher of settler descent, and currently a Vice Chancellor's Postdoctoral Fellow at RMIT School of Art, Naarm (Melbourne). She has presented art projects across Australia and internationally, including at Australian Centre for Contemporary Art (ACCA), Monash University Museum of Art (Melbourne) and the 2015 Vienna Biennale. She has also published widely, including co-editing *Let's Go Outside: Art in Public* with Charlotte Day and Callum Morton for Monash University Museum of Art (Monash University Publishing, 2022) and co-authoring the book, *Art/Work: Social Enterprise, Young Creatives and the Forces of Marginalisation*, with Grace McQuilten, Kim Humphery and Peter Kelly (Palgrave Pivot, 2022). Most recently, she was awarded a 2024 Australian Research Council Discovery Early Career Researcher Award (DECRA) to examine non-Indigenous artists' engagements with truth-telling Australia's colonial past through creative practice.

# Contributors

**Arlie Alizzi**  University of Melbourne, Naarm/Melbourne, Australia

**Paola Balla**  Moondani Balluk Indigenous Academic Unit, Victoria University, Naarm/Melbourne, Australia

**Tony Birch**  University of Melbourne, Naarm/Melbourne, Australia

**Vicki Couzens**  RMIT University, Naarm/Melbourne, Australia

**Fiona Foley**  University of Queensland, Meeanjin/Brisbane, Australia

**Kate Golding**  Naarm/Melbourne, Australia

**Julie Gough**  Nipaluna/Hobart, Australia

**Charmaine Papertalk Green**  Yamaji Country/Geraldton, Australia

**Genevieve Grieves**  GARUWA, Garramilla/Darwin, Australia

**Dianne Jones**  Naarm/Melbourne, Australia

**Odette Kelada**  University of Melbourne, Naarm/Melbourne, Australia

**Clare Land**  Moondani Balluk Indigenous Academic Unit, Victoria University, Naarm/Melbourne, Australia

**Neika Lehman**  RMIT University, Naarm/Melbourne, Australia

**r e a**  Gundungurra Country/Hazelbrook, Australia

**Amy Spiers**  RMIT University, Naarm/Melbourne, Australia

# List of Figures

Fig. 2.1    *The Violence of Denial* (2017) exhibition curated by Genevieve Grieves installation view at Arts House, exhibiting left to right: Julie Gough, *The Grounds for Surrender* (2011); r e a, *Poles Apart* (2009); Vicki Couzens, *pang-ngooteeweeng-wanoong (we remember)* (2017). Photograph Bryony Jackson. Image courtesy of Genevieve Grieves and Arts House .............................. 24

Fig. 2.2    *The Violence of Denial* (2017) exhibition installation view at Arts House exhibiting left and right: Julie Gough, *The Grounds for Surrender* (2011) and r e a, *Poles Apart* (2009). Photograph Bryony Jackson. Image courtesy of Genevieve Grieves and Arts House .............................. 26

Fig. 2.3    Julie Gough, *Hunting Ground incorporating Barbeque Area* (2014) video stills. Image courtesy of the artist .............. 28

Fig. 2.4    Vicki Couzens, *pang-ngooteeweeng-wanoong (we remember)* (2017). *The Violence of Denial* (2017) exhibition installation view at Arts House. Photograph Bryony Jackson. Image courtesy of Genevieve Grieves and Arts House .............................. 30

Fig. 2.5    Vicki Couzens, *prangawan pootpakyooyano yoowa* (2009). Possum skin cloak, 150 × 110cm. Image courtesy of the artist ... 32

Fig. 2.6    Vicki Couzens, *pang-ngooteeweeng-wanoong (we remember)* (2017). *The Violence of Denial* (2017) exhibition installation detail depicting the mourning bags. Photograph Bryony Jackson. Image courtesy of Genevieve Grieves and Arts House .............................. 34

Fig. 2.7    Julie Gough, *The Lost World (part 2)* (2013) video still. Image courtesy of the artist .............................. 35

Fig. 2.8    Vicki Couzens, *Tarnbeere Gundidj* (2010). Digital image on paper, 90 × 60cm. Image courtesy of the artist ............. 37

xvi                                                                List of Figures

Fig. 3.1    *The Violence of Denial* (2017) exhibition curated
            by Genevieve Grieves installation view at Arts House,
            exhibiting left to right: Julie Gough, *The Grounds
            for Surrender* (2011); r e a, *PolesApart* (2009); Vicki
            Couzens, *pang-ngooteeweeng-wanoong (we remember)*
            (2017). Photograph Bryony Jackson. Image courtesy
            of Genevieve Grieves and Arts House ......................     45
Fig. 3.2    r e a, *PolesApart* (2009), video still. Image courtesy
            of the artist .............................................     46
Fig. 3.3    Dianne Jones, *found objects from what lies buried rises*
            (2017). Installation detail from *The Violence of Denial*
            (2017) exhibition. Photograph Bryony Jackson. Image
            courtesy of Genevieve Grieves and Arts House ..............     48
Fig. 3.4    r e a, *PolesApart* (2009). Installation detail from *The
            Violence of Denial* (2017) exhibition. Photograph Bryony
            Jackson. Image courtesy of Genevieve Grieves and Arts
            House ....................................................     50
Fig. 3.5    r e a, *Look Who's Calling the Kettle Black* (1992), no.5
            from the series, edition of 15. The image includes a black
            and white photograph of r e a's maternal grandmother
            c.1920s. Image courtesy of the artist ......................     52
Fig. 3.6    *The Violence of Denial* (2017) exhibition installation view
            at Arts House, exhibiting left and right: Vicki Couzens,
            *pang-ngooteeweeng-wanoong (we remember)* (2017)
            and Dianne Jones, *found objects from what lies buried rises*
            (2017). Image courtesy of Genevieve Grieves ...............     53
Fig. 6.1    Fiona Foley, *Annihilation of the Blacks* (1986). Wood,
            synthetic polymer paint, feathers, string, 204.5 × 267 ×
            85.7 cm, 13 parts. National Museum of Australia collection.
            Image courtesy of the artist and Andrew Baker Art Dealer ......     86
Fig. 6.2    Fiona Foley, *Stud Gins* (2003). Installation view
            of *Fiona Foley: Forbidden* (2009) exhibition at Museum
            of Contemporary Art, Sydney. Seven ex-Government
            woollen blankets with screen-printed lettering, each
            190 x 148 cm (irregular). Dimensions variable. Image
            courtesy of the artist and Andrew Baker Art Dealer ...........     88
Fig. 6.3    Fiona Foley, *Witnessing to Silence* (2004). Installation view,
            Brisbane Magistrates Court, Brisbane, Australia.
            Cast bronze lotus stems, etched granite pavers
            180 × 140 cm diameter, stainless steel water feature,
            laminated glass five pillars 210–350 × 25 × 25 cm.
            Commissioned by the Queensland Government. Built
            by Urban Art Projects (UAP). Image courtesy of the artist,
            UAP and Andrew Baker Art Dealer ........................     90

# List of Figures

xvii

Fig. 6.4  Fiona Foley, *Witnessing to Silence* (2004) installation view. Image courtesy of the artist, UAP and Andrew Baker Art Dealer ............................................... 91

Fig. 6.5  Fiona Foley, *Dispersed* (2008). Installation view of *Fiona Foley: Forbidden* (2009) exhibition at Museum of Contemporary Art, Sydney. Charred laminated wood, polished aluminium, blank .303 inch calibre bullets, overall 51 × 500 cm. Image courtesy of the artist and Andrew Baker Art Dealer ........................................ 95

Fig. 7.1  Dianne Jones, *L.H.O.O.Q 'ERE!* (2001). Inkjet print on canvas 111.2 × 88.8 cm. State Art Collection, Art Gallery of Western Australia. Image courtesy of the artist ....... 103

Fig. 7.2  Dianne Jones, *The Great Heads* (2017) from *The Grand Tour* series. Inkjet print on paper 53.0 × 80.0 cm. State Art Collection, Art Gallery of Western Australia. Image courtesy of the artist .................................... 109

Fig. 7.3  Dianne Jones, *Shearing the Rams* (2001). Inkjet print on treated canvas 121.9 × 182.6 cm. State Art Collection, Art Gallery of Western Australia. Image courtesy of the artist ... 110

Fig. 7.4  Dianne Jones, *Sunbaker* (2003). Digital print 38.6 × 43.4 cm. Image courtesy of the artist ................ 111

Fig. 7.5  Dianne Jones, *The Great Clock* (2017) from *The Grand Tour* series. Ink jet print on paper 53.0 × 80.0 cm. State Art Collection, The Art Gallery of Western Australia. Image courtesy of the artist .................................... 112

Fig. 7.6  Dianne Jones, *The Great Echo Chamber* (2017) from the Grand Tour series. Ink jet print on paper 120 × 180 cm. State Art Collection, Art Gallery of Western Australia. Image courtesy of the artist ....... 115

Fig. 7.7  Dianne Jones, *Lest We Forget* (2007). Unrealised design for a public billboard. Image courtesy of the artist ............ 116

Fig. 8.1  Jason Wing, *Captain James Crook* (2013). Bronze sculpture 70 × 50 × 30 cm. Collection of the Art Gallery of New South Wales. Image courtesy of the artist .................. 125

Fig. 8.2  Tupaia, *Māori trading a crayfish with Joseph Banks* (1769). Drawing by Tupaia, from 'Drawings illustrative of Captain Cook's First Voyage, 1768–1771'. Watercolour, on paper, 26.8 × 20.5 cm. British Library, London, UK. © British Library Board. Add. MS 15,508, fol. 12 ............. 130

Fig. 8.3  Kirsten Lyttle, *Death in Hawaii* (2009–2011). Hand-painted and home-sewn Hawaiian shirt. Cotton, cotton thread, paint, ink and transfers. Image courtesy of the artist ................ 134

| | | |
|---|---|---|
| Fig. 8.4 | Clare Land, Paola Balla, and Kate Golding, *Negotiating Captain Cook's Voyages* (2021). Time spiral from *Blak Cook Book*, reproduced with the blessing of Stephen Banham & Letterbox typographic design studio. Image courtesy of the authors ............................ | 138 |
| Fig. 8.5 | Kate Golding, Camera obscura illustration (2023). Image courtesy of the artist ................................ | 141 |
| Fig. 8.6 | Kate Golding, *Camera obscura (VCA), Boon Wurrung and Wurundjeri* (2016) installation detail. Site-specific installation, dimensions variable. Image courtesy of the artist .... | 142 |
| Fig. 8.7 | Kate Golding, *Camera obscura (Ballarat Observatory) Wadawurrung* (2017) installation detail. Site-specific installation, dimensions variable. Image courtesy of the artist .... | 142 |
| Fig. 9.1 | Fiona Foley, *Lie of the Land* (1997). Sandstone, 7 pillars, 300 × 100 cm. Accompanying sound component by artist Chris Knowles. The work is shown here in its temporary location in front of the Melbourne Town Hall, Swanston Street in 1997. City of Melbourne public art collection. Image courtesy of the artist, City of Melbourne and Andrew Baker Art Dealer ................................ | 154 |
| Fig. 9.2 | Fiona Foley, *Lie of the Land* (1997). Sandstone, 7 pillars, 300 × 100 cm. Accompanying sound component by artist Chris Knowles. The work is shown here in its present location in the foyer of the Melbourne Museum. City of Melbourne public art collection. Photograph by Collin Bogaars. Image courtesy of the artist, City of Melbourne and Andrew Baker Art Dealer ........................... | 156 |

# Chapter 1
# Introduction: Artists confronting the violence of denial in Australia

**Genevieve Grieves and Amy Spiers**

**Abstract** In this critical introduction, co-editors Genevieve Grieves and Amy Spiers describe a settler Australian memorial landscape that continues to celebrate colonisers while remaining silent about their theft and mass murder, as First Peoples repeatedly call for truth-telling about Australia's troubling foundations in violence. Positioning and grounding their separate research practices, Grieves and Spiers continue by identifying that the realm of art and culture has become a space to remember and mourn the profound loss of life caused by invasion and colonisation in the absence of official commemorations. It is through the spaces of art that First Nations artists powerfully resist historical amnesia and tell the truth about Australia's past, providing spaces of healing through the long overdue recognition of painful events. The chapter also describes Grieves' research that informs this edited collection, and the exhibition she curated, *The Violence of Denial* (2017), that considered the deeply restorative, place-based creative practices of First Nations artists Vicki Couzens, Julie Gough, r e a and Dianne Jones that not only disclose colonial injustices, but also heal sites of violence and revive First Peoples cultural futures.

## 1.1 A Memorial Landscape of Colonial Denial and Doubled Violence

… how is it possible that we don't consider genocide a part of colonial history? How is that possible? Why and how is that we have to argue for this when it is such a searing reality?

---

G. Grieves (✉)
GARUWA, Garramilla/Darwin, Australia
e-mail: genevieve@garuwa.com

A. Spiers
RMIT University, Naarm/Melbourne, Australia
e-mail: amy.spiers@rmit.edu.au

© The Author(s), under exclusive license to Springer Nature Singapore Pte Ltd. 2024
G. Grieves and A. Spiers (eds.), *Art and Memorialisation*, Indigenous-Settler Relations in Australia and the World 6, https://doi.org/10.1007/978-981-97-6289-7_1

> This is indicative of the sort of country we imagine for ourselves. It is a white fiction, it is a fabrication. And until we deal with that fabrication, until we have a much more open discussion about what sort of country we've been and where we're going, we will never get anywhere with the issues of so-called reconciliation and recovery. (Birch, 2023, p. 51)

> A moral engagement between past and present must acknowledge violence, and having done so, must acknowledge the moral burden of that knowledge [...] Our Australian context presses us to consider not only the justification of others' pain, but the denial of it as well. It follows that part of our moral burden is an injunction to hold the memory of violence within our texts. (Rose, 2004, pp. 13–14)

At this point in time, there is no complete cartography of the violence that occurred with the colonial invasion of Australia.[1] There is not even a final agreement as to the extent or veracity of this violence: the language used to describe it, the numbers of the dead and the existence of violent acts in moments of time is highly contested, with archival material and oral histories continuously interpreted and re-interpreted in the discipline of history. As the late historian Tracey Banivanua Mar noted, 'History' (which she delineated with a capital 'H') is 'a discipline of ordering and narrating the past' that is distinct from the 'encompassed past' (2012, p. 176). Integral in the struggles over land and possession in settler colonies, 'History', Banivanua Mar observed, is a principal site for the denial of colonial violence and erasure of Indigenous peoples (2012).

Settler colonialism is an ongoing structure that is active in disappearing and destroying First Peoples (Wolfe, 2006), permitting only certain forms of 'History' and remembrance in the memorialscapes of Australia. Today, statues representing perpetrators of mass murder, invasion and theft continue to loom prominently in Australia's public spaces unabashedly celebrating, and naturalising, white invasion and possession of First Peoples' Country (Carlson & Farrelly, 2023; Mar, 2012). Any mention of a reappraisal of history and review of such monuments provokes reactionary, hysterical commentary about 'Stalinist' cancellations of white cultural heritage (Murphy, 2017). Meanwhile, commemorative public spaces remain largely silent about the enormity of losses and devastation First Peoples and their lands, waters and skies have experienced since colonisers arrived; settler authorities are slow to establish prominent commemorations atoning for the violence of colonial invasion; as First Peoples' Country, heritage and significant sites are stolen, vandalised, slated for demolition and thoughtlessly destroyed.

There is no denying that colonial violence constituted our shared past (and is ongoing in a variety of forms), but violence is amplified in the present in the form of *doubled violence*. Deborah Bird Rose defines 'doubled violence' as a continuous act of wounding, which occurs as 'the amplification of pain through repetition and

---

[1] We acknowledge the significant efforts of Waanyi artist Judy Watson, as well as historians such as Lyndall Ryan, to map massacres of First Peoples in Australia. In a 21:59 minute HD video, *the names of places* (2016) Watson, for example, presents place names of massacre sites where First Peoples were murdered spooling like credits across maps of Australia and images of Watson's own artworks. Debates over how to define a 'massacre' or 'genocide' continue, and as settler perpetrators were often invested in obscuring or obliterating evidence of their violence, a wide range of sources including print, archival, oral and visual testimony are required to verify instances of violence (Dwyer & Ryan, 2012; Ryan, 2020).

# 1 Introduction: Artists confronting the violence of denial in Australia

denial' (2004, p. 7). The refusal to recognise and include violent histories in historical interpretation and memorial landscapes ignores and denies the pain and trauma of the past felt in the present by First Peoples, therefore enacting further violence. The trauma of violent contact is experienced on both sides of the perpetrator and survivor divide (Veracini, 2023), with the Australian nation's continual refusal to accept and incorporate violent histories in its narratives creating a psychic wound that penetrates deep in contemporary society, producing festering relations between settler and First Peoples communities that can only be remedied via an urgent reckoning with the past.

First Peoples have repeatedly called for 'truth-telling' about Australia's past to address colonial atrocities frequently silenced or denied in settler social memory and nation-building histories, such as 'the genocides, the massacres, the wars and the ongoing injustices and discrimination' (Commonwealth of Australia, 2017, p. 32). This truth-telling seeks a collective confrontation with colonisers violence and disregard of First Peoples' Country, law and sovereignty, and is asserted as a crucial step in healing, and developing a shared understanding of the past that will transform race relations between First Nations and settler communities and inform initiatives of redress such as Treaties (Appleby & Davis, 2018; Barolsky et al., 2023; Commonwealth of Australia, 2017; Yoorrook Justice Commission, 2022).

While nation-wide processes of truth-telling are yet to be initiated, Victoria's formal truth-telling inquiry is currently underway with the First Peoples-led Yoorrook Justice Commission taking submissions and holding hearings about the historic and ongoing injustices committed against First Peoples since the arrival of colonisers to the region now known as 'Victoria' (Yoorrook Justice Commission, 2022). Meanwhile, a recent report on community truth-telling describes how First Peoples have not waited for formalised processes to tell their historical truths, and instead lead advocacy for a variety of forms of recognition and truth-telling at the local level, that include creative and cultural initiatives such as memorials, public art, critical heritage interpretation, community education and storytelling (Barolsky et al., 2023). Communities are attending to difficult memories at local sites of colonial violence, with annual memorial services commemorating massacres of First Peoples at Appin and Myall Creek in New South Wales being powerful examples (Barolsky et al., 2023; Carlson & Farrelly, 2023; Dalley & Barnwell, 2023). Likewise, this edited volume underscores that First Peoples have for decades turned to the spaces of art and culture to air denied truths in public forums.

We are two artists and researchers who have come to consider the silences and violences in Australia's memorial landscape, and how artists create occasions to truthtell Australia's unsettling past, through our own separate research-based creative practices. We approach this subject and the framing and editing of this book, however, from different positionalities:

**Genevieve Grieves**: I am a Koori woman of mixed heritage. My mother's side is Worimi/Biripi, of the mid north coast of New South Wales and also Scottish settlers who colonised this Country in the 1800s. My father's side is a mix of Anglo Celtic Ancestors, the earliest who arrived to Dja Dja Wurrung land during Gold Rush times, and had a part in the devastation caused to First Peoples and Country. While my cultural frameworks are deeply embedded in the Southeast, I also have family from northern Australia. My brothers are Gurindji and Pertame, from Central Australia; my daughter is Iwadja and Malak Malak, from Coburg Peninsula, Arnhem Land, and the Daly River region. While my experience, as a fair-skinned Koorie woman, means I have a level of privilege, I have a lot of family who do not share this privilege, and I am deeply aware of the all pervasive racism of Australian society. In my life and career, I have also faced structural and interpersonal racism in many forms and am committed to resisting this through education, truth-telling and building intercultural frameworks for the collaborative work of decolonising. I was raised in both Koorie and settler Australian cultural frameworks and work across them and in between providing the skills to be an intercultural 'bridge worker' (Rowe, 2010) who creates spaces and projects for learning, understanding and justice across education and art/ culture. My Koori/Koorie cultural learning spaces during my childhood were my family and communities in Sydney, north coast NSW, Bathurst, Perth and Canberra. My mother and stepfather worked in education—in the Aboriginal and Torres Strait Islander Commission (ATSIC), Department of Employment, Education and Training (DEET) and establishing Aboriginal student centres at universities. I spent a lot of time in these contexts and was exposed at an early age to the importance of truth-telling and sharing our histories. As a young woman, I moved to Naarm (Melbourne) to take up my first professional position at the Koorie Heritage Trust Inc. under the leadership of Uncle Jim Berg, a fertile and seminal learning ground for me with the guidance of Uncle Jim and many Victorian Koorie Elders including Aunty Joan Vickery, Uncle John 'Sandy' Atkinson and Len Tregonning. This education extended my grounding in Koorie ways of doing, being and knowing. A key learning from these cultural leaders is the need for shared labour for social change, that we have to find ways to work together to dismantle colonialism and work for justice, hence my deep focus on collaboration and intercultural work.

**Amy Spiers**: I am a queer, white settler artist-researcher (she/they) currently living on the unceded lands of the Wurundjeri Woi Wurrung people in Naarm (Melbourne). I have Anglo Scottish heritage, while also being a descendent of a matrilineal line of Ashkenazi and Sephardi Jews. Despite living in areas in the Southeast that were violently possessed earliest with deadly and devastating consequences—on the lands of the Burramatta people, Dharug Country (Parramatta, NSW), of the Muwinina people in Nipaluna, Lutrawita (Hobart, Tasmania), as well as Naarm—I grew up ignorant and untroubled by histories of colonial violence and the theft of First Peoples' Country. Exemplary of settler Australia's colonial amnesia, my position-ality is inflected by the consciousness of a contradiction: while I was raised on stories of my great-grandparent's arrival to Australia as Jewish migrants fleeing antisemitism, pogroms and Nazi genocide in Europe, I was not accordingly told of my settler ancestors' contribution to a vicious colonial project of First Peoples dispossession and elimination. My research and work to counter the silences and denials rife in Australia's colonial memorial culture, and interest in artists' efforts

1 Introduction: Artists confronting the violence of denial in Australia

to raise awareness of our true difficult past, arose from a sense of profound injustice produced by this contradiction. While my Jewish ancestors have monuments acknowledging the scale of loss and pain caused by the Holocaust, Australia's public spaces and commemorations remain appallingly mute about our foundations in a genocidal colonial project and the atrocities inflicted on First Peoples. Indebted to First Nations activists, researchers, storytellers and artists—including my co-author Genevieve Grieves and many of the contributors to this book—who have opened my eyes to the full scale and consequences of this injustice, my ongoing creative research explores how the white settler community might generatively take 'ownership of and responsibility for the full knowledge of its own past' (Birch, 2020, pp. 114–115).

## 1.2 Art Holds a Space for Remembrance

Over the years First Nations artists have shown us that the realm of art and culture holds a space to remember and mourn the profound loss of life caused by invasion and colonisation in the absence of official commemoration and public acknowledgement of deep wounds that continue into the present. Exemplary of this is *The Aboriginal Memorial* (1988), an assemblage of 200 painted *dupun* log coffins, commemorating all First Nations lives lost in defence of their homelands since British colonisation began in 1788 created by Djon Mundine (Bundjalung) and forty-three Ramingining artists on permanent display at the National Gallery of Australia.[2] Meanwhile Badtjala artist Fiona Foley's bold body of work, beginning with *Annihilation of the Blacks* (1986) and continuing with *Lie of the Land* (1997) and *Witnessing to Silence* (2005), also strongly demonstrates how the public visibility afforded by the spaces of art can create uniquely compelling opportunities for remembrance and the exposure of uncomfortable truths about colonisation. Countless artists have contributed to the resistance of settler denial and the resuscitation of memory in Australia while honouring First Peoples' oral accounts, culture and ways of memorialising. This book focuses on the creative and cultural practices of a number of artists, writers and cultural practitioners leading these moves to creatively activate truth-telling—including Fiona Foley, Vicki Couzens, Julie Gough, r e a, Dianne Jones, Tony Birch, Paola Balla, Charmaine Papertalk Green, Neika Lehman and Arlie Alizzi—but there are, of course, numerous others. We attempt to begin to name

---

[2] The Aboriginal Memorial was made by Ramingining artists Djardie Ashley, Joe Patrick Birriwanga, David Blanasi, Roy Burrnyla, Mick Daypurrun 2, Tony Dhanyula, Paddy Dhatangu, John Dhurrikayu 1, Jimmy Djelminy, Tony Djikululu, Dorothy Djukulul, Tom Djumburpur, Robyn Djunginy, Charlie Djurritjini, Elisabeth Djuttara, Billy Black Durrgumba, Gela Nga-Mirraltja Fordham, Toby Gabalga, Daisy Ganyila 2, Philip Gudthaykudthay, Neville Gulaygulay, Don Gundinga, George Jangawanga, David Malangi Daymirringu, Jimmy Mamalunhawuy, Terry Mangapal, Agnes Marrawurr, Andrew Marrgululu, Clara Matjandatjpi (Wubukwubuk), John Mawurndjul AM, Dick Smith Mewirri, George Milpurrurru, Peter Minygululu, Jack Mirritji 2, Jimmy Moduk, Neville Nanyjawuy, Victor Pamkal, Roy Riwa, Frances Rrikili, William Watiri, Jimmy Wululu, Wurraki 2, Yambal Durrurringa.

some of the many creatives driving this powerful memory-work in the realm of visual and contemporary art below. While this is by no means an exhaustive review, these artists' works are representative of the vast effort and ground shifting achievements of truth-telling settler colonial Australia through creative practice.

Celebrated artists disclosing colonial violence include East Kimberly painters Rover Thomas (Wangkatjungka/Kukatja) and Queenie McKenzie (Gija). Thomas depicted the 'Killing Times' drawing on oral histories of massacres of First Peoples in the East Kimberley region, in a series of paintings made in the 1980s and 90s. A painting from this series, *Ruby Plains Massacre 1* (1985), was acquired by the Australian War Memorial in 2016 (Australian War Memorial, 2024). McKenzie's painting, *Mistake Creek Massacre* (1997), was acquired by the National Gallery of Australia in 2005 but it was rejected from inclusion in the gallery's core National Historical Collection due to disputes about its historical accuracy amidst Australia's History Wars (Daley, 2013). The painting was kept in deep storage until 2012, when it was finally incorporated in the museum's core collection for its historical significance in representing First Peoples' perspectives on settler violence. It was not put on display, however, until 2020 for the exhibition *Talking Blak to History* (Burnside, 2020).

Numerous First Nations contemporary artists have reflected on disregarded colonial atrocities on this continent, evocatively reflecting on the abominable absence of memorials to First Peoples afflicted. Yhonnie Scarce (Kokatha/Nukunu/Mirning) has researched monuments to victims of state violence and genocide overseas, and subsequently produced her own memorials to the devastating British nuclear tests conducted at Maralinga, South Australia between 1953 and 1963 that destructively contaminated Maralinga Tjarutja Country and produced long-term health impacts for First Peoples communities in the region who had contact with the radioactive fallout, including Scarce's own family. One example is *Cloud Chamber* (2020) which features 100 hand-blown glass pieces in the shape of desert yams, ghoulishly suspended in the air suggesting the toxic black cloud that appears in the aftermath of a nuclear blast. Waanyi artist Judy Watson also tirelessly uncovers effaced First Nations' histories in a multimedia practice that encompasses *40 pairs of blackfellow's ears, lawn hill station* (2008), an artwork comprised of cast beeswax ears nailed to the gallery wall—including casts of Watson's own family members' ears—that recall vile acts committed against Waanyi people by pastoralists at a Queensland homestead in the 1880s; and also, *the names of places* (2016), a video work and collaboration with the public to share knowledge and map sites where First Peoples were massacred by colonisers.

First Nations artists use a range of artistic approaches to reject colonial representations and assert the stories and presence of First Peoples in acts of cultural remembrance that are healing and rejuvenating. Yorta Yorta, Wamba Wamba, Mutti Mutti and Boonwurrung artist, Maree Clarke, for example, has undertaken extensive research to reprise Southeastern cultural practices including *kopi*, caps made of gypsum weighing up to seven kilograms that First Peoples would wear on their heads as part of mourning rites. This research has culminated in moving artworks such as *Ritual and Ceremony* (2012), consisting of large black and white portraits

# 1 Introduction: Artists confronting the violence of denial in Australia

of 84 Southeastern First Peoples daubed in white ochre face and body markings, installed alongside kopi that were made with the portrait subjects as they reflected on grief and sorrow they have experienced. *Ritual and Ceremony* powerfully provides space to honour all that has been lost and damaged with colonisation, including land, language and culture. Additionally, The Unbound Collective—a collective of South Australian women artists Ali Gumillya Baker (Mirning), Simone Ulalka Tur (Antikirinya/Yankunytjatjara), Faye Rosas Blanch (Yidniji/Mbarbarm) and Natalie Harkin (Narungga)—produce multidisciplinary artworks that intervene into spaces riven with colonial narratives. Their *Sovereign Acts* performance series starting in 2014, for example, utilises their own bodies as forms of counter-monument in performative works that interrupt sites of colonial power, such as the South Australian Museum, to assert an ongoing sovereign existence despite the devastating impacts of colonialism. In another act of resistance and remembrance, Quandamooka artist Megan Cope's monumental public artwork, *Whispers* (2023), installed 85,000 oyster shells across Sydney's iconic Opera House precinct to recall the ancestral middens and Gadigal gathering place, Tubowgule, once located there prior to colonisation. Notably in 2024, Archie Moore (Kamilaroi/Bigambul) won the Venice Biennale's prestigious award the Golden Lion for Best National Participation for his work *kith and kin*, a monument to First Nations vitality that traces Moore's genealogy chart back 65,000+ years. Drawing on reams of state documents and coroner reports, Moore included in the work a reflective pool to memorialise injustices First Nations people have experienced, including deaths in state custody. Prominent artists who have rejected colonial erasure and produced defiant reminders of First Nations' sovereign presence, include also Vernon Ah Kee (Kuku Yalandji, Waanji, Yidinji and Gugu Yimithirr), Richard Bell (Kamilaroi, Kooma, Jiman and Gurang Gurang), Gordon Bennett (Aboriginal and Anglo-Celtic descent), Christian Thompson (Bidjara, Irish and Chinese), Nici Cumpston (Barkandji) and D Harding (Bidjara, Ghungalu and Garingbal).

Scholars have noted that Australia is a nation obsessed with memorials honouring those who served the nation in overseas battlefields, especially to the ANZACs of WWI (Baguley et al., 2021). Numerous war memorials erected in every town and city are ubiquitous public reminders of Australian soldiers who have died in offshore military engagements, while only a few public monuments venerate First Peoples, particularly those who died resisting colonial invasion on their Country. It was just in 2022 that the national institution, the Australian War Memorial, conceded to expanding their permanent displays to recognise the wars fought over possession of the continent now known as 'Australia', and honour those who were killed in the conflict (Reynolds, 2022).

While there are no recent national surveys of official monuments to First Peoples— Chilla Bulbeck noted that a National Register of Unusual Monuments identified just 33 in the late 1980s (1991)—in recent years, official commemorations dedicated to First Peoples' histories have been increasing, with many prominent commissions of First Nations artists rectifying a historical absence of monuments commemorating First Peoples involvement in military conflicts (Batten & Batten, 2008; Inglis,

2008). Tony Albert (Girramay and Kuku Yalanji), for example, has produced memorials to First Peoples who served for Australia in overseas wars but on their return were not treated as equal citizens in artworks that include the commemorative public artwork *YININMADYEMI Thou didst let fall* (2015) in Hyde Park, Gadigal Country (Sydney). In 2018, artist Daniel Boyd (Kudjala/Gangalu/Kuku Yalanji/Waka Waka/Gubbi Gubbi/Wangerriburra/Bandjalung), with architects Edition Office, was commissioned by the Australian War Memorial to design the inaugural National Aboriginal and Torres Strait Islander War Memorial for its sculpture garden. The resulting sculptural pavilion, *For Our Country* (2018–19), commemorates First Peoples' service in all conflicts in which Australia's military has been deployed—including in defence of homelands—and incorporates a ceremonial firepit and a chamber containing deposits of soil from Country across the continent. Additionally, artist Jason Wing who has Chinese and Biripi heritage created *Firesticks* in 2020, a public memorial located on the banks of the Burramatta (Paramatta River) that is comprised of eight *nawi* (canoes) rendered in steel and resembling the shape of .50 calibre bullets. The nawi contain firesticks that light up at night, recalling the local Dharug practice, and honours First Nations heroes that died fighting in Homeland Wars, as well as wars overseas. Meanwhile, Wiradjuri, Ngunnawal and Celtic artist Brook Andrew has realised commemorations to Homeland Wars and colonial violence working as a curator, artist and researcher, including creating with non-Indigenous artist Trent Walter the permanent public marker for the City of Melbourne, *Standing by Tunnerminnerwait and Maulboyheenner* (2016), which commemorates two First Nations resistance fighters who were the first prisoners executed by public hanging in the early Melbourne colony; as well as leading the Australian Research Council funded project, *Representation, Remembrance and the Memorial* (2016–2019), which explored how the magnitude of First Peoples' losses and survival under colonisation might be represented through a national state memorial (Andrew, 2017).

Additionally, First Nations artists have reflected on the dearth of official public memorials dedicated to First Peoples with inventive creative commemorations that critique the ubiquity of memorials dedicated to settlers, while repurposing Western memorial forms. Addressing the Homeland Wars, for example, Wiradjuri artist Amala Groom's *Yindyamarra Roll* (2014) subverts the settler custom of honouring people who died serving the nation in wars overseas by listing their names on wooden honour boards. Groom's honour roll (*Yindyamarra* means 'to show honour, respect' in Wiradjuri) pays respect instead to First Nations warriors who died resisting invasion and fighting for Country. Kamilaroi, Gamilaroi and Gamilaraay artist Reko Rennie's repeatable site-specific sculpture *Remember Us*, encompasses large marble slabs inscribed with roman lettering in deep red. The first iteration which was installed at the Museum of Contemporary Art, Gadigal Country (Sydney) in 2023 read:

DLI
DEATHS
SINCE
RCIADIC

MCMXCI
MMXXIII

The work is dedicated to memorialising the 551 First Peoples who have died in police custody since the Royal Commission into Aboriginal Deaths in Custody (RCIADIC), at the time of the work's fabrication. Drawing on the gravitas placed on ancient roman marbles and inscriptions, the sculpture aims to lend seriousness, dignity and monumentality to this inexcusable, ongoing crisis. In a creative collaboration that provides reflection on First Peoples struggles for land rights and self-determination since colonisation, Senior Wurundjeri Elder Aunty Joy Murphy Wandin AO with Wiradjuri and Kamilaroi artist Jonathan Jones and non-Indigenous artist Tom Nicholson launched *untitled (seven monuments)* in 2019. A critical memorial artwork comprised of seven upturned, buried flagpoles with accompanying above ground brick footing and information plaques, the work commemorates the original boundary of Coranderrk Aboriginal Station, an early base of First Peoples' political organising and advocacy established in 1863 by Wurundjeri and other Southeastern First Nations communities displaced by colonising invaders. Colonial government interference and policies ultimately undermined Coranderrk and it was closed in 1924, but it remains a significant site for First Peoples.

What these diverse works demonstrate is that artists are on the frontline in resisting historical amnesia in settler colonial Australia, exploring a multiplicity of commemorative creations, acts and interventions to recall disregarded injustices and disavowed histories while amplifying the experiences of, and providing healing for, communities through the long overdue acknowledgment of painful events. The spaces provided through the medium of art and culture are employed to draw public attention to the settler nation's 'cult of forgetfulness', the unfinished project of recognising the violence of the colonial past and First Peoples' enduring resilience (Stanner, 1969). These cultural practices and creative memory-works located across galleries, sites of violence and public spaces participate powerfully in an ongoing struggle and contest over memorial landscapes in settler colonial Australia (Graves & Rechniewski, 2017), broaching a future where such histories might not be minimised or dismissed, but instead solemnly and actively commemorated by all people residing on unceded First Peoples' Country.

## 1.3 Artists Healing Wounded Spaces and Reviving Cultural Futures

This edited collection is underpinned by editor Genevieve Grieves' prior research into First Nations artists who confront colonial amnesia in deeply restorative, place-based ways that heal sites that have witnessed violence and revivify First Peoples' cultural futures. *Part I* of this book delves deep into the practices and approaches of four artists particularly—Dianne Jones (Ballardong), Vicki Couzens (Gunditjmara),

Julie Gough (Trawlwoolway) and r e a (Gamilaraay/Wailwan/Biripi)—who Grieves brought together in 2017 for the exhibition, *The Violence of Denial*, at Arts House for Yirramboi First Nations arts festival in Naarm (Melbourne). In the remainder of this section, Grieves provides insight into this research from her first person perspective.

**Genevieve Grieves**: *The Violence of Denial* (2017) was focussed on Aboriginal women and non-binary artists who work with screen-based media and interrogate overlooked colonial crimes, particularly what has come to be known broadly as 'frontier violence'. What unites these artists is the generative ways they recall traumatic histories in cultural landscapes that are largely devoid of representations of colonial violence and its aftermath, and utilise creative practice to actively disrupt the ongoing act of erasure and denial that constitutes settler colonialism. These four artists attend to wounded spaces where death and trauma has occurred and has been wilfully forgotten. They engage in the recuperative work of opposing repressive systems of closure—of time and history—to bring forth sovereign truths, voices, experiences and knowledge that confront denial and work toward realising a more just, healing and equitable future.

Yet, these artists' focus is not only toward shifting and disrupting settler colonial frameworks, they are also resisting 'aenocide'—the attempted annihilation of future generations of First Peoples, the community of memory who mourn lost Ancestors (Rose, 2004, p. 27)—restoring self, Country, story, and culture within First Nations' cultural frameworks and, in doing so, are engaged in regenerative, reparative and decolonising acts. Through this work, they interrogate Westernised conceptions of 'art', 'violence', 'time' and 'history/memory', shifting understandings of what these concepts can constitute in an intercultural context.

Part of the impetus for developing this project is that I had not yet experienced an exhibition that highlighted the depth of these artists' creative practices outside of the form of their art. I was very interested in the impact and strength of the art that they make, but even more so their practice of embodied research—discovering, unearthing and exposing the past through a *restorative* framework. Distinguished decolonial scholar Linda Tuhiwai Smith has described such practices of 'restoring' as:

> … a project which is conceived as a holistic approach to problem solving. It is holistic in terms of the emotional, spiritual and physical nexus, and also in terms of the individual and the collective, the political and the cultural (1999, p. 155).

The process of creating this exhibition was based in relationality—all of the artists are known to me across many years. I have been privileged to spend time with both Vicki Couzens and Dianne Jones on their Country, and I have been deeply inspired by the way they creatively connect with Country to excavate, and make visible, colonial violence. They both undertake deep and difficult work intersecting art and memorialisation with a layered process involving archival research, memory-work and connection to Country. Dianne is archaeological in her relentless uncovering, removing the shrouds of denial and untruths that cover the area to which she is connected near Perth. Vicki both discloses violence and provides deep moments of healing for Southeastern Victorian communities in her revival of language, culture and ceremony including possum-skin cloakmaking and ritual mourning practices, as well as through a creative practice that has also worked to expose homeland violence on her Gunditjmara Country. Similarly, Trawlwoolway artist Julie Gough's forensic examination of colonial crimes in Lutruwita (Tasmania) has also been inspirational and instructive, exemplifying a deep, never-ending commitment to disclosing and resolving the repressed histories of violence embedded across the state. Additionally, r e a has been an inspiration for many years, forging a space for emerging cultural-creatives like myself, and one of the earlier practitioners of the deep research and place-based methodologies that all these artists employ.

The exhibition was not only an opportunity to highlight the under-recognised work and methods of these artists but to create a space of connection. The work that they (we) do is emotionally challenging, onerous and difficult and often met with resistance by settler colonial Australia. *The Violence of Denial* allowed us to come together to speak of our experiences, provide support and meaning for one another as we continue the struggle of holding these painful and traumatic histories, while resisting the colonial amnesia that is central to the identity of the Australian nation state.

Each artist in their work and their creative/cultural methodologies deepen our understanding of the unique process, and transformative impacts, of First Nations art and memorialisation. In the framing of the exhibition, and my related research, for example, I struggled with the framing of all four as 'artists' which seems a woefully inadequate term for the breadth and depth of their embodied, embedded, holistic practices, which also comes at a cost. As Kelada and Clark articulate, First Nations women artists often put their 'bodies on the line', placing themselves in the frame, with all the emotional, physical and spiritual toll that this entails (2013).

Vicki Couzens also professes she struggles with the notion of herself as an 'artist', preferring to describe herself with the term 'creative cultural practitioner'. She acknowledges that the spaces of art provide convenient opportunities to undertake her creative and culturally restorative practice, but it is not always adequate in describing the full extent and purpose of her work. She has described her motivation to produce art in public spaces, for example, as primarily for 'our Mobs' to strengthen and give presence (Spiers & Couzens, 2021, p. 50). Vicki explains:

> It's an assertion, a declaration of sovereignty never ceded, of Belonging ... It's a reclamation of public space, it's resistance and most importantly it's cultural expression for no other reason than the beauty of our cultures, our Stories and our Belonging to Country/ies ... My work's intention is to very subtly but resolutely be implacable, immovable ... to influence, to bring about change and to educate. Most importantly, it is about inserting a visible point of reference: we are still here!! (Spiers & Couzens, 2021, pp. 49-53)

Vicki's creative cultural practice is deeply inspiring, demonstrating a life-long commitment to the revitalisation of her language and culture—demonstrative of a healing process of what Smith has referred to as 'restoring' (1999). In Vicki's work for *The Violence of Denial* exhibition, *pang-ngooteeweeng-wanoong (we remember)* (2017), she not only resists colonial erasure but incorporates objects she has created through this process of restoring, items whose making had been disrupted by colonial violence and were at risk of erasure from the present, and future. The work includes a possum skin cloak used in Gunditjmara funeral and burial practices that was suspended in the exhibition space. Underneath the cloak in a circle of soil was laid a series of possum skin mourning bags that Gunditjmara people use to carry a loved one's cremated remains for months while in mourning. The practice of making the bags has been revived by Vicki, and the bags created for the exhibition were made for the first time in 180+ years since British invasion. A two minute video showing Vicki gazing over her Country is projected onto the cloak, accompanied by audio of Vicki speaking in Gunditjmara language.

Dianne Jones' practice focuses on unearthing the truth of the colonial histories of her Ballardong Country, around York, Western Australia. She has created a range of works that speak to this history, bringing a First Nations lens, understanding and perspective to events that are largely presented on settler colonial terms. Part of her uncovering of York's true history has involved curating an exhibition, *What Lies Buried Rises* (2013), that explores the story of young white servant Sarah Cook, whose death in the 1830s was the catalyst for many massacres of First Nations people in Western Australia. Two Noongar men, Barrabong and Doodjeep, on tenuous evidence were convicted and hanged for her murder in 1840.

Dianne invited me to make a work for the *What Lies Buried Rises* exhibition, the result of which was a seven minute, three channel video work *lament* (2013). An active work of memorialisation towards First Peoples' healing in the face of all that has been lost, *lament* features Keerray Woorroong and Gunditjmara dancer and culture woman, Yaraan Bundle, painted in ochre and dancing in the Royal Exhibition Building in Naarm (Melbourne), one of the oldest colonial buildings in the nation, to audio recorded in York in the area where Sarah Cook, Barrabong and Doodjeep were killed. As part of the process of making *lament*, I travelled back to York together with Dianne to visit the site of Sarah Cook's death and see what more on the story we could glean from the landscape and people. I was able to witness Dianne's process through this trip. She was determined—at risk to herself—to make the town see the truth of the past, although there was little appetite for this from the townspeople. She was dismissed, shut down and ignored as she fought to uncover this story.

The work made for *The Violence of Denial* exhibition focuses on this process of Dianne's more than the history itself. In *found objects from what lies buried rises* (2017), a three minute video shows Dianne forensically examining, assembling and arranging found objects—glass shards, a rusty chain, spear fragments and pieces of ceramics—like evidence. The work represents her creative process, a painstaking and deliberate reassessment of the past. Dianne's practice is research based, scouring the archives, questioning, revising and reframing the largely white voices she finds there; as well as place-based, connecting with sites of violence and her own community to discover oral versions of events. The work reflects on a history of settler violence that has been distorted, minimised and obscured in colonial narratives, the video depicting

# 1 Introduction: Artists confronting the violence of denial in Australia

the labour in surfacing evidence of the colonial mistruths and misrepresentations, and the excavation of alternative testimony to the violence First Peoples have experienced.

r e a's practice similarly has uncovered colonial violence of many forms. The multimedia artwork I selected for *The Violence of Denial, PolesApart* (2019), speaks to colonial oppression and our individual struggles to free ourselves from these confines. A 6:55 minute silent video, *PolesApart* depicts a figure, performed by r e a, dressed in a cumbersome black nineteenth-century gown fleeing an unseen but malevolent force—stumbling, crouching fearfully, resuming flight—through a bush-fire charred forest near Daylesford in Central Victoria. The site was chosen due to its proximity to where the Heidelberg School painters, such as Frederick McCubbin, produced iconic Australian artworks like *The Pioneer* (1904). *PolesApart* animates a collective memory, held in r e a's body, of female forbears—r e a's grandmother Ruby and great aunt Sophie, but also countless other First Nations women—stolen from their families and forced into servitude by colonisers, who longed to escape and return home to family. The fleeing figure enacts the desires of such Ancestors, but also r e a's ongoing fight to escape the domination of colonial narratives that attempt to vanish these memories, efface these women and dictate how r e a themself is made visible. The video concludes as r e a's body is sprayed with red, white and blue paint. As r e a has described:

> At the end of the video work I become invisible through the spraying of these colours all over me. It seems that the harder I work to be visible the more I'm blotted out— I'm continuously running, hoping to find the freedom to create my own identity'. (cited in Nicholls, 2009)

Likewise Julie's work in the exhibition, *The Grounds for Surrender* (2011), is a video work that scours sites of violence for traces that reveal, and make sense of, the attempt at genocide of Palawa that occurred in the British colonial invasion of Lutruwita (Tasmania). A 19 minute two channel video work, that juxtaposes present day scenes of the Tasmanian regional town of Bothwell, surrounding farmlands, roads, bodies of water and picnic areas, alongside quotes from early colonial records that describe conflict with Palawa in the region and the calls made by colonisers to escalate measures to quash their resistance. The video opens with an image of an ornamental silver cup Bothwell residents presented to George Augustus Robinson in 1835 to thank him for his role in so-called 'conciliating' the First Peoples of Lutruwita, a mission which quelled violent conflict by removing surviving Palawa people, who had endured coordinated dispossession and massacre, to concentration camps on Wybalenna (Flinders Island).

Julie's practice is deeply inspirational, defying categorisation. Her forensic dedication to revealing her history, that builds an archive of knowledge, evidence, and subsequent creative reflections, to the violence experienced by her Ancestors is an extraordinary, life-long practice that exemplifies the work of this cohort of creative/cultural practitioners. This effort to summon the truth moves beyond 'art' into deeper spaces of memory, resistance, trauma, historiography, place-based interventions and healing. When I think of Julie's body of work, I think of the term 'memory-artists' coined by memory studies scholar James E. Young to describe the practice of artists who work to activate the memory of victims of traumatic atrocities and state violence, such as the Holocaust (2000). I came across it in my research, trying to find the words to articulate the impact of artists such as Julie, r e a, Dianne and Vicki. It remains not quite the right term, and the few words to frame the deep impact of their work still eludes me.

The art- and culture-making of these impactful artists exemplify the ways First Peoples creatives holistically restore memory, confront and shift settler myths, and tirelessly fight the amnesia of this country, often outside Western commemorative frameworks and discipline of history. As we discuss in our transcribed conversation in *Part I* of this book, Koori historian and writer Tony Birch has identified that many First Peoples historians work in film, art, theatre: beyond academic and historical texts, it's in the creative arts that our histories are told and shared. First Peoples creatives and storytellers have radically transformed our understanding of settler colonial Australia, persistently disclosing stories of violence in landscapes and contexts where settler histories have buried the truth. It is through the space of art that important ground has been shifted, truths told and healing has occurred.

## 1.4 Truth-Telling Memorial Art in Settler Colonial Australia

Foregrounding Genevieve Grieves' prior research into First Peoples artists who defy erasure by recuperating memory and cultural identity, this volume begins with transcriptions of a series of public talks she facilitated in 2017, as part of the exhibition *The Violence of Denial*, between herself and the artists showcased in the exhibition, as well as Tony Birch. The edited transcripts of these generous and insightful conversations between leading First Peoples practitioners focussed on truth-telling through restorative creative and cultural practices are published for the first time in *Part I* of this volume.

In *Part II: Truth-telling with creative practice in settler colonial Australia*, we assemble together a series of essays and creative texts from contributors within our community of practice: artists and scholars, the majority of which are First Peoples, who have been pivotal in informing and inspiring our own creative research. These chapters examine a diversity of creative approaches to artistic truth-telling and counter-colonial memorialisation in Australia through the perspectives of creatives and researchers with deep knowledge and experience in attending to difficult colonial histories. The collection of texts celebrates artists who strive to produce visible reminders of colonial violence and First Peoples' survival in a settler colonial context steeped in denial, while critically examining the aspects of the Australian nation's memorial culture that need urgent redress.

*Part II* begins with Yamaji poet Charmaine Papertalk Green's *The wind has not yet answered!*, a creative reflection on the lack of monuments to Yamaji people on Yamaji Country (Geraldton, Western Australia). An example in itself of creative

# 1 Introduction: Artists confronting the violence of denial in Australia

truth-telling, Green's poem provides a seething critique of the contrasts in Australia's memorialscapes that continue to prominently venerate settler conquest, including marking the first stone wall of the colony, while First Peoples' greatest monuments and achievements, many dating back thousands of years, experience, as Green notes, 'national invisibility'.

In her chapter *Remembering those who have gone before*, Badtjala artist and academic Fiona Foley provides a revealing account of how she has been confronting the lack of monuments to First Peoples' losses, producing artworks that commemorate warriors who died resisting colonisation since her undergraduate studies in visual art in the 1980s. Foley describes the many works she has created, drawing on First Peoples' oral histories and colonisers' own records, to publicise colonial atrocities of murder and massacre, asserting: 'public art is a way of putting in plain sight this history, which has been shrouded in silence and draped in settler complicity'. Foley reminds us that while artists are today emboldened by a more receptive artworld to create artworks confronting settler violence, she has been working in defiant resistance of settler silences for decades during fraught times when truth-telling artworks provoked culturally unsafe and dismissive censure from her educators and peers. Her account invites us to consider that while her numerous creative outputs compelling remembrance of difficult events are regularly assigned and appraised as 'public art' and 'contemporary art', and are often given only impermanent prominence in public spaces and galleries, these *are* memorials to First Peoples' losses and should be solemnly regarded and appreciated as such.

In *Mass Exposure: Memory Laundering, Racial Literacy and the Art of Truth-telling*, Ballardong photomedia artist and researcher Dianne Jones and settler scholar and writer Odette Kelada usefully coin the term 'memory laundering' to describe settler colonial Australia's persistent attempts to obscure and whitewash the wealth generating ties that many of the colonial figures who are enshrined in monuments, or commemorated in street and place names, have to colonial theft, eugenics, slavery and genocide. They describe how the role of omission and denial is pivotal to this process of memory laundering, with formal education as well as commemorative place-making practices contributing to the mythic construction of colonial possession as peaceful and inevitable and the invaders as heroic. Kelada and Jones' chapter explores how such 'strategic uses of forgetting' can be countered through increasing racial literacy, a critical skill that develops understanding of how race operates historically, and in contemporary contexts, to produce unequal power relations. They conclude by instructively examining how First Nations artists, such as author Jones, challenge memory laundering and develop racial literacy through decolonising creative practices that expose colonialism's violence.

Continuing this deep examination of the power of creative practices to challenge whitewashed colonial myths and lies, co-authors Wemba-Wemba and Gunditjmara artist and scholar Paola Balla, settler scholar and historian Clare Land and settler artist and researcher Kate Golding candidly describe the process they undertook to develop *Blak Cook Book: New Cultural Perspectives on Cooks' Cottage* (2021): an 'image-rich monograph' that presents First Nations' views on British explorer James Cook's life and legacy commissioned by the City of Melbourne. The City of Melbourne—evidently aware that their tourist attraction in Fitzroy Gardens, Cooks' Cottage, is offensive to First Peoples in its celebration of the 'original invader' James Cook (Foley, 2019)—invited the authors to develop First Nations' perspectives for incorporation in the Cottage's existing interpretation. In their chapter, *This full agency, this decolonised spirit: Talking Blak to Cooks' Cottage*, the collaborators insightfully describe an unease and reluctance in having their labour and knowledge co-opted by the City of Melbourne to add value to the crude colonial attraction. The authors detail how consequently they produced *Blak Cook Book* instead, a text that searingly truth-tells Cook's legacy through the wide-ranging and rich critical perspectives of First Nations artists, writers, activists and scholars. Refusing the book's integration into the 'irredeemably colonial' Cottage, the authors describe how they alternatively made the text available as a free download online and as hard copies at visitor centres, while also speculating on more substantive, imaginative ways to challenge the Cottage beyond updating interpretive displays.

In *What should the City of Melbourne do with the inaccurate and offensive John Batman memorial obelisk?*, settler artist and writer Amy Spiers also speculates about forms of imaginative visual and spatial justice that could be enacted to address contentious monuments and truth-tell the past in public spaces permeated with colonial place-making. The chapter focuses on a critical examination of the bluestone memorial obelisk to John Batman, located at the Queen Victoria Market, Naarm (Melbourne), that inaccurately describes Batman as a founder of Melbourne on a site that was in 1835 'then unoccupied'. Drawing on comparisons of other cities' (counter-)memorial cultures in Nipaluna, Lutruwita (Hobart, Tasmania) and Berlin, Germany, Spiers argues that the City of Melbourne to date has failed to provide substantive remembrances of the victims of Batman's horrific deeds that includes mass murder, deception and land theft. Addressing speculation that the Batman obelisk will quietly disappear due to a forthcoming multi-million-dollar renewal of the market, Spiers' chapter argues that the redevelopment could provide an unprecedented opportunity for the City of Melbourne to fulfil it's declared commitment to truth-telling by meaningfully atoning for Batman's memorial and legacy, and acknowledging the anguish they have caused First Peoples, through creative memorialisation.

We conclude the edited collection with an epic, incisive dialogic text between writers Arlie Alizzi (Yugambeh) and Neika Lehman (Trawlwoolway) that emphasises the need for care in monument-making, drawing on American Black Studies theorist Christina Sharpe's notions of 'the wake' and 'wake work' (2016). Continuing an ongoing conversation between the longtime friends on who monuments are for, the chapter *Exposure Therapy: Spectacles, Monuments and the Question of Care* thoughtfully examines artworks such as *Standing by Tunnerminnerwait and Maulboyheenner* (2016) by Brook Andrew and Trent Walter, as well as *Scaffold* (2012–2017) by American settler artist Sam Durant, both artworks that illicit consideration of colonial atrocities through depictions of gallows and scaffolds—apparatuses of terror and violence. Given that Bla(c)k people live, as Sharpe notes, in the still unfolding wake of historical racialised violence, with the lived effects of trauma and violence still circulating in the present, Alizzi and Lehman instructively consider

# 1 Introduction: Artists confronting the violence of denial in Australia

passed Ancestors and their survivors, and how they might be more sensitively considered in representations of colonial violence, particularly in artworks that purport to honour and commemorate those who were lost resisting colonisation.

As we assemble this volume for publication we are conscious that we have reached a contemporary moment where First Nations people are freshly wounded by settler racism and disregard, and where it feels that the doubled violence is doubling down. In October 2023, as we were close to finalising this edited collection, the majority of Australians voted 'no' in a national referendum, rejecting a proposal to recognise First Peoples through a formal advisory 'Voice to Parliament' enshrined in Australia's Constitution. The referendum process has been strongly criticised by numerous commentators as damaging and hurtful, a shameful period in Australian national politics where an onslaught of settler racism and misinformation was emboldened and publicly aired (Canales, 2023; Davis, 2023; Wellauer et al., 2023). The subsequent defeat of The Voice has highlighted for First Peoples, and their supporters, that a public discussion mired in ignorance and prejudice will not bring about meaningful political change and justice, inciting fresh appeals for truth-telling (Hinman & Heymann, 2023; McKenna, 2023; Norman & Payne, 2024). It feels timely then to conclude this book on Alizzi and Lehman's call for care in memorialisation, a care that recognises that it is difficult to mourn a violence that persists, or as American writer of Black life Saidiya Hartman observes: 'When the injuries not only perdure, but are inflicted anew?' (Hartman, 2002, p. 758).

Taken together these deeply researched, considered texts and conversations lend vital, critical perspectives on Australia's toxic settler colonial remembrance culture of ignorance and denial. This book recognises that in this highly contested, doubly violent and racist context, artists are frequently intervening—often at personal cost— to counter the denial and speak up about the truth of Australia's violent colonial foundations, creatively translating and sharing difficult knowledge while honouring and celebrating First Peoples' survival (Atkinson-Phillips, 2021). Through a range of creative means and mediums, artists and cultural practitioners are making essential contributions to truth-telling, devising evocative, sensitive ways to make the injustices committed against First Peoples not only visible and tangible, but also strongly felt and grieved. This volume demonstrates that artists are working tirelessly to envision a more representative and just memorial landscape, having already actualised countless public commemorations and memorials that produce community healing and collective recognition, while the officially sanctioned public monuments solemnly atoning to colonisation's violence and prominently honouring the vast losses are still yet to come.

## References

Andrew, B. (2017). Remembrance, representation and the memorial. In B. French & A. Loxley (Eds.), *Civic actions: Artists' practices beyond the museum* (pp. 62–69). The Rocks: Museum of Contemporary Art Australia.

Appleby, G., & Davis, M. (2018). The Uluru Statement and the Promises of Truth. *Australian Historical Studies, 49*(4), 501–509.

Atkinson-Philiips, A. (2021). Interpreting difficult knowledge: What difference do artists make? In A. Spiers, C. Day, & C. Morton (Eds.), *Let's go outside: Art in public* (pp. 70–97). Monash University Publishing.

Australian War Memorial. (2024). Ruby plains massacre 1. *AWM Collection.* https://www.awm.gov.au/collection/C2148046. Accessed May 1, 2024.

Baguley, M., Kerby, M., & Andersen, N. (2021). Counter memorials and counter monuments in Australia's commemorative landscape: A systematic literature review. *Historical Encounters, 8*(1), 93–120.

Banivanua Mar, T. (2012). Settler-Colonial Landscapes and Narratives of Possession. *Arena Journal, 37/38*, 176–198.

Batten, B., & Batten, P. (2008). Memorialising the past: Is there an aboriginal way? *Public History Review, 15*, 92–116.

Barolsky, V., Berger, K., & Close, K. (2023). Recognising community truth-telling: An exploration of local truth-telling in Australia. *Reconciliation Australia.* https://www.reconciliation.org.au/wp-content/uploads/2023/09/Recognising-community-truth-telling-report.pdf. Accessed April 30, 2024.

Birch, T. (2023). A brief aboriginal history of Victoria. In T. Birch, J. Katona, & G. Foley, *Native title is not land rights* (pp. 9–60). Common Room Editions.

Birch, T. (2020). 'The invisible fire': Indigenous sovereignty, history and responsibility. In A. Moreton-Robinson (Ed.), *Sovereign subjects: Indigenous sovereignty matters* (pp. 105–117). Allen & Unwin.

Bulbeck, C. (1991). Aborigines, memorials and the history of the frontier. *Australian Historical Studies, 24*(96), 168–178.

Burnside, N. (2020, 22 July). Queenie McKenzie's 'mistake creek massacre' displayed by national museum after years of controversy. *ABC News.* https://www.abc.net.au/news/2020-07-22/talking-blak-to-history-indigenous-exhibition-at-national-museum/12472370. Accessed May 1, 2024.

Canales, S. B. (2023, 22 October). Yes supporters say voice referendum 'unleashed a tsunami of racism'. *The Guardian.* https://www.theguardian.com/australia-news/2023/oct/22/indigenous-groups-say-voice-referendum-unleashed-a-tsunami-of-racism. Accessed May 1, 2023.

Carlson, B., & Farrelly, T. (2023). *Monumental disruptions: Aboriginal people and colonial commemorations in so-called Australia.* Aboriginal Studies Press.

Commonwealth of Australia. (2017). Final report of the referendum council 30 June 2017. Referendum Council. https://www.referendumcouncil.org.au/sites/default/files/report_attachments/Referendum_Council_Final_Report.pdf. Accessed April 30, 2024.

Daley, P. (2013, 4 July). What became of mistake creek massacre? *The Guardian.* https://www.theguardian.com/artanddesign/2013/jul/04/mistake-creek-massacre-indigenous-painting. Accessed May 1, 2024.

Dalley, C., & Barnwell, A. (2023). *Memory in place: Locating colonial histories and commemoration.* ANU Press.

Davis, M. (2023). Truth after the voice. *The Monthly.* https://www.themonthly.com.au/issue/2023/december/megan-davis/truth-after-voice#mtr. Accessed May 1, 2024.

Dwyer, P. G., & Ryan, L. (2012). Introduction: The massacre and history. In P. G. Dwyer & L. Ryan (Eds.), *Theatres of violence massacre, mass killing and atrocity throughout history* (pp. xiii–xxv). Berghahn Books.

Foley, G. [goori2]. (2019, 19 May). On captain cook [video]. YouTube. https://youtu.be/f2CKlgeUXMo. Accessed August 8, 2023.

Graves, M., & Rechniewski, E. (2017). Black wars and white settlement: The conflict over space in the Australian commemorative landscape. *E-rea: Revue électronique d'études sur le monde anglophone, 14*(2).

Hartman, S. (2002). The time of slavery. *The South Atlantic Quarterly, 101*(4), 757–776.

# 1 Introduction: Artists confronting the violence of denial in Australia

Hinman, P., & Heymann, R. (2023, 12 September). Celeste Liddle on the voice: 'Truth-telling is the first important step'. *Green Left, 1390*. https://www.greenleft.org.au/content/celeste-liddle-voice-truth-telling-first-important-step. Accessed May 1, 2024.

Inglis, K. S. (2008). *Sacred places: War memorials in the Australian landscape*. Melbourne University Publishing.

Kelada, O., & Clark, M. (2013). Bodies on the line: Repossession and 'talkin up' in Aboriginal women's art. *Artlink, 33*(3), 39–43.

Mar, T. B. (2012). Settler-colonial landscapes and narratives of possession. *Arena Journal, 37/38*, 176–198.

McKenna, M. (2023, 26 October). The need for truth-telling is more urgent than ever if we are to change hearts and minds for future referendums. *The Guardian*. https://www.theguardian.com/commentisfree/2023/oct/26/the-need-for-truth-telling-is-more-urgent-than-ever-if-we-are-to-change-hearts-and-minds-for-future-referendums. Accessed May 1, 2024.

Murphy, K. (2017, 25 August). Changing colonial statues is Stalinist, says Malcolm Turnbull. *The Guardian*. https://www.theguardian.com/australia-news/2017/aug/25/changing-colonial-statues-is-stalinist-says-malcolm-turnbull. Accessed April 30, 2024.

Nicholls, C. (2009). PolesApart. *BREENSPACE*. https://www.breenspace.com/exhibitions/r-e-a-pol esapart/009.rea_breenspace_09.jpg.php. Accessed May 1, 2024.

Norman, H., & Payne, A. M. (2024, 18 April). How can we have truth-telling without the Voice? Our research shows a way forward. *The Conversation*. https://theconversation.com/how-can-we-have-truth-telling-without-the-voice-our-research-shows-a-way-forward-226511. Accessed May 1, 2024.

Reynolds, H. (2022, 6 October). Recognising the warriors: Henry Reynolds on the war memorial's surprising change of direction. *The Conversation*. https://theconversation.com/recognising-the-warriors-henry-reynolds-on-the-war-memorials-surprising-change-of-direction-191861. Accessed May 1, 2024.

Rose, D. B. (2004). *Reports from a wild country: Ethics for decolonisation*. UNSW Press.

Rowe, A. C. (2010). Entering the Inter. In Nakayama, T. K., & Halualani R.T. (Eds.), *The Handbook of Critical Intercultural Communication*, Blackwell Publishing. https://doi.org/10.1002/978144 4390681.ch13

Ryan, L. (2020). Digital map of colonial frontier massacres in Australia 1788–1930. *Teaching History, 54*(3), 13–20.

Sharpe, C. (2016). *In the wake: On blackness and being*. Duke University Press.

Spiers, A., & Couzens, V. (2021). Making the law of the land visible: Vicki Couzens interviewed by Amy Spiers. In A. Spiers, C. Day, & C. Morton (Eds.), *Let's go outside: Art in public* (pp. 40–61). Monash University Publishing.

Smith, L. T. (1999). *Decolonising methodologies: Research and Indigenous peoples*. Zed Books.

Stanner, W. E. H. (1969) *After the dreaming; Black and white Australians—An anthropologist's view*. Boyer Lectures. The Australian Broadcasting Commission.

Veracini, L. (2023). Recognition beyond recognition! *Interventions*, 1–15.

Wellauer, K., Williams, C., & Brennan, B. (2023, 16 October). Why the Voice failed. *ABC News*. https://www.abc.net.au/news/2023-10-16/why-the-voice-failed/102978962. Accessed May 1, 2024.

Wolfe, P. (2006). Settler colonialism and the elimination of the native. *Journal of Genocide Research, 8*(4), 387–409.

Yoorrook Justice Commission. (2022). Yoorrook with purpose: Interim report June 2022. https://yoorrookjusticecommission.org.au/wp-content/uploads/2022/06/Yoorrook-Justice-Commission-Interim-Report.pdf. Accessed April 30, 2024.

Young, J. E. (2000). *At memory's edge: After-images of the Holocaust in contemporary art and architecture*. Yale University Press.

**Genevieve Grieves** is a Worimi woman from Southeast Australia currently based in Garramilla (Darwin). She is an award-winning artist, curator and content creator committed to sharing First Peoples' histories and cultures and interrogating colonising frameworks and practices. Her recent projects include *The Violence of Denial* exhibition (2017) as part of the Yirramboi Festival; *Barangaroo Ngangamay* (2016), a place-based Augmented Reality app that shares and celebrates the living cultures of Sydney Aboriginal women; and, she was the Lead Curator of the internationally celebrated permanent exhibition, *First Peoples* (2013), at the Melbourne Museum. She is a passionate advocator of decolonising and community-engaged practice and teaches these methodologies in university, institutional and community contexts. Her current role is co-founder and creative director of GARUWA, a First Nations storytelling agency.

**Amy Spiers** is an artist and researcher of settler descent, and currently a Vice Chancellor's Postdoctoral Fellow at RMIT School of Art. She has presented art projects across Australia and internationally, including at Australian Centre for Contemporary Art (ACCA), Monash University Museum of Art (Melbourne) and the 2015 Vienna Biennale. She has also published widely, including co-editing *Let's Go Outside: Art in Public* with Charlotte Day and Callum Morton for Monash University Museum of Art (Monash University Publishing 2022) and co-authoring the book, *Art/Work: Social Enterprise, Young Creatives and the Forces of Marginalisation*, with Grace McQuilten, Kim Humphery and Peter Kelly (Palgrave Pivot, 2022). Most recently, she was awarded a 2024 Australian Research Council Discovery Early Career Researcher Award (DECRA) to examine non-Indigenous artists' engagements with truth-telling Australia's colonial past through creative practice.

# Part I
# The Violence of Denial

# Chapter 2
# The Violence of Denial: Genevieve Grieves in conversation with Vicki Couzens and Julie Gough

**Genevieve Grieves, Vicki Couzens, and Julie Gough**

**Abstract** Worimi researcher, curator, artist and filmmaker, Genevieve Grieves, curated an exhibition in 2017, *The Violence of Denial*, at Arts House for Yirramboi First Nations arts festival based in Naarm (Melbourne). The exhibition showcased female and non-binary First Nations artists who work with screen-based media to disclose Australia's violent colonial past. The artists featured in the exhibition—Dianne Jones, Vicki Couzens, Julie Gough and r e a—are all engaged in regenerative acts of reviving First Peoples memory, story, culture and connection to Country to actively disrupt repressive settler colonial systems that refuse the violence of colonial occupation and erase First Peoples. *Part I* of this volume features three edited transcripts from the public talks program that took place during *The Violence of Denial* exhibition, that produced insightful conversations between Grieves and the participating artists, as well as Koori historian, academic and writer, Tony Birch. The transcripts reveal how artists resist colonial amnesia and engage in truth-telling through creative practice, while at the same time acknowledging the emotional cost of engaging in such memorial acts. In this first transcript, Genevieve Grieves yarns with artists Julie Gough (Trawlwoolway) and Vicki Couzens (Gunditjmara).

**Genevieve** I want to acknowledge the Country that we're on tonight and also acknowledge the wonderful artists of this exhibition *The Violence of Denial*. Tonight, we'll be speaking with two of its artists, Vicki Couzens and Julie Gough. It's been an incredible journey putting together this exhibition as a curator and spending time together. *The Violence of Denial* is an exhibition that I developed because I feel a passion for these stories and these histories and am also driven to respond to the

---

G. Grieves (✉)
GARUWA, Garramilla/Darwin, Australia
e-mail: genevieve@garuwa.com

V. Couzens
RMIT University, Naarm/Melbourne, Australia

J. Gough
Nipaluna/Hobart, Australia

© The Author(s), under exclusive license to Springer Nature Singapore Pte Ltd. 2024
G. Grieves and A. Spiers (eds.), *Art and Memorialisation*, Indigenous-Settler Relations in Australia and the World 6, https://doi.org/10.1007/978-981-97-6289-7_2

**Fig. 2.1** *The Violence of Denial* (2017) exhibition curated by Genevieve Grieves installation view at Arts House, exhibiting left to right: Julie Gough, *The Grounds for Surrender* (2011); r e a, *Poles Apart* (2009); Vicki Couzens, *pang-ngooteeweeng-wanoong (we remember)* (2017). Photograph Bryony Jackson. Image courtesy of Genevieve Grieves and Arts House

denial of our histories that aren't shared enough in educational institutions and across our memorial landscape almost anywhere. If anything, there's a deep resistance to these histories being told. I greatly admire the women in this exhibition and the continuous counter-resistance they undertake, often at great personal cost. They've mentored and inspired me in different ways, so I'm deeply honoured to have been able to bring them together in this exhibition (Fig. 2.1).

There's a lot of crossovers between your work, Vicki and Julie, but you're also quite different in the way that you make art. We might start with you, Julie. Can you talk just a little bit about who you are and the artwork you brought to *The Violence of Denial*?

**Julie** I'm honoured to be here on the Kulin Nation's grounds and pay respects to the Wurundjeri and Boonwurrung/Bunurong people and First Peoples all across Victoria. It's a huge pleasure and honour to be part of the exhibition so thanks to Genevieve, and creative producer Tara Prowse and everyone at Arts House. And thank you to my artist clan, you're part of it too, because that's how I feel about being in this world of art—I have my family, my extended family at home in Tasmania and I have my artist family; we work and we overlap and keep each other nourished in some way through life on this similar journey we're on.

I'm a Trawlwoolway woman on my mother's side. We've been in Tasmania for 45–50,000+ years, forever really. We are Trawlwoolway people and Tebrikunna is our home country in Northeast Lutruwita (Tasmania). My mum's family has lived around the Latrobe and Devonport region since the 1840s. Before then our family were removed to Flinders Island—it was very different circumstances for different ancestors, depending on their culture, particularly from the 1820s onwards. My dad was born in Glasgow, and his family is mostly Scottish and Irish.

I was born in Melbourne, and grew up here as a child, through the circumstances of my grandmother coming to Victoria from Latrobe, Tasmania to find work. So, my journey has been one of moving around Australia and to Tasmania as an adult. There are a lot of Tasmanian families who have moved back and forth, to and from Victoria, and mine is one of them. My mum, my dad, brother, stepmum are living in Tassie now, and it's been a series of returns and reconnections over a long period. My art-research also focusses on the same. I begin with my family, but in doing that I find our contemporary stories often mirror Ancestors before us, as well as the broader Aboriginal community.

Since 2009 I have regularly utilised the medium of video. It is a really useful way to share ideas about traversing time and place. Video assists me to understand and convey aspects of my family and community's experiences and history. Research is an integral part of the art process. For me, a great deal of the work is bringing together what families can offer or want to share about events, locations, memories and stories along with research drawn from archives. I re-connect these—place, stories, archival findings with objects that resonate, in a film or in a combined installation outcome. Sometimes reconnecting threads of stories, objects, traces on Country and in archives brings back into the light knowledge of something or someone or an event that is practically otherwise all but lost, and what seemed a dead-end becomes a new beginning.

**Genevieve** Vicki, could you introduce yourself, and your art?

**Vicki** I want to thank Arts House, Gen and my fellow artists for having us here. I feel very honoured to be included in this exhibition. I want to especially thank my family for turning up. Tonight's really exciting because we don't always get that chance for people to come and connect when we exhibit our art. Thanks for coming to listen to our stories. What underpins a lot of our work is getting these stories out, heard, shared and remembered so that they're not forgotten.

I'm a Gunditjmara woman from the Keeray Woorroong language group on my dad's side. And, again, I also have Scottish ancestry. Yes, so men in kilts are pretty cute and bagpipes—love them. My daughter Niyoka has been back over there to part of that Country where our Scottish ancestors have come from.

**Genevieve** And I've got Scottish ancestry too, so we can all go back together.

**Vicki** With the kind of work that Genevieve and I are doing on frontier violence for the museum,[1] we found out that the model used for the Native Police barracks here in Victoria was developed for the Highland clearances back in Scotland. The British

---

[1] Vicki and Genevieve both worked on the *First Peoples* exhibition, Bunjilaka Aboriginal Cultural Centre at Melbourne Museum.

**Fig. 2.2** *The Violence of Denial* (2017) exhibition installation view at Arts House exhibiting left and right: Julie Gough, *The Grounds for Surrender* (2011) and r e a, *Poles Apart* (2009). Photograph Bryony Jackson. Image courtesy of Genevieve Grieves and Arts House

created it and they came out and applied it here. So, we could go back for a lot of reasons.

**Genevieve** That's right. The Black Watch is a system that was developed by the British to control the people of Scotland, and in terms of the Australian version of this, the very first Native Police—based on this same system—were established right here in Melbourne. They were a very effective system for quashing resistance that was then used across the country.

Julie, your practice is very much engaged in history and in excavating the archive. You are constantly working through fragments, as you say, in the archive. How does your work, *The Grounds of Surrender*, fit into your practice (Fig. 2.2)?[2]

---

[2] Julie's work, *The Grounds for Surrender* (2011), is a 19 minute two channel video work, edited by Jemma Rea, that juxtaposes present day scenes of the regional town of Bothwell in Lutruwita (Tasmania), and surrounding farmlands, roads, bodies of water and barbeque areas, alongside quotes from early colonial records that describe conflict with First Peoples in the region and calls by colonisers for stronger measures to be taken to quash their resistance. The video opens with an image of the ornamental silver cup Bothwell residents presented to George Augustus Robinson in 1835 to thank him for his role in *conciliating* the Aboriginal people of Lutruwita, which effectively quelled the conflict by removing First Peoples, who had survived dispossession, murder and massacre, to Wybalenna (Flinders Island). *The Grounds of Surrender* (2011) can be viewed at Julie's YouTube channel: http://youtu.be/xSA4dAsTBPU.

**Julie** It's one of the works that involved all of those elements I mentioned because it started with an object, a silver cup. This cup was given to George Augustus Robinson who is infamous in both Victoria and Tasmania. Robinson was the government appointed *conciliator* from 1829-1842 in colonial Van Diemen's Land (Lutruwita/Tasmania) who was assigned with the task of finding a solution for the *problem* of Tasmanian Aboriginal people. His concluding determination, eventually, was our Ancestor's offshore detention on Flinders Island in Bass Strait. It is much more complex than that, but our exile was the result. And one town in Tasmania, Bothwell, gifted him this very expensive silver cup as a trophy, as a reward for his work in *conciliating* the Natives—in effect *moving them on,* pretty much. So, the cup became part of my obsession to work out the character of the town today, since I can't travel back to 1835. So, I kind of stalked the town in the film—I kept doing laps of the place in my car, sitting on hills nearby, scoping, trying to figure out why that particular town gifted Robinson this expensive cup.

The film expresses this idea that, for me, it feels possible to time travel sometimes through the archival records; the journey emerges from being there with them, as well as considering what fragments are elsewhere—in newspapers, etcetera, and trying to raise it up again into reconsideration. Associated objects seem to surface, or sometimes arrive first as something to compulsively think about, interrogate. Those colonial veils, hiding actions of absolute violence against First Peoples, lie not really that far below the surface—as far as I can see. It needs to be punctured.

Bothwell is a small town about an hour northwest of Hobart. It has a Scottish colonist history. The street signs are patterned tartan. It feels heavy and secretive. It seems a ghost town. This work, *The Grounds of Surrender* (2011), and its research led to other artworks, as is always the case, none exist in isolation but are part of a continuum. I subsequently made a video work apparently about barbeque areas called *Hunting Ground incorporating Barbeque Area* (2014)—against this absence of people, there are places to sit at picnic tables.[3] I came upon at the Clyde River at Bothwell, a sort of flood scene, a picnic table was immersed underwater, and it reminded me of this Danish television horror series by Lars von Trier, *The Kingdom* (1994-2022). It kind of confirmed my feeling that it's a sick and haunted place—all of Tasmania is—but Bothwell feels especially like that for me. Barbeque areas appear

---

[3] In a mixed media installation and ten minute video work, *Hunting Ground incorporating Barbeque Area* (2014), Julie reflects upon the seemingly innocuous barbeque and picnic areas that colonisers have erected around Lutruwita (Tasmania). By directing an estranging attention to them, Julie transforms these picturesque recreational sites into something uneasy and crude, prompting consideration on how they are erected on landscapes that are imbued with trauma, violence, loss and resistance for Palawa of Lutruwita (Tasmania). In an artist statement Julie has said of the work: 'For the love of country, Aboriginal Tasmanians fought to the death at places such as these. BBQ areas retain an uncanny independence from other built environments. They offer free fuel at the push of a button, welcoming everyone to cook anything on a stainless steel plate whose central drainage hole seems simultaneously medical and military. These sites might appear innocuous, democratic, nurturing. For me, however, they express loss of original people from country. Rarely occupied, they appear a cruel recreational, amnesiac joke. For what reason did wholesale slaughter occur across my island—for this—designated BBQ areas?' (Gough, 2014). The video work can be viewed on Julie's YouTube channel: http://youtu.be/k8peyCLLXsM.

**Fig. 2.3** Julie Gough, *Hunting Ground incorporating Barbeque Area* (2014) video stills. Image courtesy of the artist

to me to be both memorials to, and erasures of, the attempted genocide of Aboriginal people by colonists.

**Genevieve** And you've got a shot in there where you are actually in the work, in a kangaroo skin cloak. In this exhibition, all of the artists are so present in their works but I was surprised to see you in this one.

**Julie** It's my secret—my Hitchcock moment. In *Hunting Ground incorporating Barbeque Area* (2014) there is a fleeting shot of me sitting, back to camera, in a hand sewn kangaroo fur coat at a barbeque area picnic table in the town of Oatlands (Fig. 2.3). In some films, I'm attempting something I call the 'impossible return'. I have this hope—I keep trying to literally time travel. In another film *Traveller* (2013) I am hitchhiking with all the gear and trying to get somewhere—but people don't want to stop and pick you up when you're carrying spears.[4] It is a kind of pilgrimage with purpose film, I visit a range of places of historic violence towards finally burying a volume of *Friendly mission*, a compilation of journals and papers by Robinson (1966). The film consists of various sequences from hitchhiking unsuccessfully, entering a cave, laying down in a forest to rest with my furs and spears, and finally burying the book.

**Genevieve** Vicki, your practice is so broad, it's sometimes hard to describe all the things that you do and put that under the category of art. How do you see and explain your practice?

**Vicki** I was never really quite comfortable calling myself an artist for a long time. And I thought: 'I must be, everyone says I am. And I sold a few paintings and I'm in exhibitions, so I must be'. I'm back to a point where I'm not comfortable with that label because it's not really what I do. I don't make art. I haven't been to art school and I'm not trained. I prefer to use the term 'creative cultural expression' to describe

---

[4] Julie Gough's *Traveller* (2013) is an eight hour 43 minute video projection, edited by Jemma Rea. The artwork can be viewed on Julie's Youtube channel: http://youtu.be/aoWJdRBVafw.

what I do. But I do enjoy exploring different creative mediums and I've been given lots of opportunities to work in mediums like glass work or printmaking. I don't really have time to go back to school and learn how to do the whole thing, so I work with a master printer, I work with sculptors, and design public art.

**Genevieve** Your work does exist beyond the framework of *art* as it's also deeply cultural and embodied, it's not just what you do, it's part of who you are…

**Vicki** Fundamentally, I think like all the other artists in the exhibition, and a lot of people I know, in our work—it's about that reconnecting, telling those stories and keeping those stories alive and having that legacy for the future, which underpins and drives what I do in the work. I work in language reclamation as well, because our dad (Elder Ivan Couzens) started that 21 years ago. I think we need to have a celebration of that and honour him and that outcome that the Gunditjmara mob have access to our language and a language worker, someone dedicated to working on our language.

So revitalising language and possum skin cloakmaking has been a central part of what I've been doing for the last seven years working across Southeast Australia. But I'm always wanting to explore new mediums. I have a partner who does a bit of film and he's a muso and songwriter. I've been working on *Leempeeyt Weeyn*, a campfire event for *The Light in Winter* festival at Fed Square. It's allowed me to go a bit further with the mediums of projection light and sound. The work here in *The Violence of Denial* is the third kind of work, if you like, that I've made that's for an art exhibition.

**Genevieve** Can you tell us about your work in the exhibition?[5]

**Vicki** Julie, you talked about being in your work, and I am in my work—I didn't think about it, I just did it. I wanted this figure to be remembering because the work is all about remembering and honouring the stories of our people who fought and died defending Country from invaders. We actually got some other footage and then we lost it. And so we had to go out last minute and do this, which is actually perfect. Way better than what we did the first time. We added the sound with language speaking to what we remember… (Fig. 2.4).

**Genevieve** Could you share that language phrase with us?

**Vicki** *pang-ngooteeweeng-wanoong.* Or remember. We remember.

**Genevieve** So, both of you in different ways delve into history and into telling *our* versions of history and our stories. What are some of the challenges that you find in

---

[5] In Couzen's work for *The Violence of Denial* exhibition, *pang-ngooteeweeng-wanoong (we remember)* (2017), a possum skin cloak honouring Gunditjmara funeral and burial practices is suspended in the exhibition space. A two minute video showing Couzen's gazing over Gunditjmara Country is projected onto the cloak, accompanied by audio of Couzen speaking her Gunditjmara language. Eight possum skin mourning bags, which Gunditjmara mourners would wear to carry ashes of the deceased, are arranged upon a circle of soil beneath the cloak.

**Fig. 2.4** Vicki Couzens, *pang-ngooteeweeng-wanoong (we remember)* (2017). *The Violence of Denial* (2017) exhibition installation view at Arts House. Photograph Bryony Jackson. Image courtesy of Genevieve Grieves and Arts House

presenting these works, in delving into these spaces, in uncovering particularly these histories of violence and these traumatic stories?

**Julie** I think a problem if you work with history, as an artist, and are not very explicit is that viewer-visitors can miss the meaning or intention from not knowing the context and background. But if you worry too much about that, then there is a danger of allowing your creative work to change into being an educational resource. A lot of the work I've been making is shining a light on or sending back out information that is hidden in the archives, of what colonists did, what colonists said. When I'm in that mode, I need to get out more, undertake more walking, feeling and thinking to avoid being laden by the general lack of public knowledge about the cross-cultural history of this continent, and to not try to rectify it. So, I keep re-directing what I find in archives to the outside world, but try to avoid didacticism. I have some examples of works, though, where viewers didn't get the context of my references, and their reception went pear-shaped.

The first video I created was called *Driving Black Home* (2009).[6] I drove through all the counties of Tasmania—it is split up into these English-style counties, it's this crazy omelette of counties. Then I transcribed all of the land grants given to colonists in Van Diemen's Land from 1804 to 1832, the span of time by which most

---

[6] Julie Gough, *Driving Black Home* (2009) is a three hour 43 minute silent colour video, edited by Nancy Mauro-Flude. The artwork can be viewed on Julie's Youtube channel: https://youtu.be/wCR BYw5k2DE?si=D3mWOtGI_IuI90L0

of our Aboriginal Ancestors had been killed or exiled from mainland Tasmania. This land grant information became the subtitles of the film, and ran along the bottom. It detailed what land went to what names and how much acreage, and matched the video footage of the Country I drove through. The film is three hours and 43 minutes long, which only myself and the film editor suffered through. It has no real start or end point, within five minutes you witness visually and textually the vast loss of what has been taken from Aboriginal people, and by who.

The first time I showed the film was in an exhibition in a colonial home—the group exhibition *TRUST* (2009) at Clarendon House—that offered the chance to disrupt the usual mainstream reading of the colonial estate, Clarendon, on the Nile River, near Evandale, Tasmania. The film was projected in the basement and linked to the notion that things are not right in the plumbing, the underbelly of the place. I found out later that all the local landholders were coming in and spending hours proudly waiting for their ancestors' names to turn up on screen. I should have just locked them all in there, turned the volume up really loud, thrown away the key. It backfired.

**Genevieve** So, you try to uncover the scale of loss and then it becomes a celebration…

**Julie** They didn't get it. So, I need to figure out ways to change what I present and think more about where I present it.

**Vicki** Just listening to Julie is reminding me of the things that you do read and find in archives, like a letter our grandfather wrote in 1940, published in *The Warrnambool Standard*. He was writing about the same issues that we're still dealing with now around housing, government policies and government funding, and I used the letter in an artwork many years ago. I learned through these stories the importance of education, so I'm finally doing a PhD. My dad's been a big inspiration in teaching, guiding and learning things, and central to my journey of working in community and giving back.

It informed my work on battles and massacres for the *Stony Rises* exhibition at RMIT Gallery in 2010.[7] The cloak on display in *The Violence of Denial* was also part of that work, but it's morphed for the exhibition into something else to explore our mourning and burial practices (Fig. 2.5).

When there's a site of violence and people die, survivors aren't always given the chance to mourn their family properly. Mourning should be a process of healing and

---

[7] For the *Stony Rises* exhibition, Couzens developed works drawing on stories her father told her about battles and massacres that took place on Gunditjmara Country in the early days of European invasion and to acknowledge the Old People who fought and died defending their Country. For the exhibition, Couzens produced a series of white wooden crosses, creating photographs of the crosses positioned near Country that experienced frontier violence, and inscribing the memorials with the names and details of Aboriginal people 'killed by whites'. These works that include *Tarnbeere gundidj* (2009) (see Fig 2.8) respond to a white wooden cross that has been erected by the roadside near Port Fairy memorialising a coloniser: 'George Whatmore, speared by blacks 1841'. Couzens also created for the exhibition *prangawan pootpakyooyano yoowa* (2009), a possum skin cloak used in Gunditjmara funeral rites. For further information see *Stony Rises Project* information at the RMIT Gallery website: https://rmitgallery.com/exhibitions/stony-rises-project/.

**Fig. 2.5** Vicki Couzens, *prangawan pootpakyooyano yoowa* (2009). Possum skin cloak, 150 × 110cm. Image courtesy of the artist

dealing with your grief and moving on. The funeral rites of the person who has died are so important for them to continue onto their journey, and that hasn't happened in those sites of violence. So I looked into what our funeral and burial practices are from the perspective of: what are the things that we can reclaim, reactivate and revitalise and bring back into practice, like possum cloaks and language? There are some practices you might not want to bring back that emerged with the advent of Christianity and missions—the mob here will know about the song, 'The Old Rugged Cross'—it's at every funeral you go to.

When someone dies, we mostly go to a church or a chapel and it's run by white funeral directors; they sing hymns and the minister talks about everything *but* the person, and I just find it unsatisfactory. How does that help our people who have passed into their next journey? And how does that help you move through your grief and to heal? What can we do? For example, we can use whiteface (white ochre)—white is our mourning colour, not black. So what are those things and what are the songs and what are the words—the words in our language? Because those things are what resonate with us and what resonate with where you're from.

So, you made me think Julie about *why* we make the work? The massacre work was primarily made for the mainstream audience to reflect back on. But I make most of my other work for us, Gunditjmara. And I'm in an exhibition, so I get to share that with you. But I'm actually in a mode where I'm focusing the majority of my attention on us and what we need to learn and reclaim in my own family.

Kelsey, my niece, my younger sister Lisa's daughter, trained to be a teacher and might become a language teacher one day if I can no longer keep that living repository. I don't want my great-grandchildren having to go through books to learn stuff about their families or to retrieve the language. Like our dad wrote in the Keerray Woorooong and Related Dialects dictionary, what prompted him was going to meetings where he was either the only Aboriginal person or one of the few Aboriginal people in the room who couldn't say who he was or where he was from in his own language whereas other mobs could. There's healing that comes with us taking back our stories, our language and our knowledge.

**Genevieve** Your work is so deeply restoring and evident in the possum skin cloaks and the mourning bags in your piece. Can you describe what they are?

**Vicki** They're representations of mourning bags that my sister helped with, one of the practices where we would carry cremated remains around for a number of months, or over a year sometimes. I learned this from a description in a historical record. I've never seen one (Fig. 2.6).

**Genevieve** One of the amazing things we see here in Victoria in that possum skin journey that's been going for so many years now is that people are now being buried in possum skin, it's a beautiful restoration of that practice.

**Vicki** A big part of this is that we don't need anyone's permission for that. We don't need *recognition* and the constitution or anything to do those things—it might help, but we can do it anyway!

**Genevieve** Absolutely. Both of you work deeply with place. I'm really interested in these sites in the landscape—sites of violence—and how we even find them, because they're often hard to find. But then what's held within them is trauma—how do you connect with them and how do you look after yourself? How do we make them visible? Or put another way, how do we manage these places of deep trauma?

**Julie** There are two recent works I have made about *return*. For example, return is about returning stone tools to Country. So that's something I'm thinking about a lot because the *Aboriginal Relics Act* is up for review in Tasmania this year. This legislation was passed in 1975 and in effect renders anything made by Aboriginal people after 1876 as not Aboriginal heritage or belonging to Aboriginal people, including Ancestral remains. There are a few reasons why this law is ludicrous, but

**Fig. 2.6** Vicki Couzens, *pang-ngooteeweeng-wanoong (we remember)* (2017). *The Violence of Denial* (2017) exhibition installation detail depicting the mourning bags. Photograph Bryony Jackson. Image courtesy of Genevieve Grieves and Arts House

not recognising that *any* living Tasmanian Aboriginal people can make *anything* Aboriginal is way out of line.[8]

If any Tasmanian Aboriginal cultural heritage is desecrated at the moment, the fines are very small. Meanwhile, permits to destroy are being issued all the time around Tasmania when no evidence of Aboriginal occupation, of cultural heritage on the land can be demonstrated. Yet Tasmania was flooded by the hydroelectric scheme which covered up a lot of our ancestral places. As well there are tens of thousands—more than tens of thousands—of stone tools from Tasmania in museums around the world, and probably just as many held in the two museums and other institutions within Tasmania. There are quite a number of them with locations named on them, from where they were picked up. It is a concern of mine, just how to return them, and as well, document where they are held, what they are and name the places they come from, which new technology can assist with by matching stone tools to their original quarry sites.

---

[8] The *Aboriginal Relics Act 1975* was amended in 2017. Changes to the legislation included renaming the act to the *Aboriginal Heritage Act*, increasing penalties for damage to Aboriginal heritage to become on par with penalties related to non-Aboriginal heritage and the removal of a problematic 1876 cut-off date that deemed anything made by Tasmanian Aboriginal people after 1876 as not Tasmanian Aboriginal heritage. 1876 is notably the year Truganini died, a woman who was incorrectly considered the last Tasmanian Aboriginal. For further information see the Tasmanian Government Aboriginal Heritage website (2023): https://www.aboriginalheritage.tas.gov.au/legislation.

**Fig. 2.7** Julie Gough, *The Lost World (part 2)* (2013) video still. Image courtesy of the artist

I made the film *Lost World (Part 2)*[9] in 2013, following an artist residency at the Museum of Archaeology and Anthropology at Cambridge University, England. The work was presented in a simultaneous exhibition of the same name in 2013 at the museum in Cambridge as well as Contemporary Art Tasmania in Hobart. To make the work I returned to Tasmania with photographs of 35 ancestral stone tools that are held in that Cambridge collection. I filmed myself leaving photographs of the tools, that I couldn't bring back to Tasmania, at the places where I think they were from across my island. I then returned to Cambridge, England and projected the film next to the real stone tools—the idea was that those tools could hear their original homes. As an artist there is this potential to bring attention or focus to matters of concern, a strange power to make people think, hopefully (Fig. 2.7).

Walking around Tasmania, this artwork-making brings me back to Country, yet not all of it is *my* traditional Country because my people are from Northeast Tasmania. And as far as I understand it, our Ancestors are from the Northeast because the rest of the Old People were killed (or *disappeared* according to the textbooks, *elsewhere*, an alien abduction or something). So, we survivors are responsible for all of Tasmania now. And this also feels quite problematic. Like we're responsible and caring for Country. There are also dangerous places that are so full of anguish from the violence that we have to learn them anew. So, returning the tool idea—this idea of the ongoing interim of their lives in exile—has brought me to greet Country in a different way.

---

[9] Julie Gough, *The Lost World (part 2)* (2013), one hour 15 minute colour video, edited by Jemma Rea. View the artwork on Julie's YouTube channel: http://youtu.be/HGMZrZRga3M.

A good but sad update, saying: 'here I am, and I know that this tool should be here, and I'm bringing this photograph in the meantime'.

Another work I made more recently was about places of massacre. In my research into personal, media and government accounts, I easily found more than 80 recorded massacres in Tasmania (if a massacre is understood as the deliberate murder of more than one person). In the work, *Hunting Ground (Haunted) Van Diemen's Land* (2016), I printed a range of texts that described the violence against our Old People in the colonists' words and placed them in the landscape.[10] But the feeling one has is that if there are 80 that are written about that I could find quickly, there are 800 that aren't written about.

**Vicki** That is sad about the stone tools.

**Julie** It really is, and it should be necessary for heritage officers to have access to the records of tools in collections internationally, and their original locations, and say, 'well we know that from this area there's 400 stone tools in twenty institutions around the world, there is clear evidence of Aboriginal occupation in that area', and that should be reported and prevent destruction of Country.

**Vicki** But our Ancestors' remains are the priority as well—many of them are still in overseas institutions.

**Julie** Yes, shockingly. Also our cultural objects. I'm looking at the tools thinking maybe they'll come back without a struggle. I'm also aware and wary of causing any issues with what is going on with the repatriation processes for Ancestral remains. In Tasmania that's a clear process that has been happening since the 1970s. But there's always more people to be found as well. They're not all known about yet.

**Vicki** No.

**Julie** Are there places and stories, Vicki, that you've been connecting within your Country?

**Vicki** The massacre and battles work for the *Stony Rises* exhibition that I was talking about deals with a little white cross beside a road on the main highway, just outside Port Ferry. Its inscription says, 'George Whatmore, speared by blacks 1841' and there was a little plaque on it added more recently that notes that someone from Portland had been over to restore and repaint it. And I'm thinking: 'are they serious?' I really couldn't quite believe it was still there. I know there was a mob in Portland that did a big thing about it back in the eighties, but it's the first time I'd seen it.

Dad had a strong passion for memorial sites and he really wanted to see memorials to our Old People who died fighting for Country, not just to those who died in overseas wars like the Anzac stuff. So I made this series of photographic works—which wasn't in a place, I've still got to do that, but using digital prints—based on this cross. I took

---

[10] Julie Gough, *Hunting Ground (Haunted) Van Diemen's Land* (2016) is a 13:16 minute HDMI video projection, 16:9, colour, sound, edited by Angus Ashton accompanied by 10 prints, 462 × 329 mm, BFK Rives paper 280gsm, printed by Cicada Press. The video can be viewed on Julie's YouTube channel: https://youtu.be/1mBvRpGuGAI

**Fig. 2.8** Vicki Couzens, *Tarnbeere Gundidj* (2010). Digital image on paper, 90 × 60cm. Image courtesy of the artist

a photo of George's cross and I digitally superimposed the cross on photographs of sites where massacres of our people occurred (Fig. 2.8). For exhibition, I placed a burial possum skin cloak alongside these images. Genevieve and I recently went out there to look at the cross again and it's been painted, all brand spanking new.

**Genevieve** It's particularly interesting because it's the only memorial to any violence at all in the Western District…

**Vicki** It's this little white object, now lost in the grass if you don't know where it is. But that prompted that work and it was my first step towards creating a memorial with dad's idea in mind. I'm working with my cousin John Clare to look at the Murdering Gully massacre down there and trying to do a memorial on Country.[11]

**Genevieve** I know both of you in different ways are working with or searching for people from the other side, or meeting people from the other side, by which I mean descendants of the perpetrators of this violence. You both have different experiences and stories of that. Can you share some of those stories?

**Julie** Another work, *The Gathering* (2015), involves an installation of a large antique dining table gridded with wooden crosses upon it, and a video projection behind the table.[12] Each cross features the name of a Tasmanian property established between the 1820s–1830s and holds a stone I gathered from the entry area at each of those homesteads. The video shows footage I made whilst driving to these properties—a lot of driving. I stop at the gates and show the signs that name these places and link them directly back to the violence that seems otherwise silenced. The colonial land owners demanded the removal of Tasmanian Aboriginal people from our island— these colonists were heavily involved in the subsequent drawing up the 'Military Operations against the Aboriginal Inhabitants of Van Diemen's Land', the title of the official map of the campaign by Government Surveyor, George Frankland (1830) that was forwarded to British authorities in Whitehall.

Over 6 weeks in late 1830 colonists, their convict servants and retired military undertook to drive Aboriginal people southeast onto the Tasman Peninsula and into captivity. It eventually worked because 16 months later the last (then) known group of Aboriginal people remaining at large in Tasmania walked to Hobart to make a treaty (records of which have not yet resurfaced) with the Governor. To think of this as a military campaign and war is important. This language is real. And it was real not just from our perspective but made so by the colonists themselves.

A woman in Sydney wanted to meet me not long ago, who was a descendant of these perpetrators. I don't know the extent of what she knew about what had happened with her Ancestors and Aboriginal people and the place, but she was in tears. This sort of thing has happened a lot since the mid-nineties—this *moment together*. And I'm not sure what we're meant to do, but there's *something* we're meant to do which I suppose is to meet each other. It's not only been my experience that people want forgiveness, there's something else. I'd be interested to hear if your meetings with the descendants of the people that met or shot your people are the same, Vicki.

**Vicki** There are a couple of people I've met, again, when I moved back home and was working with dad. I met an amazing woman, a little tiny Sicilian powerhouse

---

[11] At Puuroyup (Murdering Gully in Victoria's Western District), 35 Tarnbeere Gundidj people were massacred by a group of colonisers led by Frederick Taylor in 1839.

[12] Julie Gough, *The Gathering* (2015), 18:13 minute HDMI video, H264, 1080P, colour, sound, edited by Jemma Rea. Installation includes a table, enamel on Tasmanian oak, 28 found stones, variable dimensions, collection of the artist. The video work can be viewed on Julie's YouTube channel: https://youtu.be/N9nPR4m1eN0.

she was. And she was married into one of the original colonising families in the region. And I've since met several of the others through her. All these women that I've met are actually really proactive in community development and reconciliation and more. And I haven't got to talking a lot, but I've had those contacts and we've been able to use them in the work we're doing now.

I was reading a book when I was 16 and I found a description of a white man who pleaded guilty and was charged for killing two Aboriginal people near Warrnambool, which is where we are from. The guy who was charged had the same family name as my mum's family. There's no oral history that I'm aware of in the family, but I'm quite interested to dig around a little bit more. There are things you want to know, but you've got your mum's family too who you don't want to upset. This history is filled with stories and gets more complex when you start to dig. I pointed this out to mum and dad at the time because none of us knew, and their response was that it was weird to now be married and to have kids—that times change.

But it's bizarre that as you get older and think about it and you learn more about your own stories and history, then actually *understanding* the impacts and that it *really* meant that you weren't considered a citizen until 1967. Because I was born prior to that in case you couldn't tell! And around that time they bought out Advance Australia Fair, so I was in the principal's office for not standing up during the national anthem at school.

**Genevieve** Any last statements from the two of you?

**Vicki** I've got my family that always keeps you going. You just have to keep the stories alive—I'm not gonna be erased from history. I draw strength from my family and my dad and my grandparents and my mum too; we've always had their love and support. So, I feel that responsibility because I'm here and able to talk to you, for and on behalf of our Ancestors.

I've made a conscious decision to make sure that what I know is handed on to my family, so the story continues. At the same time, I have been thankful that some cultural objects and things have been acquired so it's a legacy right into the future and doesn't just get lost in my great grandkids' garage. But the rest of it, I really want to share with my family. That's my priority.

But then if I'm on Country, living on Country, walking on Country, I don't have to be doing some great big ceremony to heal the Country. Of course, we can do that. And that does happen through ceremony and we do have gatherings in ceremony so that happens. But for me, just being on Country and going to visit places, that nourishes me. It's reciprocal.

**Julie** You find what you're meant to do, your path, from being unable to stop doing it. It does slowly change through time, probably when there's some learning and personal development, some progress. So, I'm on that journey of trying not to direct things too much, because a work will turn into its next iteration, something always happens and emerges, in its own time. You make what you're meant to and the idea determines what the medium is. So, I don't feel fixed, but rather more led to do each work.

I don't have kids, and my brother doesn't have kids, and we're the only two. So, it's interesting, like what is the future, and whose future do I hope I am positively contributing to? It feels a bit global. My cat's not very cultural!

**Vicki** Put him in possum fur.

**Julie** I chose Harry, my cat, because he looks like a possum! And the future unfolds. My brother works in education and with kids and making objects that people share. I find working with children exhausting, but I'm living through his experience of that world. I'm more reclusive and I'm on another parallel journey. Vicki, you are managing both ways, educating and making art, which is impressive.

**Vicki** Thanks Julie. I think we have to do it every way; things have to happen on all fronts and in every way. It's about the healing. You tell the stories, we get that out there, you meet people and you create healing for people and Country. So that's one of the things that keeps me going.

**Julie** The more I think about and read and access archives, I notice how little there is by Aboriginal people in Tasmania—either published or oral and archived histories. I look for family stories and so many have gone with people who have passed. There's this sense of: 'they knew some things and they died last year'. I have an anxiety that I'm often stuck in the colonial archives of the 1820s and 30s but I probably should also be attending to *now* and our living archives.

## References

Gough, J. (2014). Artist statement. *Gallery Gabrielle Pizzi*. http://www.gabriellepizzi.com.au/art ists/gabriellepizzi_julie_gough.html. Accessed July 7, 2023.

Robinson, G. A. (1966). *Friendly mission: The Tasmanian journals and papers of George Augustus Robinson, 1829–1834*. In N.J.B. Plomley (Ed.), Tasmanian Historical Research Association.

Tasmanian Government. (2023). Legislation: The aboriginal heritage act 1975. *Aboriginal Heritage Tasmania*. https://www.aboriginalheritage.tas.gov.au/legislation. Accessed January 25, 2024.

**Genevieve Grieves** is a Worimi woman from Southeast Australia currently based in Garramilla (Darwin). She is an award-winning artist, curator and content creator committed to sharing First Peoples histories and cultures and interrogating colonising frameworks and practices. Her recent projects include *The Violence of Denial* exhibition (2017) as part of the Yirramboi Festival; *Barangaroo Ngangamay* (2016), a place-based Augmented Reality app that shares and celebrates the living cultures of Sydney Aboriginal women; and, she was the Lead Curator of the internationally celebrated permanent exhibition, *First Peoples* (2013), at the Melbourne Museum. She is a passionate advocate of decolonising and community-engaged practice and teaches these methodologies in university, institutional and community contexts. Her current role is co-founder and creative director of GARUWA, a First Nations storytelling agency.

**Vicki Couzens** is a Keerray Wooroong Gunditjmara woman from the Western Districts of Victoria, Australia. Vicki acknowledges her Ancestors and Elders who guide her work. She has worked in Aboriginal community affairs for over 45 years and her contributions in the reclamation, regeneration and revitalisation of cultural knowledge and practice extend across the arts and creative, cultural expression spectrum including language revitalisation, ceremony, community arts, public art, visual and performing arts, and writing. Vicki is Senior Knowledge Custodian for Possum Skin Cloak Story and Language Reclamation and Revival in her Keerray Wooroon Mother Tongue.

**Julie Gough** is a Trawlwoolway (Tasmanian Aboriginal) artist, writer and curator. She is Trawlwoolway through her maternal family, and her Traditional homeland is Tebrikunna in far north eastern Lutruwita (Tasmania), with her extended family living in the Latrobe/East Devonport region since the 1840s. Gough's research and art process involves uncovering and re-presenting often conflicting and subsumed histories, some referring to her family's experiences as Tasmanian Aboriginal people. Gough completed a PhD, University of Tasmania (2001) and MA, Goldsmiths College, University of London (1998). Since 1991, Julie has exhibited in more than 20 solo and 180 group exhibitions and her work is held in numerous state and national collections.

# Chapter 3
# The Violence of Denial: Genevieve Grieves in Conversation with Dianne Jones and r e a

**Genevieve Grieves, Dianne Jones, and r e a**

**Abstract** Continuing *Part I* of this volume is the second of three edited transcripts of the public talks program that took place during *The Violence of Denial*, an exhibition curated by Worimi researcher, curator, artist and filmmaker, Genevieve Grieves at Arts House for Yirramboi First Nations arts festival, Naarm (Melbourne) in 2017. In this second talk transcript, Genevieve Grieves discusses artworks from the exhibition, *PolesApart* (2009) and *found objects from what lies buried rises* (2017), with artists r e a (Gamilaraay/Wailwan/Biripi) and Dianne Jones (Ballardong) and the creative processes and stories of colonial violence that informs them.

**Genevieve** So it's been my absolute honour to be a part of this exhibition, *The Violence of Denial*, and to bring together these incredible women and non-binary artists who I admire and who I've learned from in so many different ways. This is a gathering with friends really. I'm excited that you are going to have a chance to hear from a couple of them tonight. I'm going to hand over first to r e a to talk a bit about their work, and then to Dianne.

**r e a** I just wanted to pay my respects to the Wurundjeri people and to the Boon Wurrung as well. It's been an amazing time here at the Yirramboi Festival and I'd like to thank them for welcoming me here to their Country. I think one of the things that Indigenous artists really struggle with is when we are invited to go to festivals, we're not sure if there's going to be an Indigenous delegation there to welcome us or if there are people we can connect with from Country. It's always great when there is an Indigenous presence, we know that we are part of something, like this really great Yirramboi festival. I'm just going to connect some of my earlier works

---

G. Grieves (✉)
GARUWA, Garramilla/Darwin, Australia
e-mail: genevieve@garuwa.com

D. Jones
Naarm/Melbourne, Australia

r e a
Gundungurra Country/Hazelbrook, Australia

© The Author(s), under exclusive license to Springer Nature Singapore Pte Ltd. 2024
G. Grieves and A. Spiers (eds.), *Art and Memorialisation*, Indigenous-Settler Relations in Australia and the World 6, https://doi.org/10.1007/978-981-97-6289-7_3

to this particular work, the *PolesApart series* (2009), that I am showing as part of *The Violence of Denial* exhibition.[1] And then engage in dialogue around the work and the context of the show that we've been invited by Genevieve to be part of here at Arts House.

I've known all of these artists at different times and during different periods of my practice, but I've never been in a show like this in my 28+ years of practice. I'm saying 'no' quite a lot to showing the *PolesApart* series at the moment, it's a bit overexposed, and most people think it's just a video work, but it's part of a larger body or work. However, in the context of this show, it was important to participate because it is profiling video work and it's also looking at the content in relation to what *PolesApart* is about (Fig. 3.1).

The first piece of work that I made back in 1992 when I was emerging as a new media artist was called *Look Who's Calling The Kettle Black* series.[2] My grandmother is in this series, she is the yellow kettle. She's an important matriarch in my family, the person who I had a really special relationship with. Even though she was part of the Stolen Generation, she had a strong connection to her Country, her family, and she carried this heritage with her. This creative work is fitting in the context of this show, and important in relation to violence because I watched my grandmother, and most of the women in my family, suffer domestic violence. And when they weren't actually dealing with domestic violence, they were dealing with the violence of institutions and organisations.

The interesting thing about that particular work, *Look Who's Calling The Kettle Black,* is that, when I first made it, I invited my grandmother to the show—she was still alive then. When she came to this —my first show —she wouldn't come into the gallery. She came in briefly saw the work and she wouldn't come back in. I just thought she didn't really like the work. My mum was there and I asked her, 'what's happening?' And she said, 'Nan won't come in because she's worried that if the police turn up and see that work on the wall, that they're gonna arrest us all'—because the work was actually profiling the women in their working roles. The women in each

---

[1] *PolesApart* (2009), is a multimedia artwork by r e a featuring a 6:55 minute silent HD video of a figure—played by the artist r e a—dressed in a black nineteenth-century gown running through a bushfire-blackened forest fleeing or escaping something not shown but clearly malevolent. The video work is often accompanied by four triptychs of large-scale C-type photographs also depicting the figure trying to find their way out of the forest, alongside the gown r e a created collaboratively with Melbourne designer, Amanda Fairbanks. Grieves has noted that the fleeing figure in *PolesApart* 'could be caught in time, the ghost of an Ancestor escaping the violence of settlers—an all too common story in our nation's history'. At the video's culmination, Grieves notes, 'we are shifted into an entirely different paradigm as [r e a's] body is repeatedly splattered with red, white and blue paint', and is a commentary on the whiteness of Australian art that attempts to paint Aboriginal people out of the landscape. Grieves has observed, the video was filmed 'in a landscape in Victoria, near the region where the famous "Heidelberg School" artists painted. Their popular depictions of the Australian pioneer experience omitted any representation of Aboriginal people or life, creating a white fantasy of possession and belonging. [r e a] runs through this Country to reject this. To say, I am here, we are here and you can't deny our existence any longer' (Grieves, 2020).

[2] *Look Who's Calling The Kettle Black* series (1992) is an artwork comprised of a series of digitally generated prints that combine brightly coloured images of domestic appliances, including an iron, a toaster and a kettle, with historical black and white images of First Peoples in domestic service and dictionary-style definitions of terms associated with domestic servitude.

**Fig. 3.1** *The Violence of Denial* (2017) exhibition curated by Genevieve Grieves installation view at Arts House, exhibiting left to right: Julie Gough, *The Grounds for Surrender* (2011); r e a, *PolesApart* (2009); Vicki Couzens, *pang-ngooteeweeng-wanoong (we remember)* (2017). Photograph Bryony Jackson. Image courtesy of Genevieve Grieves and Arts House

of the single images, were all women from Cootamundra Aboriginal Girls' Home.[3] Nan was of that generation (c. 1915) where you couldn't really expose this kind of history in the way that I was in 1992.

I was invited to make a new body of work titled: *EYE/I'MMABLAKPIECE* for my first major festival solo exhibition for Adelaide Festival in 1996.[4] Later that year my grandmother passed away. This work was about paying homage to the *loss* of identity and the *loss* of growing up without culture for my grandmother, who didn't have the opportunity to grow up on Country before colonisation, her life would have been so different, our lives would also have been different.

---

[3] Cootamundra Aboriginal Girls' Home located in Cootamundra, New South Wales was a place where Aboriginal girls, who had been forcibly removed from their families, were trained to become domestic servants for wealthy families from 1911 to 1968.

[4] *EYE/I'MMABLAKPIECE* (1996) was comprised of an installation and four-part digital photographic series that traced colonial history inscribed on the blak female body. Three images in the series depicted a headless black mannequin wearing a floral dress and a necklace of varying materials. The floral dress is typical of those worn by Aboriginal women in outback communities and represents the body as the site of various colonial constructs, from 'Traditional' (represented by a wooden beaded necklace), 'Christianity' (a necklace of rosary beads and a cross) to 'Civilization' (a pearl necklace). 'Blakpiece', the fourth image in the series, presents a subversion of these oppressive codes, and depicts the artist stepping into the frame to take control of their image, the camera and their representation.

**Fig. 3.2** r e a, *PolesApart* (2009), video still. Image courtesy of the artist

There is deliberately no body in *EYE/I'MMABLAKPIECE* because the blak body has been 'whited' out of the Australia landscape. The layers reflect on what I'm left with as an Indigenous artist, this work is the beginning of a new story for the next generation in my family. I am the blak piece (body) putting these new pieces together. The images don't have much colour in them—they are kind of black and white—but if you've been out to Indigenous communities, you'd know that Indigenous women wear really highly coloured frocks. I didn't celebrate these works with colour, because it wasn't about a celebration of colour, it was about the loss of it.

Then down the track, I made the *PolesApart* series in 2009, which is a video installation with four photographic triptychs. You experience the photographic work before you get to the video work. So, the photographic work is really about my grandmother trying to find her way back to Country. She's lost, she's sitting, she's resting, she's not sure where she is, she's in someone else's Country and she doesn't know how to get back home. She starts to panic and that's when she starts to run. The work has a number of layers to it, but really it is about the violence of denial. As Indigenous people, every time we go back to Country, we experience a colonial violence of denial. Before I can make a connection, I have to first understand the disconnection. And I think that this particular work, created a few years down the track in 2009, brings a whole lot of fragmented stories together, which creates a sense of belonging (Fig. 3.2).

I grew up in community and on Country, and I learnt through art history and landscape painting—the Heidelberg School of Art. *PolesApart* is making a comment about the blak body, how it has been left out of Australian landscape painting. So, I bring into focus a reclamation of belonging through introducing the blak body back into view in the Australian landscape, as a way to pay homage to my grandmother and to all those Indigenous women who were left out of the history of this land. I've come across many women from all walks of life, who've found themselves in front of *PolesApart* and they have talked about how they felt this energy of loss and violence—about their grandmothers or their mothers who were also forced into servitude through the colonial powers of the time. Another layer in this work highlights how the early colonial painters participated in creating both a nationalist and European view of the Australian landscape. One of the many paintings that played a part in the layering of this work is Frederick McCubbin's *The Pioneer* (1904). I'm attempting to smash that idealism and nationalism apart to create my own reclamation of sovereignty into the present, a new lens that positions the blak body back in the landscape!

**Genevieve** There's so much to unpack from that…

**r e a** It's big.

**Genevieve** Thank you, r e a. It's such a gift to have the *PolesApart* video work in the exhibition because it's such a powerful work. You were talking last night about the difficulty of connecting with it in some ways cause it's quite overwhelming. Like I had quite a physical reaction to the work—but it's so important that we have works that do that, that actually create that sense of horror that comes with colonisation. I want to pick up from one thing you said, because it connects us with Dianne's work really strongly, and that's the blak body in the landscape. That's a really strong feature in a lot of your work, isn't it Dianne? Dealing with the absence of blak bodies in representation in paintings, in photographs.

**Dianne** Or particular type of representation.

**Genevieve** Can you talk a little bit about how that's informed you?

**Dianne** I think my work has often been about repositioning representation. So often it's really negative—whenever you hear or see anything about Aboriginal people, it's so kind of degrading in the language. And often I read this stuff and I think, well that's okay because I know that this is traditionally from some racist person writing this and they're dehumanising people that they're talking about. So I thought, well, why don't I try to change it and talk about people that I know and try to change that instant effect that you get when you look at something? So I thought, this is great, let's talk about positive images. The unfortunate thing was that I didn't wanna tell another sad story, but I noticed these other complex stories were getting told and they weren't getting told in a way that was respectful.

And I thought, how would I tell these stories? And it's traumatising to even read these stories. I want to tell these stories but I have to also protect myself. And if I can manage this respectfully within the community, then I know that this is going to be something that we can look back on and say, 'oh, at least that story got told'. And that's why we went on those trips, Genevieve and I, for the particular work in the exhibition, *found objects from what lies buried rises* (2017), to look at found objects (Fig. 3.3).[5]

---

[5] Dianne Jones' artwork for the exhibition, *found objects from what lies buried rises* (2017), involved a 3 minute video showing Jones forensically examining and arranging found objects, that include pieces of glass, a rusty chain, spear shards and fragments of ceramics. In her artist statement for *The Violence of Denial*, Jones offers context: 'In the month of May, 1839, there was a murder of a young white woman and her baby in the wheat belt town of York in Western Australia. Her name was Sarah Cook. When the reports started to spread throughout the colony, outrage and fear erupted

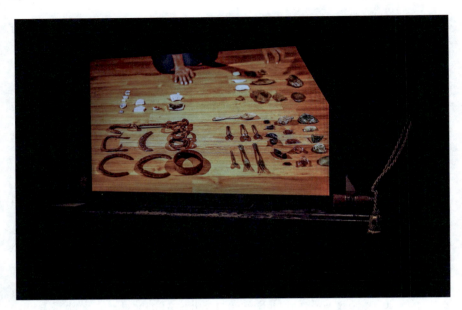

**Fig. 3.3** Dianne Jones, *found objects from what lies buried rises* (2017). Installation detail from *The Violence of Denial* (2017) exhibition. Photograph Bryony Jackson. Image courtesy of Genevieve Grieves and Arts House

**Genevieve** r e a's work has been really important to me as a younger Koori artist growing up and being interested in new media and film. And your work, Dianne, has been really important to me in another way because the work I did with you for the *What Lies Buried Rises* project has informed this whole exhibition. I travelled with Dianne over to York in Western Australia where she invited me to make a video work, and the whole project's grown out of that, hasn't it?

**Dianne** Yeah. It was a real turning point actually because, how do you tell a story about the first white woman, Sarah Cook, to be murdered in 1839 by two Aboriginal men? That's the story. How do you tell that story? I was actually advised by both Indigenous and non-Indigenous people in Western Australia to not tell this story. It's an awful story. Forget about it. And then I thought, okay, but then *that story disappears*. But how do I tell that story and actually emphasise that there were Frontier Wars at the time, and if they did kill this woman—and with further research, I was actually convinced that they didn't—but if they did, then the number of Aboriginal men, women, and children that died in reprisals in Sarah Cook's name,

---

and vigilantes rebelled by shooting any Aboriginal person they saw. In 1840 two Noongar men, Barrabong and Doodjeep, "confessed" to the murder of Sarah Cook. Without an adequate trial, these men were convicted and punished by death—they were hanged from a Gum Tree near the murder site. This series of works has been made to excavate a story of violence and retribution. It examines the role of art and how it can engage with storytelling, history and memory to investigate critical events in colonisation and bring mistruths and misrepresentations to the surface' (cited in Grieves, 2017, p. 3).

as well as were killed before she died, was four or five times that number. So these are the kind of issues that emerge through these research projects.

I don't want to celebrate her death, but I don't want to pretend it never happened. I don't want Barrabong and Doodjeep—who were hung for Sarah Cook's murder—not remembered for their part in the Frontier Wars, you know?

The more I dug into this story—and *literally* digging in the ground and finding objects where she lived—apparently the murder was so traumatising that people never built or lived in that area again. So we found things at that site that had been there since 1839 and it was highly likely that they were hers. The place where they hung Barrabong and Doodjeep, the point was to create fear. The perpetrators decided that if you're going to kill a white woman, then we are going to hang Barrabong and Doodjeep by chains and leave their bodies hanging; we are going to make a point that you will never be able to bury them. And there were so many levels—you can't even bury the dead who are fighting the Frontier War.

What do we do with that? I get emotional when I think about it. And maybe that's how Sarah Cook's family felt: that she was in Australia working as servant, that before her marriage she was Sarah Farrell and she would've been removed from her family in Ireland. They don't know what happened to her. Or maybe they heard that she was murdered. And I didn't want her story to be forgotten either. So, we deal with these kinds of stories and we try to tell them in a way that it's not just another sensational story or another dehumanising or degrading story. And that's the trick.

**Genevieve** And we spent a lot of days driving around looking for that site too. We had warnings from Dianne's dad, he told us 'you're either gonna get bogged or shot', because we were trespassing on white land, you know, settlers' land. When we finally found that site, the camera batteries were flat and we couldn't take any photos. I had a sound recorder, I got a tiny bit of a sound, and we weren't allowed back to that site.

**Dianne** So it's actually on an area that isn't recognised as historical land at all, as a historical memorial. We spoke to this man, the farmer, that night and he yelled abuse at us…

**Genevieve** 'How dare you go on my land'.

**Dianne** And this land is where my ancestors are from… I'm actually trying to work out what happened here on *my* land.

**Genevieve** And we explained that we're artists, we're not going to do anything, just take photos. And that didn't help cause we didn't get back there again. That's part of the conversation we were having last night. We're talking about the *violence of denial*. We've got these spaces in the landscape where things have happened, where violence has occurred, and we can't even access them. Where did you film your work r e a? How did you negotiate it? (Fig. 3.4).

**r e a** Dianne, that's an interesting piece of work.

As some people know, I'm Gamilaraay/Wailwan from the Central West New South Wales, and my father's a Biripi man from the mid-North Coastal NSW. I made the video and photographic images in the Hepburn Springs area of Victoria. I'd been going out to that country for quite a while, and there was something about that landscape that felt like my grandmother's spirit was there. I have a connection

**Fig. 3.4** r e a, *PolesApart* (2009). Installation detail from *The Violence of Denial* (2017) exhibition. Photograph Bryony Jackson. Image courtesy of Genevieve Grieves and Arts House

to this part of Victoria through her because she was sent across the border from Cootamundra Girls' Home to work in different homesteads in Victoria. She worked for this General—I don't know his name because I haven't had the opportunity to do that research—but the General used to have Dame Nellie Melba stay with him and she took a liking to my grandmother. Every time she'd go stay there, she'd always make a request for my grandmother.

My grandmother never really stayed anywhere permanently, but she'd always go back to Cootamundra. My grandmother had these relationships, and she always said that she never had any bad stories about her experiences. I don't know whether she just decided to repress them, or she had a really interesting and happy life managing—I think she accepted it all. She was one of those people that had that spirit that was always happy. I think that was just how she managed the situation.

So, if it was difficult: she didn't take it on, she didn't internalise it, she didn't have to go to therapy. Like the generation that I come from, she didn't seem to have this baggage of pain that we carry with us. But, unfortunately, it's there. I'm thankful I'm an artist, otherwise I probably wouldn't be alive today. It's the way that I've learned to tell those stories, to carry those stories, to find ways to understand a history that isn't taught in schools, but a history that I've been taught by my family, and then I find these links, like all of us do. As much as I hated my early education, it has been the way for me—to become a researcher of history, an academic working in a university, teaching and making work, always Aboriginal. I teach Indigenous history, creative arts and gender studies.

It's nice to feel like you can get to that point where you feel like you have some sense of power. But it's not real. In *PolesApart*, the land, the burnt landscape, was really haunting. And the sad thing about that piece of work—I made that work at the exact same time that other parts of Victoria were burning down and I was struggling with this kind of internal discomfort around it, and I felt like maybe I should stop making the work.

We also started to realise that people were watching us on the site where we were filming, in the way that people would be watching strangers hanging out in the bush. So, I realised that I had to get some big white paper and write a couple of signs so that they would know that we were a film crew filming on this site. Once we put the signage up people would just blow their horns and wave as they were driving past—they felt safe, and we felt safe too because you never know how people are going to react.

The interesting position for me as the artist, is being in the work—it's probably the most difficult thing I've ever done as an artist—to be visible. Because my body is about representing those that have come before me. I'm only visible through them. So, to make this work and put it out there in a contemporary arts context, it puts you in a different position, and it kind of validates the 'I', the individualistic role. But I don't really have one of those roles. I have a 'we' role and this positioning sometimes complicates things. I felt that the embodiment of this work was really important—I wanted this sense to come through my body physically.

In this particular work, it wasn't only one of the most emotional pieces of work that I've made, it was also physically hard because I fell down that hill a lot [laughs]. I smashed my knees, I had black knees, and I couldn't get up every time I fell over because I had a corset on. I was literally strapped in. And as you know, you can't actually bend your body, you can't get up—you have to get people to pick you up. I think that the embodiment of history comes out—it is expressed in the pain and discomfort that I personally experienced in my body. Even in the work Dianne that you were talking about, and even in the work that you make Gen, you cannot be an artist and not cross those boundaries, unpack those boxes: roles and structures are constructs that are put up there for us.

We work across the curatorial, in museums, in academia, in many areas that feed into the kind of works that we make. Some stories push themselves out more than other stories. I have lots of things that I'd like to make work about, but some just become really dominant. They push themselves out front (Fig. 3.5).

**Dianne** Yeah, I've noticed that.

**Genevieve** Yeah. It's funny because all five of us are all involved in research, so there's that space we're all inhabiting, eh?

**Dianne** It's like the story wants to get told. That's how I voice. I don't know what that is. It resonates. You have to think about how you do that. Definitely something that's resonating at the time politically, how you're seeing things.

**r e a** Different triggers provoke the work.

**Dianne** I think that's what happened with this work for the exhibition, finding these objects and thinking: Where is this from? Who used this piece? And just creating little stories about each one of them so that when they're all together, I'm

**Fig. 3.5** r e a, *Look Who's Calling the Kettle Black* (1992), no. 5 from the series, edition of 15. The image includes a black and white photograph of r e a's maternal grandmother c.1920s. Image courtesy of the artist

hoping it's like a puzzle that's getting put together and I can find the truth in that. I think the truth is the biggest thing that I'm trying to find. I always feel like I'm sifting through to get past all the lies, all the untruths, so that I can actually work out who did kill this person. Why is there this cover up? What purpose did this serve?

When Sarah Cook was murdered, the laws were changed a year later in response to her murder so that her death wasn't just another death—it had an impact. And why did it have an impact? You can just get stuck down this road, trying to work it out, and it's almost impossible. Because what is written in the records is tough to read and it's telling a story from this white settler person's perspective. I might not agree with this person, as I often do, so the writing is kind of like *rewriting*. Or writing what we know is more likely so that we can talk about it and give it some truth.

**Genevieve** I love seeing you hold all those objects. Every object you picked up that had a story, you knew exactly where it came from and what it fitted into in terms of the bigger picture. What does art do for you, do you think? What is it about it? What draws you to be an artist and to tell stories in that medium?

**Dianne** I think that's kind of a difficult question because I often think if I wasn't an artist, I'd be pretty depressed. Art makes me feel like I have a voice and it feels like all this stuff that I know or all this stuff that I'm hearing from the relatives or that I read, I can actually just put something else out there. Growing up, hearing one particular story in school and knowing that it wasn't how it was.

# 3 The Violence of Denial: Genevieve Grieves in Conversation with Dianne …

**Fig. 3.6** *The Violence of Denial* (2017) exhibition installation view at Arts House, exhibiting left and right: Vicki Couzens, *pang-ngooteeweeng-wanoong (we remember)* (2017) and Dianne Jones, *found objects from what lies buried rises* (2017). Image courtesy of Genevieve Grieves

Where I grew up in Western Australia, there were a lot of Aboriginal kids in the classroom with me. I remember one particular instance where the teacher put up a picture of some Northern Territory people based in Alice and said, 'so this is what an Aboriginal person looks like'. We were sitting there going, 'why are you saying that?' And that's that silence, because if we say something, then we're a bit of a troublemaker for speaking up, but if you don't say something it just becomes invisible. It's as though, well, you're not the *real* ones, they're up there.

So, let's get these stories out there, let's talk about it. It's probably really uncomfortable a lot of times, but God, we're not gonna die from it, from telling some truths or trying to uncover what happened. But that's the feeling. Sometimes I feel like we'll get so shut down, like when we went to York—which is a small country town in Western Australia where I grew up. Trying to find out what happened and going to the historical museum. First I rang the museum to learn what happened to Sarah Cook, which is a whole big story. After this conversation on the phone, I turned up with my parents to the museum and the staff present claimed they didn't know anything about Sarah Cook. And I thought, 'is that because we're obviously Aboriginal? Because you said something different over the phone'. And they say 'it must've been the *other* lady'. It's not that they won't tell you, they just tell you to come back tomorrow. So there's always this resistance to the truth and that just drives me nuts. It just makes me want to find out more (Fig. 3.6).

**Genevieve** It adds fuel to the fire. The turnaround is quite quick. That violence of denial that we're talking about in this exhibition is that *resistance to truth*, isn't it? It's a resistance and it's overpowering because it's in so many sectors of society and it's not just education—it's the memorial landscape, it's policy, it's government, it's a denial to actually accept the past. I've been really interested in the role of artists in that, and how work like yours, and r e a's and Vicki Couzens' and Julie Gough's work, is shifting that landscape.

**r e a** I think the interesting thing for me is that I ended up in education despite how I truly hated teachers and hated education. I couldn't wait to get out of school. But the one thing that I loved was history. And it was really sad because when I was about 8 or 9 years old, I realised that they were telling me a history that *I wasn't in*, so I thought: I'm not learning it anymore. Fuck Captain Cook. So, I ditched the one thing I was good at.

Some of my Ancestors out there think it's funny because they've led me right back to education. I was 25 and I thought it was all over—I thought I'd go to the Eora Centre in Redfern and hang out for a while and figure out what I'd do next. And I just happened to be in the right place at the right time, and I spent a year there and that led to studying at CoFA, the College of Fine Arts, UNSW, where I started my undergraduate degree. I struggled that first year, because again, I came up against Westernised, white-washed history and theory, and I thought: Is there any way I can do this degree without doing theory? Because I'm not learning anything.

What was really interesting is that I had a group of non-Indigenous friends who said to me, if you actually change the way you see theory and theorists, you will find the more you know about art history and theory, then you can critique them. I finished the degree even though, I never thought I was going to stay in the uni system or in any institution. What was good about CoFA was that it wasn't on the main campus: it was over in Paddington. It was a small campus, you could get to know people, and there were three other blakfellas there who I connected with: Gordon Hookey, Nikki McCarthy and Jason Mumbulla.

The four of us all worked in different mediums, but we crossed over in Aboriginal art and history, which was delivered by this Irish guy, John Fitzpatrick, who decided that it was really important to make Aboriginal history part of the Arts degree at CoFA. So, he went to La Perouse, an Aboriginal community in coastal Sydney, and connected with the Elders, and got them to establish the program. And we went through this course but we were at that stage where—and it's probably still like this now for some young blak kids at school—that when they ask questions, the white fellas look at you for the answer but we're learning too! Because we don't always know the broader Indigenous political history.

I learned from those experiences and I went on to question everything, including why people in the Australian contemporary arts scene haven't written me into this history—which, is why I did a PhD, so that I could write about the history that I was part of. I'm one of those artists that emerged in the early nineties in the digital experimental scene that was being established in fine arts colleges in this country. It's why my work got picked up early, and why it got exhibited nationally and internationally, before I had even finished my undergraduate degree. It wasn't because I was a painter, it was because I was a new media artist who was exploring a multi-layered interdisciplinary practice. And, because I'm Indigenous, I was only being written about as an Aboriginal artist in the context of identity politics. So, now *I'm* writing my own history.

For me, what's happened—and I think this has happened to a lot of Indigenous artists, particularly the 'urban' arts mob—you start exploring your ideas in one area, but then you find yourself somewhere else. If you remain open minded, an experimental practice will take you on a journey beyond the rigid constructs and frameworks in which the Australian contemporary arts scene will place you as an Indigenous Artist. I'm an artist who works with ideas, I set out to be a painter, but I realised that painting was going to be too limited. I was incredibly lucky that new media arts was available at the right time for me to change my artform. In an experimental practice the medium is found wherever the idea takes you. You find your way into the right space, unravelling the best sensorial experiences, and you find what is it about your work that brings people into a space and gives them a personal experience of their own.

**Dianne** I don't really feel okay trying to educate people. I grew up in a born again church. My dad was a preacher. And I can remember growing up and being told how to think and what to do—don't go to the cinema, don't listen to music, don't dance—because it was sinful and lustful. There were so many rules that I would control my mind so that I would not have a sinful thought, just in case that was the moment that the *rapture* happened. If I missed the rapture then I was going to hell and my family was going to leave without me. So I left the church because I decided to join the gay groups, the lesbian groups. The church hates them and tried to pray the lesbian spirit out of me, which didn't work.

I had this feeling that if I try to tell people things in a didactic forceful way, it felt like I was back in the church trying to get people to convert and then I would be leaving one church for another. It was rigid and there were racists there and I was having the same sort of feeling. I thought, hey, I just left this church that's really rigid; now I'm here and now I'm in the art world, and it's kind of the same thing. It's like everybody's putting you in a box. People need to think for themselves. That was my thought. I feel like, you can't tell me what to think and I'm also not going to tell *you* what to think. You have to think for yourself.

**Genevieve** Can you tell us more about your Sarah Cook research? That story is interesting too, because you came to it because they were going to memorialise Sarah Cook.

**Dianne** I get obsessed with the story of Sarah Cook. She arrived in 1831 in Western Australia and was a servant on this boat with a captain who was known as disgusting to both men and women. I can't imagine what her treatment was like because she was a young Sarah *Farrell*, she was a young Irish girl. There is no information about where she was for at least five years. Then she marries a man called Elijah Cook and has a baby. Two years later she's found speared three times and her house is burnt down—the remains of the house are still there, which we went to. And a year later, settler authorities found Barrabong and Doodjeep and said 'you must have done this because we found glass tip spears near her body, and you guys are known to use glass tip spears'. This flimsy connection meant that they would be hung by chains.

I get really obsessed with this story and stories where I think: what happened here? How did these glass tip spears get on the property? And then I find out that Sarah was in a really isolated place and she was actually known to be friends with all the local Noongars. And so she was a lonely person. We went to this site and it was still really isolated today. There are so many aspects of this story, like who was this violent captain who owed a lot of money to the Western Australian government and who was expelled from the state because the government didn't want anything to do with him. I get stuck in these aspects of the story and then when people start to get interested, I'm like, 'oh cool!' This is our history. Let's get obsessed about this stuff. Let's not put it in the past. It's here, it's still very much here all the time.

The reason that I got into the story was pure coincidence. I was in Perth at the time visiting my family and the historical courthouse in Western Australia were having a memorial. They were looking at the first five cases that went through the courts back in the 1800s. An artist had agreed to do it but had dropped out a couple of weeks before and they quickly invited me to do the work. They handed me the story and I said, 'Wow, this is where I grew up. Am I related to the guys that killed her? Am I related to this woman who was killed? What is the connection? How had I not heard about this story when I was growing up?' It was just pure chance, where I was at the time.

There is a mystery to the story. I haven't let go of it because I still wasn't able to completely prove that Barrabong and Doodjeep didn't do it. That requires a lot more time, but I'm doing my PhD on my grandfather who shot a man in 1955 in Swan Hill. My grandfather was friends with this guy who was a publican of a pub and the night before, he asked him for bullets to go rabbit shooting. At eight o'clock in the morning, my grandad shot him at point blank range with a sort of shotgun. Grandad died in the eighties and I was too young to question him, and I want to know what happened. The story that we grew up with was what grandad shot a racist in Melbourne—that's the reason I decided to make it my PhD. As a kid, it was cool. And then I began thinking about what actually celebrating this as an empowering thing meant, when the reality is that he actually shot a man and killed him. Why did he ask him for the bullets the night before? So I'll look at that, and my grandfather's 14 years in prison, which is fascinating in itself. I didn't know that the Aboriginal prisoners were often unofficially put into one cell and in an area that was much worse than the others. So that's been kind of eye-opening because you can't catch a break. You get into these stories and it keeps going and going.

**r e a** I remember when I made my first solo work called *RIP Blak Body* (1995)—which really meant 'ripped into pieces', not 'rest in peace'. I began the research around some difficult ideas concerning national and international institutions who were, and still are, part of a culture of theft, stealing Indigenous artefacts from all over the world. When I was doing the research, I learned about 'The Angel of Black Death' in an article I was reading, a German woman who was sent here in the 1860s by a German museum to bring back Indigenous human remains, including skins. I couldn't sleep, and I had nightmares. After this, I started to tell people about this history, but I advised them not to read it at night, read it when you wake up in the morning, so that you can process it throughout the day because it is a difficult read, a heavy read.

What's been hardest for me about moving into the area of academia and teaching Indigenous history to non-Indigenous and Indigenous students, is that even though I had a personal understanding of Indigenous knowledge that I grew up with, and I had experienced blak street politics when I moved to Sydney in the late sixties, I have since learnt that our true history is extraordinarily painful and that you're going to come across some stories and archives that you didn't know existed and that triggers trauma, and forces you back into the past—you feel the pain of our ancestors.

When I first started teaching, I was teaching and not making any work and I was getting sick and bouncing off walls left, right and centre and I was really angry! Then I started to realise that I needed to balance out my teaching. So, I did a semester teaching and a semester of making work because I needed to process all the new information that I was experiencing. That's how I learned to move on and grow into my academic career. There's no support network set up for Indigenous people coming into that area or any area—even in the museums or in art galleries—and yet you still have to do the research to unveil this hidden history to tell the truth.

You're going to come across stuff that you don't know and you're going to have to digest it—just like everybody else here if you're researching your family history. That's how I heal, by making work as an artist. It keeps me alive. It took me a while to figure that out in the context of the education system. You think you can do two years of teaching and then get out and make some work, but the system locks you in, as most academics know. You've got to find ways to buy yourself out of teaching, otherwise you don't get to make any work.

Personally, it comes back to how you work in your family, how you operate in your family, how you share information. I've come to understand that I've learnt this knowledge without knowing how to actually articulate it to my family, because it's my journey and my experiences. I share it with my family when I understand what I have learnt. So, the only way that I can actually bring them into my world is through my art. That's the only way. And they have some of their own personal experiences and that's a way of sharing experiences for me.

**Dianne** This reminds me of a story I was reading that was made up of firsthand accounts of a white guy at a massacre. He wrote, 'I'm at the end of the massacre and there are dead bodies lying everywhere, dying and dead'—and I apologise to everybody—he then describes seeing this little *piccaninny* standing there with a shocked look on her face. And I searched those archives because I thought: *What happened to that little girl?* There's nothing you can do, but you have to process that.

You have to walk away from that, and I did for a few years, then I thought, do I keep walking? I wanted to make some work about that particular story, but I didn't describe it directly in the works, it just started to come through in some works that I was making where I used my niece in different stories. I was trying to say that, 'you are here and you are safe'. I don't know what happened to that kid and I hope she was okay, but this is what happens. Making work helps process it.

And I don't have to talk about it for me. I can just make it and go, 'that's it'. And sometimes I talk about it, but I'm happy with the work. It's all poured into that particular piece of work or it comes out in a few different works and then I hope that I've embodied that. I get really sick sometimes and I have to block it all out, and then I go back and make some great work. I could walk away from it, I could not come back to this stuff. But then who's telling these stories? I want this history to be remembered.

**Genevieve** This exhibition, *The Violence of Denial*, came about because a space was made for us at the Yirramboi Festival by director Jacob Boehme. He was interested in an exhibition of Aboriginal women and non-binary artists who work with screen, and I said 'yes please!' because, in fact, it doesn't happen enough. There's not enough space for those works and we're not always given the space that we need or the resources we need to do things the way that we need to do them. As we talked about, you often get invited to an exhibition and they'll take your work, but you don't get to be there. This has been amazing because we are all here together and spending time together, talking and sharing, because we're all going through this in different ways and there is such a strength in coming together and connecting.

**r e a** That's why I accepted the invitation and came here because I haven't actually had an opportunity to really connect. I might run into these artists at different points, or at different places, but I haven't exhibited with them for a while and I haven't exhibited in this context; and this is part of a healing process for all of us. Being here, talking about our experiences and sharing our work, making connections with each other and having that validation; and it's a reminder that we're still here.

We only have those peers that have gone before us. Because you must remember that the seventies were just the beginning of Indigenous education and it took a long time for Indigenous people to trust institutions. So, I'm doing my PhD when really I probably should have done it 20 years ago. But that's just the way that life has turned out, you get to it when it's the right time. And when you have something important to say a PhD is a good way to document that process.

**Genevieve** Yes. I'm deeply honoured to have the two of these artists here tonight to share these stories and provide their wisdom, generosity and heart. The stories you heard are really what this exhibition is about. It's about holding these histories and remembering them—as difficult as this may be. I think sometimes people deny our history because they find it too hard to go into these spaces—to face the violence and trauma of our past. We've got to let ourselves go into these spaces and not just have artists like these ones hold these stories—we all need to be holding them together.

**r e a** And, thank you for bringing us together because this is not just a screen-based show. It's actually Indigenous women and non-binary artists exhibiting with an Indigenous woman curating. That's important because we don't get to have this space very often. So, thank you.

## References

Grieves, G. (2017). The Violence of Denial. *Arts House*. Retrieved from https://www.artshouse.com.au/wp-content/uploads/2017/08/The-Violence-of-Denial-by-Genevieve-Grieves-Show-Program.pdf. Accessed 25 January 2024.

Grieves, G. (2020). r e a. In N. Bullock, K. Cole, D. Hart, & E. Pitt (Eds.), *Know my name* (pp. 304–307). National Gallery of Australia.

**Genevieve Grieves** is a Worimi woman from Southeast Australia currently based in Garramilla (Darwin). She is an awardwinning artist, curator and content creator committed to sharing First Peoples histories and cultures and interrogating colonising frameworks and practices. Her recent projects include *The Violence of Denial* exhibition (2017) as part of the Yirramboi Festival; *Barangaroo Ngangamay* (2016), a place-based Augmented Reality app that shares and celebrates the living cultures of Sydney Aboriginal women; and, she was the Lead Curator of the internationally celebrated permanent exhibition, *First Peoples* (2013), at the Melbourne Museum. She is a passionate advocator of decolonising and communityengaged practice and teaches these methodologies in university, institutional and community contexts. Her current role is co-founder and creative director of GARUWA, a First Nations storytelling agency.

**Dianne Jones** is a Nyoongar artist whose photo-media work deals with Indigenous identity and cultural history. Dianne completed a Masters of Visual Arts at the Victorian College of the Arts and is currently undertaking a PhD. Her work has been exhibited in numerous exhibitions in Australia and overseas, and is included in the collections of National Gallery of Victoria, Art Gallery of Western Australia, Monash University Museum of Art and the National Gallery of Australia.

**r e a** is a descendant of the Gamilaraay, Wailwan and Biripi peoples. For over three decades they have worked at the forefront of Australian Indigenous new media theory and practice in Australia and internationally. An artist, curator, activist, researcher and cultural educator, r e a explores themes of Indigenous identity, representation and the post-colonial experience across mediums, including photography, digital media, film, video and installation.

# Chapter 4
# The Violence of Denial: Genevieve Grieves in Conversation with Tony Birch

**Genevieve Grieves and Tony Birch**

**Abstract** Concluding *Part I* of this volume is the final of three edited transcripts from the public talks program that took place during *The Violence of Denial*, an exhibition curated by Worimi researcher, curator, artist and filmmaker, Genevieve Grieves at Arts House for Yirramboi First Nations arts festival, Naarm (Melbourne) in 2017. In this third talk from the series, Genevieve Grieves in conversation with Koori writer, academic and historian Tony Birch, considers the impact of the works in the exhibition, the absence of memorials to First Peoples, and the means by which First Nations creatives resist the colonial psychosis of denial to produce recognition of Australia's foundation in violence.

**Genevieve** I just want to acknowledge some of the artists from the exhibition who are here: Vicki Couzens, Julie Gough and r e a. Dianne Jones sent her apologies. These artists are a big part of why this exhibition happened. I'm part of a cohort of incredible Aboriginal women and non-binary artists who make work that deals with the past and interrogates the violence of denial, the title of this exhibition. If I went all the way back to where this began for me, it started when I was a child travelling up and down the coast and hearing stories and visiting sites of violence—feeling those stories and understanding their weight as a child. And understanding a bit better, particularly when I got older, that there weren't markers to those sites. There were no statues, there were no memorials, and no spaces to mourn and to remember. That awareness has grown over time.

So once upon a time, I was a student of Tony Birch's at the University of Melbourne. I learned a huge amount about history in that space. I also learned our Koorie history at the Koorie Heritage Trust, working with Uncle Jim Berg, Len Tregonning, Uncle Sandy Atkinson, Aunty Joan Vickery and Uncle Wally Cooper, and all the people who taught me there. It's a part of our lives, as First Nations

---

G. Grieves (✉)
GARUWA, Garramilla/Darwin, Australia
e-mail: genevieve@garuwa.com

T. Birch
University of Melbourne, Naarm/Melbourne, Australia

© The Author(s), under exclusive license to Springer Nature Singapore Pte Ltd. 2024
G. Grieves and A. Spiers (eds.), *Art and Memorialisation*, Indigenous-Settler Relations in Australia and the World 6, https://doi.org/10.1007/978-981-97-6289-7_4

people, that we hear these stories and we know them. I'm travelling around Victoria with Vicki Couzens at the moment, visiting sites of violence in the landscape in the Western District. We're going to massacre sites, sites of remembrance, of war, of resistance, trying to find ways to share some of those stories in a museum project.[1] We're seeing again a consistent lack of recognition, lack of commemoration, the absence of opportunities for people to remember, to mourn and to heal.

So this is deep within me, this need to tell these stories and to bring awareness to these histories. I started research a few years ago where I'm writing about all of these things. Tony has been an advisor on this research. We were actually on a panel in a conversation like this and Tony said that during the History Wars, so many people were asking where are the Aboriginal historians? Where are they? Why don't you have any Aboriginal historians? He said, 'we do. We have so many Aboriginal historians. We have our artists, our filmmakers, our storytellers, our dancers. These are where our histories are told'. That's what I'm trying to write about in a way, how we share these stories and create opportunities for the recognition of this violence.

**Tony** That's so telling. We certainly don't want to bore people with the details of the History Wars, but to retrace our steps a little bit: it was largely what we might call an 'academic discussion'. And I use the word in inverted commas deliberately—the discussion was between public intellectuals and a very narrow and exclusive discussion in that sense. While I was both invited into that discussion—and for a while felt a political and intellectual need to answer back to colonial discourse—I realised very quickly how narrow it was, how much energy was lost doing it, and how it had no impact, no effect, and no value for Aboriginal people.

I seriously think it's indicative of what's on show here tonight, the sorts of other conversations you can have. When I made a decision to opt out of the History Wars discussion, I actually made a concerted decision: I'm going to work with new people. And most of those people were younger and concerned with the same issues, such as critiquing colonial history but finding different, creative and sometimes confrontational ways to deal with them. Such people are energetic, they're forward thinking, and they're engaging a younger generation of people who don't want to listen to a group of tired old white men defend a discipline essentially reliant on the appropriate footnote. One of the first people I worked with was artist Tom Nicholson, a non-Aboriginal fella who works around the whole idea of interrogating memorials. I didn't know him that well, but we had a couple of conversations, and I thought: this fella is someone I want to spin off, in a way. So, we did some work.

Returning to what you said about driving up and down the coast with stories of violence—this certainly comes out in Julie Gough's work, which we'll talk about in a moment. What struck me about r e a's work, *PolesApart* (2009) is that there's something so poignant and at the same time quite frightening about it. It really displaces you. It seems indicative of what we face, when you look at that work, that there's this absolute presence of this violence, but it's evasive at the same time. It's eluding you at the same time. To use Marcia Langton's term, it is the 'Australian psychosis'. It's so appropriate here. When people drive and walk these landscapes with this secrecy

---

[1] *First Peoples*, an ongoing exhibition at Bunjilaka Aboriginal Cultural Centre, Melbourne Museum.

of what happened there shadowing them—it's as if you have something silenced, but it's always there. So, people are dealing with these dualities or oppositions where someone's saying, well, this is a land of *terra nullius*, and this is a land waiting for our (white) arrival, but everyone also *knows* what they're *not* supposed to know. So, when you are thinking about the work, it seems odd. You are interrogating a secret, but a secret that's right there in front of you the whole time.

**Genevieve** Psychosis is a good word for it, or amnesia. Consider what happens in terms of constructing national narratives: there is so much money pumped into producing certain histories as with the Anzac myth; in remembering these selective histories as foundational stories, as Raymond Evans has articulated, you silence others. The history of the blood spilled by the Anzacs negates the blood spilled here, remembering and forgetting become political. If someone wasn't able to face their personal truths or the reality of their own history this way, you'd say that they were very sick or extremely unwell.

This national and discursive interplay of remembering/forgetting is expressed in place-making. Only on rare and peripheral occasions do you encounter the violence of Australia's past travelling across the country. Where and how a history is remembered is crucial. For example, I've seen r e a's work a number of times, but it wasn't until I experienced it in a large space in Adelaide that I really felt it so strongly. The size and placement lent itself to a heaviness and visceral experience, so you were able to feel it deeply and feel the damage. When we first installed it in this exhibition space, it was overwhelming. We had to find the right placement for it because of the power it holds; we had to give it a little bit more space just because it couldn't actually sit in the centre of the room.

**Tony** Another thing is that if we think about the damage that secrecy and lies do: we know how and what damage, including violence, is done to our community. It also reflects on the conversation with Bruce Pascoe last night about how to engage people, and how to take a conversation beyond our own community. We are talking about a mainstream community that is itself extremely damaged by that process. We would think that there should be a greater capacity amongst leaders to overcome that. But in fact, every time we raise this issue, of violence, of secrecy, it's suppressed even further by those with the authority to initiate change.

**Genevieve** Yes. There is a deep resistance that rises when you try to push against those colonising histories. If you erect a statue, someone will cut off its head or deface it with graffiti. It's not just governments and those in power that enforce this forgetting—*individuals* will do that, they're invested in this colonial project. They'll deface Uncle Koiki (Eddie) Mabo's grave, they'll desecrate rock art. When Gariwerd National Park was changed back to its proper name, people fought and said, 'no, it's called the Grampians. That's what it's called. It's not Gariwerd' (see Birch, 2010). So there's a resistance that's enacted constantly and at different levels of society. Like in Tasmania, when they're talking about actually erecting a memorial to Aboriginal people who were killed by colonial violence, the mayor of Hobart effectively says, 'but I didn't do anything, why should I be sorry?'[2] We fight by asserting our past and the reality of our history, but we're met with this overwhelming urge to preserve colonial and colonising histories, both at the level of society and the individual...

**Tony** That's the scary part because I think it shows how close to the surface the damage is. A really good example is that when I did teach the Aboriginal history of Melbourne and Victoria at Melbourne University, I would've thought that fairly open-minded young people came to do that history because they would say, 'we do want to learn, we do want change'. I still remember an incident around an essay I'd written on the Gariwerd name restoration dispute (Birch, 2010). If anyone's ever been to Bunjil Shelter, which is the most significant Aboriginal rock art site in Southeastern Australia, we know that when you go there—it's a terrible site to see—the shelter is behind a barbed wire cage. And that's a necessary *protection* because of the level of desecration and violence done to the work.

Now, what I knew was through oral history, and also what I learned in the research process, is that this desecration started in the late nineteenth century. The first desecration of Bunjil Shelter was in 1896. There are records of this in the local newspapers such as the *Stawell Times*. It's hard to get your head around this because the Black Range Scenic Reserve is where Bunjil Shelter is located. In the old measurements, that's about six miles from Stawell. People were so determined to vandalise Bunjil's Shelter, they actually used to get a can of paint, put it on the handlebars of a push bike, and ride out six miles to the site.

Based on the research I did, it had been happening for about 100 years. This is a *colonial tradition*. Not simple mindless vandalism, although, we know it's mindless. I explained to my students that it is a concerted tradition to erase and destroy Aboriginal life. And those students, who up to that point had been with me intellectually, became immediately reactionary. They were deeply offended by the notion that these acts be labelled a *tradition* of their culture. They couldn't simply dismiss the vandalism as acts of an individual racist, and didn't like it. And it's such that in the township of Stawell—and this might really shock people—people used to print postcards relating to sites of desecration that you could go and visit. If everyone's been to the Sisters Rocks outside Stawell, which is covered in graffiti, it's a major colonial tourist attraction. It is also a very important Indigenous site.

So Genevieve, when you start to address these ideas, and with your artists in this exhibition addressing them through the works, to what extent do you find a more open-minded engagement with the work as opposed to people who may be initially open-minded closing down again once confronted?

**Genevieve** All we can do as artists and curators is create the spaces—without telling anyone what to think. We can intervene at the level of the denial, and this amnesia we've talked about, by creating awareness and evidence that counters the historical omissions.

**Tony** We did something, not as sophisticated as Julie Gough's work, when we put up the initial Bunjilaka exhibition at Melbourne Museum, *Koori Voices*. One

---

[2] The mayor of Hobart in 2016, Sue Hickey, believed non-Indigenous people should not be made to feel guilty by a memorial (Wahlquist, 2016).

of the ideas we came up with was to show picture postcard images of the Western District, places like the Twelve Apostles and other iconic postcard images. And then we accompanied it with statements, not by blackfullas, but by whitefellas like Chief Protector of Aborigines George Augustus Robinson that documented the reality of colonial violence. Above the screen we put a gun and then we did a bit of eavesdropping. People were really offended and angry that we had put this in the space. The gun was eventually removed. And what was interesting about that is that we wanted to say—Julie's work does this so well—that this is the documented history of your forebears, of the Chief Protector of Aborigines himself. Even in that space, where the evidentiary statement was produced by white history, not Aboriginal history, people still wanted to deny the reality before them. So, I'm interested in that relationship to Julie's work and the conversation that took part around it. How did you see Julie's work fitting into that notion of colonial violence that you had considered?

**Genevieve** Julie is a prolific artist and has done so much work engaging with this history. She says she's obsessed; she's in the archive and she's constantly reworking it to find clues. Julie is a detective who can't let go of these narratives; of acknowledging them, remembering, repairing, reconnecting, of healing. She's someone who's inspired me a lot and her work has really helped me to frame my understanding of what it is we do as people who are responding to history, intervening in history, reframing the way historical conversations are even happening—what James. E. Young describes as *memory -artists*. I'm deeply inspired by the work that Julie does and the fact that she actually writes about it is an incredible legacy. I'm trying to find the language to articulate the power of this work in my research at the moment.

So, I'm not only reading but *writing* this history, through exploring the power of Julie's work and a chapter on Vicki Couzens. As I was writing one night, I reflected on the role I was playing in continuing western-colonial knowledge; history-makers, even myself, are very susceptible to writing into colonial histories because the system of knowledge itself is colonial, it reproduces itself through conventions you have to write to and the expectations of the academy. My response was to reframe everything; I've got to turn it upside down because that's what Vicki's doing, it's what these artists are doing and it's how I need to write it.

**Tony** Let's talk about Vicki. I'd seen part of Vicki's work at the 2016 *Sovereignty* exhibition at ACCA. We were earlier talking about the fire in the middle of *The Violence of Denial* exhibition that Julie brought across from Tasmania. Vicki's also got the cremation bags, or the bags with the cremated remains in them. One thing I love here is that you've got this symbiotic relationship to a national fire: ashes and memory. There's a beautiful act of commemoration there. Going back to r e a's work, looking at the video and some of those trees in the landscape artist runs through, they're clearly burnt. There's that fire too. What's so powerful there is the notion of fire as a productive and energetic and reproductive element rather than fire as a destructive element (see Figs. 3.1 and 3.4).

**Genevieve** And a healing element…

**Tony** Yeah. So, was that part of the initial idea to have that connection?

**Genevieve** I didn't realise it exactly the way I wanted to—I had an idea and not enough time to develop it. So, I had a fire and I remembered and I thought about the future and I thought about what I wanted to see happen, and sent this quick email to the artists and said, if you have time, can you also have a fire of remembrance and bring the ashes with you. I had envisaged that part of the experience would be an invitation to visitors to add ashes to the fire of remembrance collected from their own fires at home; this would mark their contribution to a collective shift into the future, the flame of a collective energy... The work and the experience represents sadness, violence and darkness and all the things that we carry and the artists carry. But it is not despairing—these are always transformative moments of healing and hope.

**Tony** It's interesting because I've been almost obsessed with the whole notion of mourning and remains in ashes. In my first book, which was written now 11 years ago, I had a story called *Ashes*, which is based on the cremated remains of the lover of an old woman (Birch, 2006). It's based on my grandmother who's now passed. When my grandfather died, they bought a plot at Melbourne Cemetery for him. And then when my uncle was murdered quite young, he was buried there with his father. Then my grandmother was going to be buried there. But later in life she had—as we know in the trade—a star boarder who lived out the back of her house, technically at least. But he crept up to her bedroom every night and then moved into the bed when he was very sick. On his death, my grandmother had his remains cremated. And on her deathbed, she called my sister and I into St. Vincent's Hospital and said, 'as my coffin goes down, you gotta sneak these in the grave'.

So, at the funeral my sister's trying to pour the ashes into the grave without anyone seeing. That restlessness of the spirit of people is so important to Aboriginal people. My grandmother wanted peace for her old lover. My book that's coming out in August also has a story about remains. I read an article in the newspaper when I was sitting with my mother about five years ago in Raven's Funeral Palour—which is now in Queens Parade. Raven buried all our family for decades when it was in Smith Street, Fitzroy. They hold the uncollected ashes of people going back to the 1930s—I saw a photograph of them in the newspaper, all on the shelves. And my mother was genuinely horrified and saddened by the notion that people didn't have their loved ones' remains with them. So I witnessed this in Vicki's work of commemorative possum-skin pouches containing ashes when I wrote for the *Sovereignty* exhibition (Birch, 2016).

It's one of those essential elements when you're talking about Country—whether it's Julie's film of the road trip, r e a's work, Vicki's work with the bags of ashes, and I'll get onto Dianne's work with objects in a moment. Another linking aspect of memory and truth around this work is that we need to commemorate our place in Country. That's where ashes, whether it be from a fire or the remains of our loved ones, comes in. It's so important for us to have our place in Country recognised. It's not surprising going into the issue of denial that people may or may not know this: when Aboriginal people's loved ones left the reserve or mission to go to hospital, Aboriginal people were never allowed to visit those people. And a lot of those people who died outside the reserve mission were actually never returned home to Country. It's a refusal to allow Aboriginal people to mark place. This exhibition is a remarkable recovery project in that sense.

**Genevieve** What a connection to place communicates cannot be overstated. Being out on Vicki's Country alongside her for my research has added layers to my understanding of her work and expanded her relationship to me as a teacher. Vicki's been involved in reviving the practice of making possum skin cloaks in over 70 communities across the Southeast—there is healing in the stitch and design of each and every cloak. In this iteration in the exhibition, playing a role in burials, the cloak also invokes the innumerable people who weren't mourned, remembered or buried according to tradition because of colonial violence. Vicki's concerned with the complexity of healing and keenly aware that it takes place at the levels of people, place, community.

Yes, I've been privileged to spend time with Vicki on her Country. She's an incredible teacher for me and I've learnt so much from her over the years. But actually being out on her Country with her, connecting with sites of violence and memorialisation, has added a whole layer of understanding for me as to the depth of her work. Her connection to place has created this proliferation of works—from sharing stories of violence to revitalising designs from her Country to the incredible work of the revitalisation of possum skin cloaks. The healing that has come from this recovery of an important cultural practice cannot be overstated—she has worked with over 70 communities across the Southeast to bring this back to us. The cloak she displays in the exhibition holds this power of healing, but the figure painted on it adds another layer of meaning. It could represent the ancient burial practices of her people but also all those people who didn't get to be buried or mourned, all those cultural practices that were disrupted by invasion and colonial violence. Vicki's work is concerned with healing on so many levels and her practice of healing, through her work, is profound.

We've had many conversations about the descendants of both sides of colonial violence—those harmed and those perpetrating harms—and we've been collaborating on a museum project together that integrates both journeys into a project of healing. As we know, healing can come when the violence is acknowledged and recognised. There are people coming together this way in events like the annual Myall Creek Massacre Memorial.

It recently happened at the Appin Massacre commemoration in Campbelltown, NSW. The descendant of an infantryman who was a part of this massacre 200 years ago appeared at a recent commemoration for the first time. She was having nightmares and knew that something had happened in her family, but she didn't know what it was. This happened in the context of the 2016 *With Secrecy and Despatch* exhibition curated by Tess Allas and David Garneau, which shined a light on this history and there were numerous news stories. From this, she realised that she'd descended from a perpetrator of the massacre and asked for permission to attend. That moment of healing was only a beginning, but it was profound to witness.

**Tony** That's remarkable. I want to ask about the challenges of that healing, but it is also a theme for the exhibition. I'm not saying Vicki's is more explicit, but with Julie Gough's and r e a's work, you feel an unease once you start to ask the big questions around that work. What's happening here? What does this say about us as a wider society with Julie's work? If you're talking about a particular stretch of road and how that equates to something that happened there on a particular date. As difficult and confronting as that is, that is in fact what the healing process is about—going through that confrontation. What you just mentioned there about bringing people together, that's a big challenge, isn't it? So why are you doing it?

**Genevieve** I'm not doing it just yet, but I am really interested in this space and the possibilities of healing. It started when I witnessed the power of people coming together at Myall Creek: acknowledging that history publicly and ceremonially every year. I heard an elderly white man and his grandson repeat, 'I am so sorry for what my Ancestors did'. They're not only acknowledging the violence of the past, they are teaching the next generation this history. You walk around the site and there are a series of plaques that tell the story of what happened there. When you stop at one, Koori kids and non-Indigenous kids will tell you the story and then say in unison, 'we will remember them'. This embrace of history, together, in a way not often seen in regional Australia, is profound. I'm convinced these divides can begin to be conquered with recognition.

**Tony** It's quite interesting because we go through this every Anzac Day. It's about who's remembered, who's not remembered, which wars are declared wars and commemorated. The idea that we've never spilled blood on Australian shores is ridiculous. It is profound to see when that shifts. I've recently finished an essay on the 10 year commemoration of Camp Sovereignty.[3] The Thorpe family, the descendants Robbie and Marge Thorpe today—are the great-grandchildren and grandchildren of many people who were in the services—and have relatives who are buried in France. Robbie was accused of sacrilegious acts, of having this protest camp when Anzac Day's coming up. It was considered an affront to the memory of our fallen soldiers, even though again, his grandfather had served and died in France. And our friend tabloid journalist Andrew Bolt wrote in the *Herald Sun* press that he hoped on Anzac morning that the Anzac Diggers confront those Aboriginal 'stragglers' and 'barbarians' and remove them. After the dawn service, a group of Vietnam veterans marched from the eternal flame at the Shrine of Remembrance down to Camp Sovereignty's sacred flame, and there's a whole troop of photographers running after them wanting to get the shot, hoping no doubt to witness and document violence.

They reach the camp and one of them walks up to Robbie and says, 'can we share in the commemoration of Aboriginal war dead, both on this land and in service?' They all joined arms around the flame in a spontaneous moment that really worked towards healing. And then, of course, as you move on, all you get is recalcitrant politicians and media. What frustrates me is in those moments where people come together and attempt to initiate change, others feel a need to crush them. They don't want healing. What's happening there?

---

[3] In 2006 as Melbourne hosted the Commonwealth Games, Aboriginal activist group Black GST (Genocide Sovereignty Treaty) held a protest camp, Camp Sovereignty, at the Kings Domain to draw attention to Indigenous political struggles. The protest was initiated by senior political campaigners, including Margorie Thorpe, Gary Foley and Robbie Thorpe (Birch, 2018).

4 The Violence of Denial: Genevieve Grieves in Conversation with Tony … 69

You see something that has so much potential for change, yet there are so many people who will refuse that opportunity and prefer for us, all of us, to continue to be damaged.

**Genevieve** The problem with denial is that it squashes everything; squashes all the complexity, squashes all the opportunities for people to actually speak their truth on both sides of history. It means these things remain static and unable to transform or change. Vicki and I were part of a meeting of the Yulendj Group[4] recently at the Melbourne Museum, which built the *First Peoples* exhibition with Elders from across the state of Victoria. We're talking to them about these histories, and what we can share and can't share, and the Yulendj Group had so many stories of white families coming to them and saying they were sorry for what their Ancestors had perpetrated. There were many more stories than I had thought. I've heard of these bigger stories nationally, but I didn't realise how often this is happening at the local level.

There are people already coming forth and saying: this was wrong, and my family was involved. So what then is stopping the next layer? Melbourne is such an incredibly progressive city. But if you look at the memorial landscape and what's represented, there are 520 statues in Melbourne and 510 of them are white men. Figures like Burke and Wills and Matthew Flinders: dead, white men from our history books. Where's the complexity in that? I'm sure that the City of Melbourne is aware of this… But what do we do with these relics? Do we pull them down to make way for more complex representations of our past?

**Tony** 510 whitefellas. That's a lot of statues. Within that, they are so many fictionalised accounts. There could be another take on this history. The Burke and Wills story is a Monty Python comedy—it's so crazy! We're going to start out at Royal Park in Melbourne, we've got these camels and we're going to go to the top of Australia and back—what a great idea. But there is another story there. Ian Clark and Fred Cahir co-wrote a book on Aboriginal engagements with the Burke and Wills party. It's a remarkable story and one of tragedy because of white ignorance. Aboriginal people are saying to Burke and Wills' party. 'eat this, this is good food, I'm eating it and I'm okay'. And they're saying, 'no, I'm not eating that!' Indigenous observations of that party and Aboriginal engagement with Europeans is not just the story about how we might think differently about each other, but also stories of the incredible depths of Aboriginal knowledge.

It's interesting because I think about your point about denial crushing everything. Bruce and I talked last night about how in climate change work a similar thing is happening, because if you say to people, look, a big reason for Australia's contribution to this global crisis of climate change is what we call colonial agriculture and how destructive it was. And if you look at the spread of colonialism across the world since about 1600, it's one of the major contributors to the problems we are dealing with

---

[4] 'Yulendj' is the name for the Bunjilaka Community Reference Group, comprised of a group of 16 respected community members and Elders from across Victoria, that generously shared their knowledge and experience to shape the *First Peoples* exhibition at Melbourne Museum. 'Yulendj' is a Kulin word for 'knowledge and intelligence'.

today. Really destructive forces of both genocidal acts against Indigenous communities, and then engaging in these wide acre practices of destructive agriculture, et cetera. The industrial revolution that goes on and on into the twenty-first century. But if you just say to people, well, this notion of colonial expansion was a really bad idea for the ecology and environment, it caused the problems we're dealing with today, and we have to face the fact that we have to do some things differently, because terrible mistakes were made —that knowledge is too much for people to cope with because what they've got to understand is, in fact, the notion of *European progress* is a false notion. It's another fiction. So, you're really battling with people sometimes.

I want to talk before we take questions about Dianne Jones's work. I've done a fair bit on found objects and I'll tell a little story about John Batman. And like with Julie's work and the archives, it's almost like getting a jigsaw puzzle and putting all the pieces together and creating the true story. It's tactile in that sense, isn't it?

**Genevieve** Yes, they are both amazing at excavating both the archive and place. I was really lucky to be able to do this work with Dianne on her Country. She invited me to make artwork for an exhibition she was curating at Linden in 2013, *What Lies Buried Rises* (see Jones, 2012). We travelled to York (Western Australia), this amazing historical town, as she searched for a particular site of violence central to her work—the place where a settler, Sarah Cook, was murdered, a crime for which two Aboriginal men, Doodjeep and Barrabong, were hanged for a year later at the same location. Dianne's Dad warned us as we got in the ute: 'you're either gonna get bogged or shot'. Luckily, neither happened, despite having to jump some fences!

We wanted to make work that connected to the site of their deaths, which we managed to find by the grace of this young woman who was house sitting. Dianne's camera was flat, so we couldn't take any photographs, but we recorded some sound and left some details for the landowner—we explained that we were artists, that we wanted to return to take some photos and that we weren't trying to stir up any trouble. He called us half an hour later, indignant—'how dare you trespass on my land'. It was evident that he knew the story living there in the ground. He didn't want people coming out of fear that they might claim his property. We actually found a piece of Sarah's pottery at that site. Dianne collected all the other found objects (in her artwork) on her Country. We jumped another fence to enter a different old building and I watched nervously while Dianne's digging away, getting bits of glass and chains; she knows the story of every one of those objects and exactly where it came from. She's putting these things together to tell a story that hasn't been recorded. The only histories that are written about her Country are biased, to say the least.

In a way, Dianne is another detective (like Julie) who's trying to understand the truth of the past—because the evidence around Sarah's murder didn't add up. She scoured the archives and tried to piece together what happened but the evidence did not point to those two Aboriginal men having killed her. Dianne's work asks, how do we use the objects and the archive to inhabit that space and understand what happened in that moment? How would Sarah Cook feel? She was a friend to Aboriginal people, and she was murdered, and then Aboriginal people were massacred in her name, all across Western Australia…

# 4 The Violence of Denial: Genevieve Grieves in Conversation with Tony …

**Tony** I don't need an answer to this question because historically, there's a strong history of Aboriginal women collecting found objects and sometimes for utilitarian reasons, turning them into implements. But there is something evidentiary about this work. I don't know if people know this story, but the first people that John Batman ever met when he came to Kulin Land was, was a group of Wathaurong women. So, again, it's a bit like Monty Python, because John Batman, he's got these forged treaty documents that Joseph Gillibrand drew up in Hobart. And he gets off the boat down there, at current day Indented Head, and he's thinking: 'where are the people that will sign this bogus treaty?' You know, this bodgy document?

And Batman sees a group of Aboriginal people in the distance. This is all recorded in his diary. Batman's party chase after these women and they've got these rolls of treaties. As they get closer, the whitefellas see that it's a group of Aboriginal women and children, no men. They're on Country these strong women, they're digging around, they're obviously farming, they're working. And they have what Batman describes almost like little backpacks—Vicki might know about them more than I do. But what's interesting is that what John Batman does, he gets out the trinkets and beads he has in his possession and says, 'look what I've got for you', like some whitefella trickster. And the women refuse the offer. When they open their bags, they have European implements fashioned into tools. I was intrigued when I looked at Dianne's work because of the crockery shards. The Wathaurong women also had objects to fashion into spearheads later. They were engaging with European society, engaging with European objects, and in a way reclaiming them for use. Batman is so bemused. I'm convinced that the women were saying: 'hang on, we've met you fellas already—this is our evidence, look at this stuff you've left behind, we don't need your trinkets'.

People might know a tarnuk or a water bowl, often made of eucalypt. Some are utilitarian. Others are highly decorative. They are valuable and have strong customary value. Batman thinks he's going to give away a bit of gear, some trinkets and beads, and that he might then get his signature on the treaty. The women present him with a tarnuk and he's not sure what's going on. I think what they're doing is using objects to say that what we have here is of greater value: 'by giving it to you we're showing that we owe nothing'. It's like a process of saying: 'you're only here for a short time, take this with you'. John Batman did not have a good time of it. And this was before his pox-ridden nose fell off, by the way.

**Genevieve** When curating the *First Peoples* exhibition at Melbourne Museum, Vicki and I didn't get to finish what I'll call the 'Frontier Conflict' section of the exhibition.[5] Everyone understands what I mean by that term, but I'm not entirely comfortable with that terminology. Uncle Larry Walsh says we need to call it 'homeland violence' as the idea of a frontier isn't ours.

Vicki and I travelled out to the Western District of Victoria together. Being from there, she took me to sites and introduced me to people and we actually were doing

---

[5] This work was later completed with the creation of the film, *Black Day, Sun Rises, Blood Runs* (2016) that shares stories of colonial violence from across Victoria. It is currently installed in the *First Peoples* exhibition, Bunjilaka Aboriginal Cultural Centre at Melbourne Museum.

seven projects at once; we had a few days together and she's doing her PhD research, I'm doing my research, she's doing an exhibition, I'm doing this exhibition. So we managed to do a lot. Many of the places we travelled to connected to homeland violence in this space.

We went to Camperdown, where one of the local early white settler families were the Manifolds. There's a clock tower in Camperdown, erected by the Manifolds because someone died in their family and bequeathed the money to create it—that object dominates the whole town. Behind it is a brass statue of James Chester Manifold, which stated that he loved his fellow men, that he was a great man, and a kindhearted man. But of course, this family has a whole history of violence.

In contrast to this, in Camperdown Cemetery, there is a monument to an Elder man, Wombeetch Puyuun, which was erected by James Dawson, a friend to Aboriginal people. But Dawson had to fight for that to be erected. He had to fight for his friend to be buried in the graveyard and not outside of it as a heathen, non-Christian person. Vicki and her cousin are now fighting to get the monument registered as a heritage site.

It's very culturally and historically significant for someone like Dawson to commemorate an Aboriginal person this way. So many powerful gestures like this are obliterated in retelling the history of places—there are people who don't want to recognise the potential of figures like Dawson to influence wider social healing, so they need to erase its significance as a site of history and a positively charged historical monument.

Vicki also took me out to a deeply significant cultural site on her Country which I won't go into detail about because it's a site that her Ancestors visit. The only heritage interpretation of that site—which dominates that space—is a memorial to WWII soldiers who died, erected by the local rotary club. It's not even an Anzac story; it's actually a story of men whose patrol plane crashed near there. So here is an opportunity to share important Gunditjmara history and culture and, of course, something else is dominating the landscape and blocking that opportunity.

**Tony** Going back to the Gariwerd days, I was doing work around Aboriginal Country around what became Lake Lonsdale. I've taken the piss out of the Giant Koala quite a bit at Dadswells Bridge: that colonial fantasy of erecting giant things to commemorate empire. One thing you work out very quickly was that some of the sites that Europeans occupied gave them access to water. They're clearly sites that are also important to mob. And what you find is these quaint little places dotted around the countryside and the stuff that we think of as just crass tourist attractions, they were previously really significant Indigenous sites of occupation because of the fertility of Country and availability of water. If you look at the evolution of those regional towns, they're often also sites of massacres that again are completely obliterated, in a narrative sense.

When you talk about travelling around, this goes to a strange relative issue when Karen Jackson[6] and I did the Oxfam 100km charity walk in the Dandenong Ranges

---

[6] Karen Jackson is Executive Director of Moondani Balluk, Indigenous Academic Unit at Victoria University.

with Charlie Solomon, a wonderful young blackfulla who does remarkable work with environmental ecology. What struck me was the importance of exchanging stories and knowledge for blackfullas when you're on Country. A lot of what you learn about Country is in the conversations you have while walking around.

**Genevieve** It was really hard to get my university to support the work I did with Vicki (see Grieves, 2019). I wrote up my field work application exactly as it was: going on Country with artists, to which the university responded that it wasn't very 'anthropological'—which it isn't. It's not intended to be anthropological. But it was the only bucket of money that I could access to do this generative—but not extractive—work of spending time with people on Country and yarning. We had to fight to be able to access these funds. We started this, but I'm not done yet with understanding her and her process, connecting to these stories and these places and where her creative and cultural work comes from. We did get monitored…

**Tony** You got marched off the police barracks…

**Genevieve** We got removed. Auntie Eileen Alberts negotiated to get us back so we got back. It's a constant theme of this work: to be excluded from these places that you need to visit to remember, to even try to piece the history together. Everywhere you go, that's the theme.

**Tony** I've always been the first one to admit what the issue is about colour, being a blackfulla. I was in the township of Stawell when I did the Gariwerd work, and I went into the store to buy a newspaper and explained I'm a student from Melbourne University. The bloke started to tell me about growing up on the farm and what his old man taught him: If you come across a spearhead or a stone tool: don't give it to your museum, throw it in the river. If that implement is on your land, that's evidence that the rules have changed. We're on somebody else's land. So, the first thing you want do is get rid of evidence of prior occupation. The whitefella was telling me all this stuff thinking I'm also a whitefella, and then after the weekend is over and I'm leaving town, I run into him at the coffee shop. When I tell him what I was doing and who I am, his heart sinks. I hadn't lied to him, I just didn't say any more than I had to.

**Genevieve** Our mob talk about *Deep Listening*; not just listening with your ears, but listening with your body, heart and mind. This is actually a responsibility, or it creates a responsibility, because when you hear something fully—more than intellectually—you have an ethical obligation to respond. And these works in the *Violence of Denial* exhibition invite responses in that way. They're deeply moving. A few people have said to me that it's quite heavy, and I think I'm used to that, and we're used to that. I'm not uncomfortable in that space because I'm used to holding those things. Actually, I feel there's lightness in there, too. The artworks themselves are memorials in different forms and they position the audience to remember; the exhibition is reflective of the need for spaces to mourn, remember and heal, to think about tomorrow, or what's next.

**Tony** It might seem strange to close with what is an issue sometimes of frustration. Because one thing I love about going to see artwork and what I'm moved by is that I often go back and back again. You become so attached to the space and the work and it continues to teach you. One of the things I've learned through Vicki's work, and first speaking to Vicki about this many years ago in New Zealand as part of Creative Victoria's *South* project, is that you increasingly become attached to someone's work and then one day you go back to the exhibition space and it's gone, it's over, and you miss it.

**Genevieve** It's temporary. That's the difficulty I have. We need permanent memorials in our landscape…

**Tony** It's interesting because when you talk about memorialisation, in relation to the body, your own human body, you have to find a way to carry your reflections with you and not forget them. So, in that positive way, it's a call to remember. It's a call to really soak it in and not let your experience be fleeting. Even though the space changes and there'll be another exhibition created here, you've got to find a way to carry that work with you.

**Genevieve** We also need to shift the landscape so we can have more work with permanence.

**Tony** There is a counter-argument that we don't need these permanent monolithic monuments. In some ways they are a constant reminder and narrow our thinking. If you think of Vicki, Julie and r e a's work, the temporary nature of the space is asking you to do the remembering. Meanwhile the colonial statue is going to be there next week and the one after. I think what this is doing is transferring the responsibility of that memory.

I remember when I went to Hiroshima and witnessed the prefecture building with the dome top missing that is so famous. I used to teach writing on Hiroshima—how you write about memory and how you write about mourning. I wanted to go there for many years and that building is the iconic image of Hiroshima. It was a profound experience and people were really respectful. I'm a runner, and the second day, I thought, I shouldn't run past it. I stopped and I looked. I ran past within a few days and I'd forgotten that it was there because you're just doing your stuff. But then I watched school kids make those beautiful kites about the issue of atomic violence, and you don't forget watching those kids. And it's doing something very tactile, like making a cloak. These were little paper kites that were going to disintegrate, get washed away. I never forgot that. Or the determined look on the faces of the children.

**Genevieve** I made a thousand paper cranes by myself in primary school. It probably laid the foundation for me to be thinking like this. I agree with you, but I also think that we need to transform the space, because at the moment it is white and colonial. These spaces reflect back to us who we are as a society and as a people. What's being reflected at the moment is white men of power. So shifting that memorial landscape—the actual physical landscape—is important.

**Tony** I agree with you, if they're going to have their 500, we want our 500. But yeah, I can see by faces in the crowd here, there are clearly people here who are not blackfullas as in Aboriginal blackfullas of Australia. I can see that. The other issue then is to find ways for communities that have come here, to Australia, to find their place here in a way that allows them to remember where they came from and not just be consumed by a sense of memory of this place.

**Genevieve** Because that has no complexity, no diversity. It's ugly.

**Tony** A great friend of mine, her mother was buried today. Her mother made a decision in 1951, a young woman living on an island in the middle of the Mediterranean to leave her whole family and come to Australia because they lived in a poverty-stricken existence. And when she came to Australia, you're going be Australian, you're going be assimilated, she believed. Never met blackfullas, never been introduced to Aboriginal culture. Most of those migrants were told, without saying it directly, you've got to forget where you come from, and forget about this place too. And part of thinking about finding other ways to remember is also to think about people who come as refugees. We want you to find ways, when you come to Aboriginal Country, to continue to remember where you've come from. That's something that blackfullas can be centrally involved in.

**Genevieve** That recognition and acknowledgement of feeling, of pain, of trauma. There's this beautiful memorial in Utøya, Norway where all those teenagers were shot by that gunman. They cut a piece of land out of an island; they actually removed Country physically because of the gravity of this act of violence. They felt that they had to remove a place from the earth to acknowledge the pain of this experience. That's how we need to start considering commemorating violence in our country, we need to be expressing the depth of pain that has been felt and continues to be felt.

We've come to the end of our event and I want to thank Tony. He's the only man who's come into this space. As Karen Jackson has said: 'a lot of men call themselves feminists, but Tony actually is a feminist'. He knows the rules. And we're happy to have you. We wouldn't invite any old man, but we invited Tony.

**Tony** One of the things that I have learned through family experience, but also working as a historian, is that the only way to understand where we are today as a community that have survived, is to understand the authority of Aboriginal women. It's the only way. Karen Jackson would have talked before about the work that I've done on Aboriginal women's writing: when so many things were going wrong, when there was so much despair about what was going to happen in particular parts of the country—and I'm not talking about Aboriginal women as nurturers, I'm talking about in the front line—it was Aboriginal women, historically, who kept the fight going, who stood up. So, the proof is in the pudding. That's where the strength of the community lies. With Aboriginal women. Bruce Pascoe talked about this last time in regard to Country and environment. If you don't understand the authority of women, you don't understand the respect you have to have for Country. It's pretty simple.

# References

Birch, T. (2006). *Shadowboxing*. Scribe.

Birch, T. (2010). Nothing has changed': The making and unmaking of Koori culture. *Meanjin, 69*(4), 107–118.

Birch, T. (2016). 'Our red sands dug and sifted': Sovereignty and the act of being. In P. Balla & M. Delany (Eds.), *Sovereignty* (pp. 19–25). Australian Centre for Contemporary Art (ACCA).

Birch, T. (2018). Rise from this Grave. *Overland* (p. 230). https://overland.org.au/previous-issues/issue-230/essay-tony-birch/. Accessed 24 July 2023.

Grieves, G. (2019). Just tick the box: A Koorie woman's experience of negotiating the university's ethics process. In K. MacNeill & B. Bolt (Eds.), *The meeting of aesthetics and ethics in the academy: Challenges for creative practice researchers in higher education* (pp. 101–109). Taylor & Francis.

Jones, D. (2012). What lies buried on my land rises. *Artlink, 32*(2), 38–39.

Wahlquist, C. (2016, December 12). Hobart mayor says Indigenous memorial shouldn't be 'guilt-ridden'. *The Guardian.* https://www.theguardian.com/australia-news/2016/dec/12/mayor-told-to-apologise-after-saying-indigenous-memorial-shouldnt-be-guilt-ridden. Accessed 17 July 2023.

**Genevieve Grieves** is a Worimi woman from Southeast Australia currently based in Garramilla (Darwin). She is an awardwinning artist, curator and content creator committed to sharing First Peoples histories and cultures and interrogating colonising frameworks and practices. Her recent projects include The *Violence of Denial exhibition* (2017) as part of the Yirramboi Festival; *Barangaroo Ngangamay* (2016), a place-based Augmented Reality app that shares and celebrates the living cultures of Sydney Aboriginal women; and, she was the Lead Curator of the internationally celebrated permanent exhibition, *First Peoples* (2013), at the Melbourne Museum. She is a passionate advocator of decolonising and communityengaged practice and teaches these methodologies in university, institutional and community contexts. Her current role is co-founder and creative director of GARUWA, a First Nations storytelling agency.

**Tony Birch** is a writer and historian. He holds the Boisbouvier Chair in Australian Literature at University of Melbourne. He is the author of four novels, five short fiction collections, and two poetry books. In 2022 his book, *Dark As Last Night* was awarded the Christina Stead Literary Prize and the Steele Rudd Literary Award. The book was also shortlisted for the 2022 Affiliationids : Aff1, Correspondingaffiliationid : Aff1 Affiliationids : Aff2 Prime Minister's Literary Award for fiction. His most recent book is the novel, *Women and Children*, (UQP 2023).

# Part II
# Truth-Telling with Creative Practice in Settler Colonial Australia

# Chapter 5
# The Wind Has Not Yet Answered!

**Charmaine Papertalk Green**

**Abstract** In this poetic response written in February 2024, Yamaji poet Charmaine Papertalk Green reflects on the contrasts in settler colonial Australia's memorialscape, the toppling of Cook statues by activists in Naarm (Melbourne), the blindness of settlers and the ongoing invisibility and absence of memorials to Yamaji on their Country in Geraldton, Western Australia.

*And,*

*Cook statues are toppled in Naarm yet their visibility remains through the national news,*

*Whilst our greatest monuments of thousands of years steadily hold national invisibility.*

*I scream into the wind, 'When is the Geraldton's memorialscape going to include Yamaji?*

*When are all the Cook statues going to be toppled on all First Nations lands?'*

### *'When is Geraldton's memorialscape going to honour Yamaji?'*

In the middle of Geraldton there is a small park dedicated to colonial first contact displaying shipwreck timelines, a statue, a stone wall boasting claims it's the first Australian colonial structure!

### *Turning invisibility to visibility to wipe away colonial silence!*

I have been annoyed, sad, upset, frustrated, concerned, angry, mixed emotions, curious, wild, seeing Yamaji people remain invisible and silenced in the Geraldton story memorialscape.

---

C. P. Green (✉)
Yamaji County/Geraldton, Australia
e-mail: tjaarmaan@hotmail.com

© The Author(s), under exclusive license to Springer Nature Singapore Pte Ltd. 2024
G. Grieves and A. Spiers (eds.), *Art and Memorialisation*, Indigenous-Settler Relations in Australia and the World 6, https://doi.org/10.1007/978-981-97-6289-7_5

*Yamaji men led the settlers to fresh water—the 'native' dug wells for them to survive!*

Instead, there are statues of Europeans, war memorials, religious icons, settler named streets and parks; a statue of a Dutchman called Wiebbie Hayes stands like he is the ancestor of our shorelines.

*Our invisible monuments are the same right across Australia, why is the settler still blind?*

Monsignor Hawes, an English architect turned Catholic priest, is honoured in a statue with his duthu, for his contribution to the catholic memorialscape, but what about the Yamaji Traditional Owners?

*Religions rode in, bible in hand, a genocide tool to erase Yamaji culture, to build churches!*

I always think about the Bluff Point Shell Middens, evidence of Yamaji occupation well before colonisation, yet the site signage was never made in the right materials to honour site, people, and culture.

*Shell Midden sites, memorials to a long existence of survival only to be crushed for roads!*

You should read the 'Butterabby Hangings' story, out near Mullewa Devils Creek way, and how the Yamaji were rounded up to be taught a brutal lesson by being forced to watch barbaric hangings!

*Water hole poisonings, massacres, hangings, shooting of Yamaji. Bootenal Springs is remembered!*

Where are the celebrations and honour for the Yamaji stockmen who worked this land in harsh conditions laying foundations for settler family riches whilst they only received flour, sugar, and tea?

*Yamaji Stolen Wages is indeed a thing along with Stolen Labour and Stolen Land, yes indeed!*

Last night a granddaughter asked me online 'what about my nanna trees at the Old Geraldton Town Reserve, that's a memorial isn't it?' Yes, it is a historical memorial with signs cracked and faded.

*Aboriginal town reserves on the town fringes deserve their rightful recognition and honour!*

My energy shifts from Geraldton to Canberra walking from the Aboriginal Tent Embassy to Old Parliament Courtyard café bouncing thoughts of memorialscape contrasts with each step.

## 5 The Wind Has Not Yet Answered!

*Aboriginal Tent Embassy Canberra—monumental to our people's existence!*

The Aboriginal Tent Embassy was eerily quiet and cordoned off with a sign 'camp closed', quite a difference to my many other visits here to sit with the fire that I could see with smoke still rising.

*Ongoing resistance, presence and visibility through the sacred fire smoke continues!*

So, instead my jina takes me across to the Old Parliament house searching for a coffee inside the guts of a building painted so white it stands out like an alien British Empire era colonial elephant.

*Old Parliament House—a settlers monument sitting like the big colonial intruder it is!*

I asked myself 'what am I doing here inside this very white space searching and trying to write about the Geraldton memorialscape?' Yet the contrasts between the two sites evoked many reasons.

*The shifting contrasts between monuments reflects life throughout Australia, still now!*

How often do we First Nations think of the memorialscape of culture and country not including us? I know many Yamaji people are on the survival track and perhaps cannot think beyond that just yet.

*And,*

*Cook statues are toppled in Naarm and the wind has not yet answered!*

**Charmaine Papertalk Green** born in Eradu, is a proud Wajarri, Badimaya and Wilunyu woman of the Yamaji Nation. A poet, storyteller and social science researcher, she shares her cultural knowledge in many different spheres. Charmaine has written five books, won several awards including the prestigious Australian Literary Society Gold Medal, and her poetry is studied as part of primary and school curriculum. Involved with the Yamaji Art Centre in Geraldton for over 22 years, she is currently their Chairperson. Charmaine was awarded the 2022 Magabala Fellowship 2022 and 2023 Red Room Poetry Fellowship and is a member of the national First Nation Aboriginal Writers Network.

# Chapter 6
# Remembering Those Who Have Gone Before

**Fiona Foley**

**Abstract** In this chapter, Badtjala artist and scholar, Fiona Foley, describes her effort to counter public silences concerning the violent occupation and orchestrated brutality that occurred on Queensland's colonial frontier through a committed public and contemporary art practice that started during her undergraduate studies in the 1980s. Foley argues that public art is a way of putting in plain sight a history that has been shrouded in silence and complicity since colonisation of Aboriginal Country in Queensland, Australia began. This chapter discusses key commemorative works from her practice to date including *Annihilation of the Blacks* (1986), *Stud Gins* (2003), *Witnessing to Silence* (2004) and *Dispersed* (2008). It also describes Foley's strong wish to see a public memorial commemorating the 1851 massacre of Badtjala people on K'gari (Fraser Island) in her lifetime.

## 6.1 Introduction: Silence and Complicity

Currently in the state of Queensland in Australia there exists an historical amnesia in public memory and public spaces about the war and violence carried out on the colonial frontier. Public art is a way of putting in plain sight this history, which has been shrouded in silence and draped in settler complicity. Silence was a weapon employed, and complicity was its companion, on the frontier. They went hand in hand when colonisers carried out violent occupation and orchestrated brutality on Australian soil. There were no Aboriginal prisoners when the state and squattocracy mounted raids that resulted in massacre.

Leading historians Raymond Evans and Robert Ørsted-Jensen have identified that this frontier violence was a series of prolonged wars colonisers fought against Aboriginal people over land and sovereignty, despite the fact this conflict had no officially recognised name or status among the colonising forces. As Evans and Ørsted-Jensen observe, this was an underhand war fought with:

---

F. Foley (✉)
University of Queensland, Meeanjin/Brisbane, Australia
e-mail: f.foley1@uq.edu.au

© The Author(s), under exclusive license to Springer Nature Singapore Pte Ltd. 2024
G. Grieves and A. Spiers (eds.), *Art and Memorialisation*, Indigenous-Settler Relations in Australia and the World 6, https://doi.org/10.1007/978-981-97-6289-7_6

> ... no declarations of hostilities, no agreed rules of engagement, no careful body-counts, no conventions for the treatment of prisoners, no armistice, no surrender, no settlements, no treaties, indemnities or reparations and, afterwards, no recognition of a gallant foe. (Evans & Ørsted-Jensen, 2014, p. 6)

When expanding empire, early colonial Queensland was a lawless society. Settler men in the districts gathered in small parties and went out on horseback hunting Aboriginal people of their own volition, or in the company of the Native Mounted Police consisting of Aboriginal troopers under the command of white officers. Korah Wills, Mayor of Bowen in 1867 and MacKay in 1876–1877, illustrates the silence and complicity required in the men mounting these raids when he noted in his memoir: 'Volunteers were men whom [the commanding officer of the Native Mounted Police] thought he could trust for pluck and a quiet tongue after all was over' (Wills, 1895, cited in Poignant, 2004, p. 44).

In the following decades after the establishment of the Queensland Native Police Force in 1849 official reports as early as 1874 were identifying islands on the east coast of Queensland as places to relocate surviving Aboriginal people as prisoners (Drew et al., 1874). This was a new strategy in the treatment of the remaining, decimated Aboriginal populations after relentless warfare. There is an inherent assumption in this premise that Aboriginal people were purveyors of some sort of pre-destined criminality.

As a child growing up, I wondered why there were none of my people, the Badtjala, living on our Country of K'gari (Fraser Island, Queensland). For a five-year old it was a deep question that played on my mind. It really puzzled me. I may not have had all of the language to articulate what I knew intuitively but I understood we were the rightful owners of K'gari but physically separated from it.

As a sovereign nation, the Badtjala people have undergone many years of derivational longing for our island. The last official act, in a long list of injustices, carried out by the state and Anglican Church was the removal of the last Badtjala people off the island to Aboriginal missions and reserves on the mainland in 1904. Badtjala people living on the mainland at Hervey Bay with K'gari, the largest sand island in the world, in plain view but inaccessible has rendered us—the traditional landowners—invisible on our own Country for many decades.

Theorist Rosi Braidotti has described a mode of 'double consciousness', whereby historically marginalised people possess both an awareness of oppression alongside a creative force and vision that strives for transformative, just alternatives (Braidotti, 2011, p. 32). I grew up with an awareness that a profound injustice permeated Australian society and this double consciousness sparked my interest in wanting to know more and reveal the truth. There are still many unaddressed gaps and silences in Queensland's public memory, which disregard the dispossession of Aboriginal people and the numerous wars fought on the frontier.

Sometimes you come across a small statement that shifts your thinking. This occurred for me when reading historian Henry Reynolds assertion that, 'the warriors were patriots and saw themselves in that way' (Reynolds, 2021, p. 35). As a nation, what do we know of the many Aboriginal warriors who resisted the invasion and stood strong on their sovereign lands? What strategies did our freedom fighters employ before battle commenced? What was the Aboriginal use of language around engagement? This continent finds their voice absent from the vast majority of historical writings and musings. Yet they were worthy opponents that outmanoeuvred the British in early battle grounds.

## 6.2 Annihilation of the Blacks

Whilst completing my education in Sydney I would only receive a one-week history lesson on Australian Aboriginal people in the curriculum at Asquith Girls High School. This was a general history about Central Australian Aborigines taught in year 7. It was a history that negated issues around race and invasion, conquest of land, or any real factual detail except to claim, *Aborigines look like this, hunt like this and made dwellings like this.* In the process of completing six years of formal tertiary education between 1982 to 1987 I resolved to educate myself. It was a slow grind of reading many publications by historians from 1985 onwards. I was active in seeking out historians who wrote about Australian history pertaining to the Frontier Wars and how this colony was established.

I had also been working with an aspect of oral history that had been handed down to me by my mother, Shirley Foley, about a massacre on the Susan River in Badtjala country. The Susan River flows into the Mary River at River Heads in the Great Sandy Straits. The Mary River flows from what local writer Lindsay Titmarsh describes as a 'source in the beautiful high country upstream of Conondale in the Sunshine Coast hinterland' (Titmarsh, 2014, p. 9). The current of the Mary River is fast flowing and the surrounding mainland is skirted by thickets of mangroves. My traditional Country as a Badtjala person takes in the following landmarks on the Fraser Coast, encompassing the Susan and Mary Rivers: *Fraser Island, Double Island Point, Tin Can Bay, Bauple Mountain and north to a point at the mouth of Burrum Heads.* I grew up with this knowledge.

George Furber established the settlement of Maryborough on the Mary River in 1847. The Mary River was instrumental in developing Maryborough's trade as a port town, along with three timber mills, and was the basis for daily settler conflict with Aboriginal people in the Wide Bay district. Maryborough was the site for many Aboriginal killings in broad daylight. Journalist David Marr has noted how these killings were regularly discussed in local newspapers, including a Moreton Bay Courier article in 1861 that reported: 'Young Snatchem, an excellent and industrious black, was driven into the river, near the public wharf—scores of men, women, and children stood by, and Lieut. John O'Connell Bligh stationed himself in the bow of a boat, …. and forty or fifty shots were actually fired…' (cited in Marr, 2019). Both the Mary and Susan Rivers were locales for indiscriminate murders, reprisals and massacres of Aboriginal people.

In 1986, when I was a third-year art student in the sculpture department at Sydney College of the Arts (SCA) I created, *Annihilation of the Blacks.* This free-standing sculpture depicts the oral history given to me: nine black figures are suspended from a wooden structure whilst one white figure stands on the ground casting a long shadow. It was created to keep the memory alive of what happened to the Badtjala people on the Susan River and constitutes the definition of what a memorial is meant to do: it is a sculpture designed to preserve the memory of people lost in war and serve as a public reminder of a painful historical atrocity that should not be forgotten. The sculpture was exhibited at Willoughby Workshop Art Centre in 1986 for the exhibition titled, *Urban Koories*.

I was to receive unfavourable comments from my three lecturers in the sculpture department on site at Willoughby. Like three black crows they would chime in with one more demoralising comment, ganging up on some unsuspecting prey: 'What you are doing is a five-year passing fad. Your work didn't say anything and was just a full stop. You should have burnt the figures not painted them black' (Foley, 1994, pp. 8–10) (Fig. 6.1).

Their insensitive and ignorant comments would ring in my ears for days and years after. I felt validated that the work was historically significant when during the exhibition *Annihilation of the Blacks* was bought by the National Museum of Australia to join their permanent collection. It was the Museum's first major acquisition of a city-based, contemporary Aboriginal artist. Curator and writer Timothy Morrell has noted, 'The National Museum of Australia recognised the significance of Foley's

**Fig. 6.1** Fiona Foley, *Annihilation of the Blacks* (1986). Wood, synthetic polymer paint, feathers, string, 204.5 × 267 × 85.7 cm, 13 parts. National Museum of Australia collection. Image courtesy of the artist and Andrew Baker Art Dealer

# 6 Remembering Those Who Have Gone Before

work before the institutional art world and acquired her sculpture *Annihilation of the Blacks* (1986) while she was still a student' (Morrell, 2009).

I had been so unsupported in higher education and hung out to dry by my lecturers that I didn't attend my graduation ceremony to receive my Bachelor Degree in Visual Arts. My teachers could not comprehend that history was being made at their institution or indeed in their course. In the mid 1980s I was ostracised for my groundbreaking endeavours to visually speak up and tell the truth about Australia's Frontier Wars through sculptural works before it was widely acceptable in Australian art to address colonial violence in this way.

*Annihilation of the Blacks* is the first sculptural memorial to my knowledge made by an Aboriginal artist to honour an Aboriginal massacre in Australia. The work's unflinching commemoration of Aboriginal losses that breaks the silence on colonial frontier violence led to a request for its removal from view at the National Museum during the Howard-era History Wars (Kelly, 2016). The earliest work featured in *With Secrecy and Despatch*, a major 2016 exhibition by curators Tess Allas and David Garneau showcasing artworks by Indigenous artists exposing colonial massacres, its memorialisation of Badtjala losses commanded centre stage.

## 6.3 Red Ochre Me

Another important exhibition in my early career looked at frontier violence in Australia and was titled *Red Ochre Me*, 2003. This research-led exhibition was held at Dell Gallery, Griffith University. It was at the opening of *Red Ochre Me* that I was also awarded an appointment as Adjunct Professor to Queensland College of Art, Griffith University.[1] Since that time I've written about the injustices of the colonial project in Australia. Specifically in *Biting the Clouds: A Badtjala perspective on the Aboriginals Protection and Restriction of the Sale of Opium Act, 1897* I described the *Red Ochre Me* exhibition and the response to the works exhibited such as *Bone Boxes*, *Stud Gins* and *Massacre*. All three works lifted a veil on a brutal historical past, exploring uncomfortable horrors and sexual abuse on the colonial frontier. All three, however, were negated and passed over for any potential acquisition. As I noted in *Biting Clouds*, the works were received with silence:

> I was unaware that I created powerful work that could not be spoken about. On a number of levels a public rebuke was conveyed to me. I learned many lessons about Queensland and its representatives that year. I learned how a society can shun you through absolute silence. I learned about institutional shunning. I had overstepped some invisible mark. As an Aboriginal in Queensland I didn't know my place. I was being spoken to through a wall of passive resistance. Silence. (Foley, 2020, p. 114)

For the entirety of the exhibition's duration, I was left confused by a tacit societal refusal to acknowledge this important body of work. In her major essay for

---

[1] The former Dell Gallery is now called the Griffith University Art Museum and is located at Queensland College of Art, Griffith University, South Bank, Brisbane.

the exhibition brochure, author and academic Anna Haebich remarked upon the works' uncompromising take on Australia's past that produces discomfort in a settler public committed to denial. She states, 'Foley's installation slices through these charmed circles; her works dissect and expose the facts, fantasies and frauds, they force us to look into the abyss of our imaginings; and, finally, they thrust us out into expanding frontiers of human relationships where we encounter ever more uncertainties' (Haebich, 2006, p. 21). The works' slicing of charmed circles to directly expose the predatory acts of colonisers, it appears, was too unpalatable to be considered for acquisition.

*Stud Gins* (2003), for example, highlighted a history of sustained sexual violence that has rarely been discussed publicly in this country: the brutalising force of marauding white males on the bodies of Aboriginal women and girls during the Frontier Wars. These viscous acts, while not openly discussed in polite society, were referred to using euphemisms. In *Trauma Trails*, Judy Atkinson describes how a complete language evolved around the pursuit and sexual violation of Aboriginal women, with the words *gin busts, gin sprees, gin jockeys, gin shepherds*, and so on alluding to the abuse of women as though it were sport (Atkinson, 2002, pp. 61–62) (Fig. 6.2).

*Stud gins* was another term used in the colony to dehumanise Aboriginal women's bodies. My work, *Stud Gins*, comprised of a seven-part blanket series with a word

**Fig. 6.2** Fiona Foley, *Stud Gins* (2003). Installation view of *Fiona Foley: Forbidden* (2009) exhibition at Museum of Contemporary Art, Sydney. Seven ex-government woollen blankets with screen-printed lettering, each 190 x 148 cm (irregular). Dimensions variable. Image courtesy of the artist and Andrew Baker Art Dealer

printed on each blanket: *Aboriginal, Women, Property, Defiled, Ravished, Shared* and *Discarded*. *QG* was stamped in a corner of one of the blankets, demarcating an original Queensland Government blanket. A trophy of sorts for the previous decimation that may possibly have been handed onto an Aboriginal in the mid to late 1800s. Blanket distribution for surviving Aboriginal populations was implemented by the state government at various locations, and is depicted in a pen and wash sketch by Donald Sydney Thistlethwayte, *Distribution of blankets to Indigenous people in Brisbane* (1863). During the exhibition period at the Dell Gallery, I offered *Stud Gins* to the Queensland Art Gallery to have the first option to purchase. They declined. *Stud Gins* was an important work that referenced the state but could not find its way back into a Queensland state institution. The seven-part installation was packed up and put into my storage unit where it stayed hidden from public view for years.

I started to register a pattern developing throughout the years both within the state of Queensland and nationally. A calculated form of writing out important political works by institutions was evidenced by choices not to acquire certain work, producing notable gaps in state collections. It called to mind the comments made by eminent race scholar Aileen Moreton-Robinson on *disregard*. On the ABC program, The Drum, in 2020 the distinguished professor pointed out, 'disregard is one of the ways in which racism works in this country' (Moreton-Robinson, 2020). I have experienced this *disregard* when valuable works addressing uncomfortable truths are overlooked by institutions, thereby denying the public important additions to their state collection. This is another layer of silencing that goes on unremarked in the arts.

I've experienced *disregard* throughout my practice as an artist. So much of my work in this space of bringing difficult frontier histories to the public eye has been written out by Indigenous and non-Indigenous scholars and curators, leading me to keep reinserting my art and monuments back into national discussions around frontier memorials. This is particularly true of my work addressing the abusive treatment of Aboriginal women. The sidelining and disregard of Aboriginal women continues.

Eight years passed and in recognition of the importance of the installation, I offered to donate *Stud Gins* to the National Gallery of Australia, Canberra. My donation was formally accepted on 22 June 2011 from the Chairman Rupert Myer AM under the Directorship of Ron Radford.

## 6.4 Witnessing to Silence

In late 2004, *Witnessing to Silence*, a bold, permanent work of public art was revealed outside Brisbane Magistrates Court, near to Emma Miller Place on Roma Street, Brisbane. The work unveiled comprised of several elements; long stemmed lotus lilies cast in bronze, emerging from a mist generated by a misting device; a series of stainless-steel columns rising from the ground containing glass panels embedded with ash; as well as a series of granite pavers, etched with place names, surrounded the installation. The commissioners were originally told the work addressed the extremes

**Fig. 6.3** Fiona Foley, *Witnessing to Silence* (2004). Installation view, Brisbane Magistrates Court, Brisbane, Australia. Cast bronze lotus stems, etched granite pavers 180 × 140 cm diameter, stainless steel water feature, laminated glass five pillars 210–350 × 25 × 25 cm. Commissioned by the Queensland Government. Built by Urban Art Projects (UAP). Image courtesy of the artist, UAP and Andrew Baker Art Dealer

of nature, such as bushfire and flood, but this was not the work's real subject (Figs. 6.3 and 6.4).

*Witnessing to Silence* was one of the most difficult commissions I've ever undertaken. I wanted to create a contemporary monument that revealed and commemorated sites in Queensland where massacres of Aboriginal people took place through a public artwork situated prominently outside an institution of law and justice where the commissioner was the State of Queensland. In order to do so, a number of covert strategies were employed to see the work through to completion. Primarily I had to remain quiet about the real meaning of the work for two years as the process of commissioning, fabrication and installation unfolded. The true significance of the work was kept hidden as it is unlikely if known this ground-breaking memorial—the first public artwork to tackle the magnitude of this subject in Queensland—would have been approved for commission outside such a prominent location.

Unbeknownst to the commissioning team on the project, I began the commission by employing a researcher to find out all the Aboriginal massacre sites discussed on the public record in Queensland. The final list was not an exhaustive or complete tally for Queensland but the ninety-four sites the researcher uncovered was a comprehensive first start. In addition to a list of the identified place names engraved in granite pavers indicating where the massacres occurred, the sculpture also comprised of two main elements involving ash and water. These key elements signified hard truths

**Fig. 6.4** Fiona Foley, *Witnessing to Silence* (2004) installation view. Image courtesy of the artist, UAP and Andrew Baker Art Dealer

not about bushfires or floods, but that both bodies of water and fire were methods employed by colonising perpetrators during the Frontier Wars to conceal evidence that a massacre of Aboriginal people had taken place. Since the work's installation, disappointingly I don't think anyone has further investigated this list of ninety-four massacre sites in Queensland as I've never had anyone ask me a question in relation to it. Certainly, the Queensland Government has never made any inquiries. The massacre sites commemorated are:

> Christmas Creek

Morinish Station
Rockhampton
Dawson River
Eurombah Station
Rochedale Station
Cockatoo Station
Jundah Station
Toowoomba
Hornet Bank Station
Rockhampton
Logan
Comet River
Rainworth Station
Nogoa River
Condamine
Long Lagoon
Redbank Station
Whitesides Station
Kilcoy
Maryborough
Susan River
Manumbar Station
MacIntyre River
Warrego District
Cape River
Christmas Station
Tenthill Creek
Apis Station
Cardwell District
Fraser Island
Pine Tree Station
Glenmore Station
Flagstone Creek
Rockingham Bay
East Maranoa Region
Keppel Islands
Bentinck Island
Moreton
Normanton
Flick Yard Station
Burketown

## 6 Remembering Those Who Have Gone Before

Lawn Hill Station
Camooweal
Mitchell River Region
Cape Upstart
Balonne River
Surat
Battle Mountain
Irvinebank Station
Cressbrook Station
Carbucky Station
Dalby
Mt Larcom
Burnett District
Planet Creek Station
Widgee Widgee Station
Rolleston Station
Archer River
Somerset
Bullo Downs Station
Mt Madurana
Bellenden Plains
Cloncurry River
Moonah Creek
Hinchinbrook Island
Green Island
Palmer River
Battle Camp
Endeavour River
Normanby River
Double Island
Murdering Lagoons
Cooktown
Woonamo Waterhole
South Cook
Waterview Run
Hebel
Mongaree Station
Bones Knob
Gunpowder Creek
Wills River
Mapoon

Dulcie River

Batavia River

Nocaboorara Waterhole

Teviot Brook

Laidley

Pigeon Creek Run

Yamboukal Station

Goulbolba Hills

Hughenden

Mackay

Laura River

Moreton Bay Area

Cape River

I actively continued my reading on this grave subject matter and generated new ideas for work that had the potential to further educate Australian audiences about their dark colonial history. For example, it was the in-depth historical accounts of frontier violence contained in *The Secret War: A True History of Queensland's Native Police* by Jonathan Richards and *Frontier Justice: A History of the Gulf Country to 1900* by Tony Roberts, that informed my thinking when creating *Dispersed* in 2008. *Dispersed* is a large-scale word sculpture made of charred wood and aluminium letters spelling out 'Dispersed', with the letter *D* bristling with bullet cartridges. The work reflects on the word *dispersed* that was used in government reports to act as a euphemism for violent and murderous acts carried out by the Native Mounted Police and their commanding officers. As academic Fiona Nicoll explains in the MCA's *Forbidden* catalogue, 'euphemisms are terms used as substitutes for those which might offend delicate or naïve sensibilities and are a vehicle through which popular acceptance of racist values, understandings and policies has been achieved' (Nicoll, 2010, p. 61) (Fig. 6.5).

Driving my artistic practice is further new evidence surfacing about the scale of the brutality of the frontier in Queensland. Leading historians, for example, are revising the numbers of the death toll from frontier violence, especially in Queensland where there were mass murders and open carnage waged on Aboriginal Nations as the frontier moved in time and space. Ground-breaking work by Evans and Ørsted-Jensen painstakingly puts forward new figures from losses on the Queensland frontier that claim, 'two totals of Native Police and settler inflictions amount to 61,680 in 6000 attacks' (2014, p. 5). The researchers also make the chilling point, that 'no perpetrator was ever legally punished for killing an Aborigine in Queensland frontier conflict' (Evans & Ørsted-Jensen, 2014, p. 4).

**Fig 6.5** Fiona Foley, *Dispersed* (2008). Installation view of *Fiona Foley: Forbidden* (2009) exhibition at Museum of Contemporary Art, Sydney. Charred laminated wood, polished aluminium, blank .303 inch calibre bullets, overall 51 × 500 cm. Image courtesy of the artist and Andrew Baker Art Dealer

## 6.5 A K'gari Memorial

Research on colonial crimes that took place on my Country K'gari continues to be brought to light, supporting Badtjala oral histories. Native Police Forces on occasion mounted raids joined by the districts' vigilante groups, and this was the case with a massacre that took place over 11 days on K'gari in 1851 killing Badtjala men, women, and children. Before the actual attack that commenced on Christmas Eve of that year, its leader Native Police Commandant Frederick Walker referred to Badtjala people in dehumanising terms as the '"charcoles" of Fraser Island' (Evans & Walker, 1977, p. 53). When the violence unfolded, Commandant Walker was joined by a Native Police Force of 24 troopers, as well as Lieutenant Marshall, Sergeant Major Dolan, four local squatters, and the captain and crew of the schooner Margret and Mary. Raymond Evans and Jan Walker write about this intended invasion of K'gari under the direction of Commandant Walker who, 'considered that anything short of three sections, thirty-six men, would be useless at Fraser Island' (1977, p. 53). Prior to the massacre on K'gari, Aboriginal resistance fighters who were sheltering on the island were issued with warrants, 'accused by European settlers of "murder and felony"' (Evans & Walker, 1977, p. 52). The names of these warriors are as follows:

> Neddy, Jacky Jacky, Iourning, Nosy, Boomer, Mr. Bunce, Ineway, Grassoom, Bobby, Iangara, Ben Bullen, Jimmy, Pepo, Coola-Coola, Wanauinga, Perika, Charlie, Bungalee, Tom, Old Athlone, Old Diamond, Peter, Puckemale, Toby, Tilar, Boney, Paddy, Tommy, Doughboy,

Lawley, Big Diamond, Peter-with-one-eye, Athlone, Woolga and Diamond. (Evans & Walker, 1977, p. 53)

Bridging the gap between historical fact and the silence pervading contemporary Australian society is a challenge. The range of accounts of this contentious 11-day act of violence with intent provides enough evidence, in my view, that it is worthy of a public memorial commemorating the massacre on K'gari. As an artist who wants to see change in my life-time I was keen to initiate dialogue with the state on this matter. In 2019 I wrote to the Hon Leeanne Enoch the Minister for the Arts in Queensland with regard to creating a K'gari memorial that acknowledged this 1851 11-day massacre involving many from the organised Native Police Force and squatters from the district.

Part of my letter to Minister Enoch stated the following: 'I propose a site at Indian Head (Takky Wooroo) for the memorial. This is an area that currently attracts large visitor numbers and would be a fitting place to reflect on another aspect of the island's history and turbulent early race interactions' (F. Foley, personal communication, 19 February 2019). My letter received a reply from Senior Policy Advisor, Angus Sutherland, some 3 months later and not from the Honourable Leeanne Enoch to whom it was addressed. Sutherland wrote, 'your proposal for a memorial on K'gari will require endorsement by the Butchulla Aboriginal Corporation before we could consider it further' (A. Sutherland, personal communication, 2019). This deferral to the Traditional Owners and registered Aboriginal Corporation was clearly an evasion tactic and obfuscation, the irony being that I was a member of the Badtjala nation, and actively involved with establishing the Butchulla Aboriginal Corporation as a founding Director after our consent determination in 2014.

As a Badtjala artist I can envisage a major public sculpture at Indian Head on K'gari to commemorate the 1851 massacre of my forebears. This could constitute another significant step forward in the process of truth-telling that is taking place across Australia. The issue of who shall fund such a memorial, however, is not far from everyone's mind especially within the Fraser Coast Regional Council. In 2020, the state government allocated millions towards funding Queensland Tourism initiatives for the designated Year of Indigenous Tourism, which was extended into 2021. It is rather telling that none of these funds were used for creating new memorials on Aboriginal Country to remember our dead from historical massacres.

Other forms of creative expression, most notably film, have addressed frontier violence and impacted the psyche of Australians more broadly. A recent example is the 2020 film entitled *High Ground*, starring largely an Arnhem Land cast and addressing a massacre of a group of Yolŋu in the Northern Territory. Academic Chelsea Watego has made an important observation regarding *High Ground* and other recent films: 'rarely do we see films of the massacres of mob along the east cost of the continent where so many of the settlers reside, and where so much of the violence was enacted' (2021). From *The Tracker* to *The Proposition*, Australian films often present massacre narratives shot in rock escarpment Country and sandy creek beds skirted by eucalyptus trees, desert she oak and spinifex. These films present violent histories in monsoonal, semi-arid, and arid landscapes, places that Watego suggests situate frontier violence 'in a faraway place in a faraway time' (2021). This can have the effect of convincing the public that massacres happened 'out there somewhere else' (Watego, 2021) not here in one's own Country on the east coast—this is despite the very real violence that did occur here in opening up Country for invasion by the British. Aboriginal sovereign Nations on coastal terrains took huge losses from British weaponry, disease and settler descendants over decades. Along with sculptural monuments commemorating losses on site, I look forward to seeing a feature length film that tells the truth about massacres and the colonial disruption carried out in the Wide Bay region and K'gari (Fraser Island) one day.

## 6.6 Truth-Telling

In Australia today, it is common to encounter in public discussions in the arts and academia expressions of strong support for truth-telling about our violent history and a collective desire to counter historical denial through public memorials that commemorate Aboriginal deaths on the colonial frontier. In public forums, such as *The Boiler Room Lecture: Walking on Bones, Empowering Memory* that took place at the State Library of Victoria in 2018, researchers often note that currently there are few public memorials to Aboriginal losses in Australia (Foley, 2018). While truth-telling must occur and certainly more memorials must be built, it is imperative that these calls do not overlook the persistent work of countless artists, like myself, who have been engaged in countering national ignorance and creating public reminders and memorials to these difficult pasts for many decades when it was not readily embraced. It is important to remember that when I started out creating art in the 1980s, in my early career and over the successive four decades, telling my historical truth was not supported or encouraged in the visual arts but actually shunned. In fact, my ventures into making work about Aboriginal massacre sites brought me painful encounters from my Aboriginal and artistic peers, and I was left feeling ostracised on many occasions. This is the difficult price I've paid for being a forerunner in this field, as someone who has used their voice to steadfastly bring to light unpalatable and confronting frontier histories when it was not accepted or celebrated. I now see many Aboriginal artist's working in this area and it's become a topic that is more readily discussed by receptive Australian audiences. I have tirelessly worked in this area to honour my Badtjala warriors who fought a twenty-year resistance on their Country against white invaders. I continue their steadfast resistance to this day through forms of uncompromising art that breaks the silence on frontier violence.

# References

Atkinson, J. (2002). *Trauma trails: Recreating song lines.* Spinifex Press.

Braidotti, R. (2011). *Nomadic theory: The portable Rosi Braidotti.* Columbia University Press.

Drew, W. L. G., Gregory, A. C., Coxen, C., & Hausmann, J. G. (1874). *Aborigines of Queensland: Report of the Commissioners.* Queensland Legislative Assembly. James C. Beal, Government Printer. https://aiatsis.gov.au/sites/default/files/docs/digitised_collections/remove/92128. pdf. Accessed 1 June 2023.

Evans, R., & Ørsted-Jensen, R. (2014). 'I cannot say the numbers that were killed': Assessing violent mortality on the Queensland frontier. *Social Science Research Network, 2467836,* 1–11. https://doi.org/10.2139/ssrn.2467836

Evans, R., & Walker, J. (1977). 'These strangers, where are they going?' Aboriginal-European relations in the Fraser Island and wide bay region 1770–1905. In *Occasional papers in anthropology no. 8.* Anthropology Museum. University of Queensland.

Foley, F. (1994). Traditional boundaries: New perspectives. *Periphery, 18,* 8–10.

Foley, F. (2018, July 6). The spectacle of Aboriginal Frontier War memorial research. *ArtsHub.* https://www.artshub.com.au/news/opinions-analysis/the-spectacle-of-aboriginal-frontier-war-memorial-research-256020-2360000/. Accessed 5 June 2023.

Foley, F. (2020). *Biting the clouds: A Badtjala perspective on the aboriginals protection and restriction of the sale of Opium Act, 1897.* University of Queensland Press.

Haebich, A. (2006, May 2–27). Fact, fantasy and fraud on Australian frontiers. In *3 Projects,* Casula Powerhouse Arts Centre.

Kelly, M. (2016). Art & massacre: the necessary memory of loss. *RealTime,* p. 133. https://www.realtime.org.au/art-massacre-the-necessary-memory-of-loss/. Accessed 1 June 2023.

Marr, D. (2019, November 18). Blood, brains and foul murder: Evidence of Australia's massacres is in its newspapers. *The Guardian.* https://www.theguardian.com/australia-news/2019/nov/18/blood-brains-and-foul-the-evidence-of-australias-massacres-are-in-its-newspapers. Accessed 1 June 2023.

Moreton-Robinson, A. (2020). The Drum Wednesday July 7. *ABC News.* https://www.abc.net.au/news/2020-07-03/the-drum-wednesday-july-3/12422190. Accessed 1 June 2023.

Morrell, T. (2009) Collector's Dossier: Fiona Foley. *Art Collector Magazine,* p. 50. https://artcollector.net.au/fiona-foley-collectors-dossier/. Accessed 1 June 2023.

Nicoll, F. (2010). No substitute: Political art against the opiate of the colonising euphemism. In *Forbidden: Fiona Foley.* Museum of Contemporary Art.

Poignant, R. (2004). *Professional savages: Captive lives and western spectacle.* Yale University Press.

Reynolds, H. (2021). *Truth-telling: History, sovereignty and the Uluru Statement.* Newsouth Publishing.

Titmarsh, L. (2014). *Mary and Susan: Sister rivers of the Fraser coast.* Jinglestix.

Watego, C. (2021, February 3). When Collingwood Football Club take the high ground, literally. *IndigenousX.* https://indigenousx.com.au/when-collingwood-football-club-take-the-high-ground-literally/. Accessed 29 August 2022.

**Fiona Foley (Batjala)** is an Associate Professor and Principal Research Fellow at University of Queensland's School of Historical and Philosophical Inquiry. Fiona has a national and international profile as a leading contemporary artist and historian. Her work has produced substantial new knowledge around the *Queensland Aboriginals Protection and Restriction of the Sale of Opium Act* (1897), and her numerous exhibitions have shared this knowledge with audiences across the globe. Fiona has exhibited over 50 solo exhibitions and 175 group shows, created 14 public art commissions, and her art works are held in 23 collections including The British Museum and the Hood Museum of Art in New Hampshire, USA. Her monograph *Biting the Clouds: A*

*Badtjala perspective on the Aboriginals Protection and Restriction of the Sale of Opium Act* was awarded the Queensland Premier's Award for a Work of State Significance in 2021, alongside a Highly Commended in the 2022 NSW Premier's Literary Awards. Fiona was awarded an Australian Research Council Discovery Early Career Researcher Award (DECRA) for her project, 'Investigating the Agency of Aboriginal Frontier War Memorials'.

# Chapter 7
# Mass Exposure: Memory Laundering, Racial Literacy and the Art of Truth-Telling

**Odette Kelada and Dianne Jones**

**Abstract** In this chapter, Odette Kelada and Dianne Jones argue that attempts to obscure the connections between colonial celebrated names and places from their origins in acts of slavery, eugenics and genocide, can be understood as a form of what they describe as 'memory laundering'. There is a correlation between the laundering of *dirty money* and the morphing of historic figures through a sequence of distortions and erasures to enable them to emerge *white-washed*, as elevated and revered fixtures foundational to a sacralised national landscape and imaginary. They explore this idea in relation to the factual transmission of nation building wealth having roots both in the profits of slavery money from the British Empire through the transatlantic slave trade, and the slavery of First Nations Peoples; as prisoners, as domestic labour, and enslaved in industries including pearling and sugar. The role of omission and denial in education and the visual colonising through statues, street names and commemorative practices in place making, are pivotal to this process. Kelada and Jones explore how this strategic use of forgetting may be countered through increasing racial literacy, drawing on art by Jones and other First Peoples artists as examples of creative interventions and decolonising practices that refuse this constructed ignorance and expose historical crimes through truth-telling.

## 7.1 Introduction

Feminist author and Black Lives Matters facilitator, Adrienne Maree Brown describes the work of 'all the black speculative fiction writers' who influenced her, as bending 'the world into fractals of truth and justice to help us see ourselves' (Maree Brown, 2019). This description comes to mind when attempting to convey the power and critical importance of the work of Indigenous artists who are exposing the crimes of

---

O. Kelada (✉)
University of Melbourne, Naarm/Melbourne, Australia
e-mail: okelada@unimelb.edu.au

D. Jones
Naarm/Melbourne, Australia

© The Author(s), under exclusive license to Springer Nature Singapore Pte Ltd. 2024
G. Grieves and A. Spiers (eds.), *Art and Memorialisation*, Indigenous-Settler Relations in Australia and the World 6, https://doi.org/10.1007/978-981-97-6289-7_7

past and ongoing violence and denial in this country. Their art fractures and reveals the distortions and contortions that have gone into the white mythology of colonial benevolence that constructs *heroic pioneers* and *peaceful settlement*. They are the ones doing the work of mass exposure given the range, sophistication and prolific scale of Indigenous art that continually points to the buried truths and refuses to back down. It is an honour to be part of a book that recognises and acknowledges these artists, their creativity, courage and the relentless labour of bending the world to draw on Brown's lyric description. This idea of creative practices that can help us see, conjures the imagery of disrupting the linear through shaping and forging fractals, splitting the gaze to hold up mirrors, reflecting and challenging perceptions. Creative interventions can open our vision to dimensions that exist beyond presumed narratives and dominant stories taught and inherited through generations.

We coin the term in this chapter 'memory laundering' to describe colonial memorial practices, as there is a correlation between the laundering of *dirty money* and the morphing of historic figures through a sequence of erasures to enable them to emerge sanitised and *white-washed*. Through commemorative practices from statues to place names, and public symbolism, these figures emerge as elevated and revered fixtures foundational to a sacralised national landscape and imaginary. This elevation is dependent on forgetting the inconvenient and unpalatable facts of colonial violence and exploitation. When we speak of money we make reference to the factual transmission of nation building wealth having roots both in the profits of slavery money from the British empire through the transatlantic slave trade, and the slavery of First Nations Peoples; as prisoners, as domestic labour, as pastoral labour, as sexually exploited and enslaved in industries including pearling, cotton and sugar. We explore how this strategic use of forgetting may be countered through increasing racial literacy that foregrounds truth-telling.

The term 'racial literacy' emerged in the early 2000s through the critical legal scholarship of Lani Guinier writing on racial segregation in education (2004) and in Britain through the sociological work of France Winddance-Twine on inter-racial families (2004). Racial literacy has since become influential in race scholarship across a range of disciplines and pedagogies. We have written about racial literacy in more detail in our article with Brown et al. (2021). In this article, we discuss a course on racial literacy that we teach and argue for the importance of increasing race education and awareness in Australia. Racial literacy can be understood as:

> … the development of literacy skills specifically designed to enable critical understandings of race and how race operates in contemporary contexts. The skills required for racial literacy involve learning and communicating through multiple modes, with an awareness of power relations influencing identity formation, social practices and institutionalised systems. (Brown et al., 2021, p. 85)[1]

Understanding the impact of representation is key in racial literacy approaches. This chapter draws on the work of Indigenous artists, with a case study of the art practice of co-author Dianne Jones, as artists are actively countering this constructed

---

[1] Our article drew on the work of racial literacy theorists including Guinier (2004), France Twine (2004), Rogers and Mosley (2006), and Johnson (2009).

ignorance through creative interventions and decolonising practices (Fig. 7.1). Artists are challenging the colonial legacies of racist representations and offer a vital reimagining of how power can be subverted and truths about the past exposed. The prolific output and scale of this artistic contribution and the activism from Indigenous voices are what we refer to as a 'mass exposure', given the degree of concealment and memory laundering involved in creating sanitised and heroic nations on the bones of the colonised and unceded sovereign land.

Resistance against conventional commemorative practices is evident in the actions to remove statues that represent these oppressive histories. At the time of writing, radical and transformative images continue to surface fresh from global scenes of decolonising and Black Lives Matter protests where statues are stained with red paint to represent the blood that famous figures shed and heads rolled literally; Colston toppled forcefully into the Bristol Harbour, Rhodes lifted by crane from his pedestal in Cape Town, the statue of an enslaved man kneeling at Lincolns feet removed in Boston, Canada's first Prime Minister John MacDonald taken down after a unanimous vote in Charlottetown. The list continues to grow internationally, from plantation slave owners and traders to politicians, generals, architects, leaders of residential schools and proponents for eugenics and genocidal policies. Australia is yet to add significantly to this list, however the statue of former Premier of Tasmania, William Crowther, was voted to be removed in 2022 after years of campaigning by Indigenous

**Fig. 7.1** Dianne Jones, *L.H.O.O.Q 'ERE!* (2001). Inkjet print on canvas 111.2 × 88.8 cm. State Art Collection, Art Gallery of Western Australia. Image courtesy of the artist

activists led to the Hobart council vote. Crowther, a surgeon and politician, was involved in exhuming bodies and stole an Aboriginal man's skull to send the Royal College of Surgeons in London (Australian Associated Press, 2022).

In response to the protests, governments and lawmakers retaliated globally with a hyper-vigilant safeguarding of symbols that included heavy-handed punitive laws for protestors and produced surreal images of protection with statues wrapped and sealed, some caged behind wire, others bandaged in the confederate flag. In Sydney's Hyde Park, uniformed officers formed a circle around the statue of Captain Cook with a police presence diverted from supposedly protecting the public to protecting a colonial symbol. In the US, following attempts by demonstrators to pull down the statue of former president Andrew Jackson—a slave owner who was instrumental in the genocide of Native Americans—by throwing rope around the statue's neck and the horse it was mounted on, Trump threatened imprisonment of protesters in a tweet stating, 'I have authorized the Federal Government to arrest anyone who vandalizes or destroys any monument, statue or other such Federal property in the U.S. with up to 10 years in prison' (Sprunt, 2020). The UK brought in new laws with The Police, Crime, Sentencing and Courts Bill which multiplied the penalty time for criminal damage to a memorial, from one year to ten years. This is double the penalty time for rape. This lead the UK Labour opposition shadow justice secretary, David Lammy, to make the point: 'Why are we saying that pulling down a statue is more important than a woman's body? That's the question you should be asking the government' (Sky News, 2021).

To understand why white male bodies represented in stone, concrete or bronze are worth more than living people and certainly worth more than women, is to understand something about the stakes involved in warping history and then protecting the signifiers that manifest that history into embodied narratives. Himself a figure who's statue was splattered in red paint and sprayed with the words 'Black Lives Matter' and 'was a racist', Winston Churchill exemplified this with his famous line 'I consider that it will be found much better by all Parties to leave the past to history, especially as I propose to write that history myself' (Churchill, 1948). He also said 'We shape our buildings, and afterwards our buildings shape us' (Churchill, 1943a). However, Churchill likely would not have foreseen what that meant for his own monument. His statue outside Parliament Square was completely entombed in a futuristic looking steel box after continual activist interventions (otherwise referred to in some media as 'vandalism' and 'defacement'). The boxing of Churchill was a pre-emptive move by officials in trepidation of a planned race protest in London. Imperialism requires internal as well as external domination as Churchill knew well, given he also stated 'The empires of the future are the empires of the mind' (Churchill, 1943b). The fight over these figures and memorial landscapes is still an imperial battle and it is one where the stakes are not as much about the past, as the future. This is one of the reasons why artists are so important and often on the front lines as creators of possible futures—of what can be imagined, envisioned, destroyed, illuminated and exposed.

In Australia, the education system is prime territory in the fight for future empires through shaping the *empires of the mind*. The absence of public sites telling truths about colonisation and First Peoples sovereignty, presence and stories, alongside curriculum and pedagogy that fails to adequately educate allows a toxic ignorance to be inherited across generations and transmitted to those arriving to this country. As a student, Leela Gray, in an essay for our racial literacy subject describes:

> As a young student immigrating to Australia, I wasn't aware of Aboriginal and Torres Strait Islander peoples until my second year living in Melbourne. How could I have been completely unaware of the custodians of the land I was living on for a whole year? There were no political statues, billboards, or dominant news media coverage that I could recall acknowledging that First Peoples existed. It wasn't until Year 9 History that I was confronted with the concept of living on unceded land, however, the delivery of this information was constrained and up for classroom debate.[2]

While there is talk of invasion, genocide, massacres and violence, the rhetorical mode contains these topics in a framework of being *debatable* and a matter or *perspectives* as opposed to factual historical truths. This is why recognition of the need for truth-telling is so important. Wiradjuri, Ngemba and Paakantji writer and storyteller Gemma Pol notes the repeated calls for truth-telling by First Peoples:

> The Uluru Statement from the Heart called for a Makarrata Commission to supervise processes of truth-telling and treaty-making. Other reports have recognised the need for truth-telling on a national scale, including: the report from the Royal Commission into Aboriginal Deaths in Custody, the Bringing Them Home Report, the Council for Aboriginal Reconciliation's final report, and the Referendum Council's final report. Each identifies steps in understanding the truths of the past to avoid repeating the wrongs. (Pol, 2021)

In April 2021, the Australian Curriculum, Assessment and Reporting Authority (ACARA) proposed changes to the national curriculum, making a commitment to truth-telling in the education system about First Peoples and colonisation, including replacing the term 'settlement' with the accurate word 'invasion'. This unleashed virulent pushback including responses by politicians and public commentators accusing them of taking a 'chainsaw to the curriculum' (Carey et al., 2021) and 'driving history through the guilt-ridden lens of revisionism' (Visentin & Baker, 2021).

In order to resist truth-telling, memory laundering is a critical part of colonising the future. We propose that memory laundering is a process by which the remembrance of violence and exploitation is erased through constant repetition of heroic mythologising practices while simultaneously denying any factual knowledge and impact of any violence. It is a play on the term 'money laundering'. The money from criminal activity is considered *dirty* and the process of laundering makes it appear clean, concealing the true source. Memories of crimes and the perpetrators can similarly be whitewashed to distort factual histories and conceal the origins of wealth rooted in past violences. Laundering connotes the conversion of illegal and fraudulent capital into forms that emerge and circulate as condoned and legitimate without the taint of its true origins. To launder memory allows those figures involved

---

[2] Quoted from an unpublished student essay, University of Melbourne Racial Literacy subject, 2020. Published with permission from the student.

in slavery and massacres to tower in stately glory above public spaces as celebrated bastions of virtue, symbolic of colonial benevolence and victorious righteousness.

Australia as a nation has been so efficient at laundering collective memory that as well as barely recognising even the basic fact of British invasion, there is little taught about Australia's connections with slavery and that it is foundational to this country. Slavery, we are taught, happened elsewhere. This view is exemplified by comments on slavery by former Prime Minister, Scott Morrison in 2020. When asked for his thoughts on calls for statues such as Captain Cook to be removed, Morrison responded that Cook was a most enlightened man and that: 'While slave ships continued to travel around the world.... there was no slavery in Australia' (cited in Borys, 2020). This remark was met with calls from Indigenous politicians and activists including Linda Burney, Pat Dodson and slavery survivor advocate, Moe Turuga, to recognise the stories of slavery here (Borys, 2020; Buchanan, 2020). The histories of South Sea Islander Peoples kidnapped in a practice known as 'blackbirding' and brought to Australia to work in sugar plantations, the 'stolen wages' of First Peoples in pastoral and domestic servitude, along with exploitation in industries such as pearling, were brought to the fore in the public backlash following Morrison's comments, to ensure these histories were not so conveniently denied. In this case, the need to educate the prime minister over his veneration of Cook and demonstrated ignorance in dismissing the impacts of slavery in Australia proved to be also an opportunity for truth-telling and racial literacy on a national scale.

The urgent need for schools to require an education on these critical histories is also evident. In early 2022, a teacher gave out an assessment task to Year 9 students at Lake Macquarie High School, a school located in regional New South Wales, on developing argumentative skills. The task gave students the option to speak from the position of either the US Minister for the Economy or Minister for Human Rights. For those that took up the option of Minister for the Economy, the task description read 'You outline the positive contribution slaves make to the economies of Africa, England and the United States'. A photo of the assessment handout became circulated on social media, igniting outrage at the idea that students would be asked to argue slavery was positive. Jagorda Manyuon, whose younger siblings received the assessment, claimed a teacher had told students that those who wrote from the perspective of the Minister for the Economy would receive higher marks for demonstrating critical thinking (Woolley, 2022). This incident exemplifies again the choice continually made in contemporary Australian society, to represent violent histories as matters of perspective that are up for debate and argument rather than facts taught as part of a comprehensive anti-racist education. In response to the disbelief and anger in the student community and wider public following the exposure on social media, the NSW Department of Education has declared that there would be an investigation.

While these examples indicate the lack of knowledge around even basic understandings of slavery and ethical pedagogy, the full impacts of this country's links to slavery require further research to uncover the stories of how capital that helped to finance the foundation of colonial Australia can be traced directly to profits from the Atlantic slave trade, from plantation ownership and payouts for property loss. Slaves were considered chattel and in order to finally pass the legislation to abolish slavery, money was given to slave owners as compensation for their loss. Australia's direct connections with those slave ships that Morrison mentioned as travelling 'around the world' but not here, are emerging in greater detail due to new research. One of the catalysts for this new research is access to a database titled 'Legacies of British Slavery (LBS)' by the University of College London, developed in 2014, which for the first time provides public access to an accessible search engine to locate all the names of those who were compensated in 1835 under the Slavery Abolition Act (2024). It is now possible to track the branches of slave wealth around the globe. An Australian Research Council funded project titled 'Western Australian Legacies of British Slave Ownership Project' is currently tracing the connections linking up the global slave trade with families that brought that capital to Australia (2021). One of the researchers on this project, historian Georgina Arnott notes:

> This story has implications for Australia. Compensation was paid to at least 150 families who settled in the Australian colonies. These included high-profile figures, such as judges, religious ministers, governors, journalists, pastoralists, financiers, commercial agents and writers. These settlers were typically born in a plantation colony to families that had accrued wealth, education and social advancement through the enslavement of people. (Arnott 2020)

The list of names often aligns with those who are currently commemorated in some form, given the conjunction of money with privilege, status and influence. Arnott and other researchers, continue to add to the roll call of such names from slave owning families including Victorian Supreme Court judge Sir Edward Williams (1813–80), Melbourne lord mayor and member of the Victorian Legislative Assembly Godfrey Carter (1830–1902), Chairman of the Melbourne stock exchange and *Age* journalist Robert Wallen (1831–93), Poet Adam Lindsay Gordon (1833–70) and Sydney University Vice-Chancellor Robert Allwood (1803–1891). The point of these names is not limited to individuals but allows for the mapping and recovering of truths never taught about the circulation and operation of imperial capital, patterns of exploitation and the connections that created the conditions today for ongoing inequities, wealth disparities, exclusion and division. The growing recognition of legacies of systemic violence shaping the lived realities and brutalities of marginalised peoples has ignited protest movements from Black Lives Matter, Indigenous Lives Matter and Rhodes Must Fall to Why is My Curriculum so White and the myriad diverse outpourings of community activism around statues, policing, education, history and justice.

## 7.2 Counter Memory Making

The art of truth-telling is central to the creative interventions and counter memory making that has exploded into public spaces through these protests. The inventiveness, and wit of Indigenous artists involved in mass exposure of colonial crimes form compelling creative testimonies. An example of one artist's fierce humour in responding to the protest of statues, can be seen in Tony Albert's video work made in 2020, titled *You Wreck Me*. In a parody of the 2013 popular music video, *Wrecking*

*Ball*, where singer Miley Cyrus rides astride a wrecking ball singing of being heart-broken, Albert flips the lyrics of what it means to be wrecked from a pop song to a commentary on the devastation of invasion and the artifice involved in raising up statues of the invaders. He straddles a wrecking ball to swing and smash down statues of Cook and the Endeavour ship with glee. As disembodied limbs and heads fly through the air, Albert embraces the explosive subversion of the trickster figure to harness the ridiculous and demolish the absurd celebration of colonial discovery (Albert, 2020). As the ship sinks and the statues are reduced to rubble, the pastiche style of the visual collage combined with Alberts comical performance of the song 'Wrecking Ball', ensures that any sense of heroism or glorification is smashed to pieces.

Artists are at the heart of exposing the whitewashing and memory laundering, employing a range of diverse creative strategies to reveal the hidden histories and pain behind the façade of nationalism and reverence at sites of commemoration and memorials. It is critical to acknowledge that Indigenous artists have been doing this activist work for many years. In 2000, a film titled *Confessions of a Headhunter* captured the irony of the violence and vandalism that First Peoples have endured whenever there has been a rare moment of recognising their presence and sovereignty (Riley, 2000). There are very few statues acknowledging First Peoples and when they have been commissioned, they are often subjected to extreme violence from bullet holes to decapitation. *Confessions of a Headhunter* was based on a short story by Noongar writer, Archie Weller, who was inspired by the repeated beheading of Yagan's statute, *Yagan* (1984), sculpted by Indigenous artist, Robert Hitchcock. Yagan was a Noongar warrior who mounted fierce and strategic resistance to invading colonial forces on the frontier in Western Australia. His own head was sent to England after he was killed in 1833. In 1997 his head was finally repatriated. That same year, the head of Yagan's statue was cut off with an angle grinder. This beheading became a repeated occurrence in Heirisson Island, Perth where the statue was situated. Weller created a story of revenge for these beheadings. Two Noongar men travel around decapitating bronze statutes of white men. They do not stop however at the point of destruction. They melt the bronze down to make a sculpture of an Aboriginal woman and child looking out over the ocean at the location where Cook landed. This transformative alchemy, in both the reformation of the metal and the repositioning of whose bodies are made into statutes and whose stories are thereby seen and remembered, speaks to the power of creativity and truth-telling.

We will now explore in detail the practice of co-author Dianne Jones in creating art that employs a range of activist strategies, from humour and counter narrative, to making space for witnessing violent histories, and explore the inspirations and challenges from her perspective as an artist. Jones' art practice is deeply engaged with racial literacy and truth-telling as she consistently asks audiences to question the conventional racist tropes and representations of First Peoples presented in colonial art, dives deeply into the historical archives to share stories of family and those who have been left out of national mythologies, and exposes the ways memory laundering of founding fathers conceals criminal complicity (Fig. 7.2).

**Fig. 7.2** Dianne Jones, *The Great Heads* (2017) from *The Grand Tour* series. Inkjet print on paper 53.0 × 80.0 cm. State Art Collection, Art Gallery of Western Australia. Image courtesy of the artist

In 2001, Jones made a work that appears now somewhat prescient of the recent spray painting on Cook's statue. She performed an act of graffiti on a portrait of Captain Cook. Referencing the moustache that Marcel Duchamp placed over the smile of the Mona Lisa in *L.H.O.O.Q* (1919) as a commentary on the hyperbole around this one image, Jones imposes a moustache on the face of Captain Cook. The title of Jones' work extends on Duchamp's own phonetic word play of the initials L.H.O.O.Q which translates to 'she has a hot ass' in French, a form of rude latrine (toilet) humour. Jones calls her work on Cook *L.H.O.O.Q 'ERE!* (2001) and was made in direct response to the announcement that the National Gallery had decided to purchase a portrait of Cook for 3.5 million dollars.

As Jones says on the catalyst for this work (Fig. 7.1):

> In 2000, I was really struck by watching the news and Australians were marching across bridges for reconciliation in every state. As an Aboriginal woman, I marched and it was heartening to see how many cared enough. At the same time, Howard was refusing to say sorry for The Stolen Generation and that there was no genocide. Then the National Gallery in Canberra purchased this work for millions which could not represent colonisation more. Cook is known for leaving a trail of blood. I am referencing Duchamp but using Noongar slang to call it out to fullas, 'Look 'Ere'. Look what they are doing buying this painting, glorifying Cook when there has been no apology for The Stolen Generation, Stolen Wages, invasion, genocide. (Personal communication, 9 June 2022)

Jones has worked for over 30 years as a political photo media artist and her practice has consistently brought attention to the skewered representations of colonial nationalist fantasies and First Peoples' perspectives and resistance. Her metaphorical

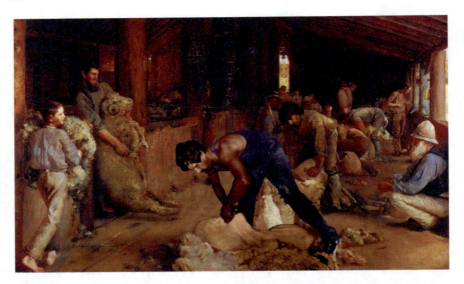

**Fig. 7.3** Dianne Jones, *Shearing the Rams* (2001). Inkjet print on treated canvas 121.9 × 182.6 cm. State Art Collection, Art Gallery of Western Australia. Image courtesy of the artist

and literal lens brings sharply into focus the role of romanticism, and myth-making in both the colonial and contemporary racist imaginary. Her early series on iconic Australian painting reframed the celebrated bush scenes and landscapes of John Glover and Eugene Von Guerard, where images of First Peoples appear as romanticised caricatures or extensions of the flora and fauna. In place of homogenous and anonymous black figures 'dancing' or 'bartering', Jones inserts up front and centre her own family portraits from her sister's wedding to a family picnic into Glover's landscapes. The quotidian and ordinary lived experiences of her childhood growing up in a Noongar family, are brought to the fore through contrast and juxtaposition to disrupt the othering gaze and unsettle the dehumanising visions of some imagined colonial idyll. In another work for this series, *Shearing the Rams* (2001) (Fig. 7.3), the white shearing team in the quintessential Tom Roberts' painting *Shearing the Rams* (1890) is replaced with Jones's own father, who was a gun shearer,[3] and her brother. The nostalgic fantasy of an Australia made rich off the sheep's back and hard sweat of white labour is unravelled to reveal the mass exploitation of First People's labour to build the wealth of the nation. True stories of no pay and stolen wages speak to the slavery buried beneath images of heroic pioneers and stoic immigrant farmers.

In a follow up series to this intervention into iconic historical imagery, Jones travels forward to the mid twentieth century and critically *vandalises* Max Dupain's photographs of bodies revered in art culture as capturing some kind of Australian

---

[3] Gun shearer is the term for a professional shearer who is fast and shears more than 200 sheep a day.

**Fig. 7.4** Dianne Jones, *Sunbaker* (2003). Digital print 38.6 × 43.4 cm. Image courtesy of the artist

essence through beach portraits such as *Sunbaker* (1937). In *Sunbaker* (2003), Jones removes the white man and places her own body on the beach towel, with head raised to stare directly down the camera in a classic embodiment of bell hooks' 'oppositional gaze' (Fig. 7.4). As hooks writes in *Black Looks*:

> ... all attempts to repress our/black people's right to gaze had produced in us an overwhelming longing to look, a rebellious desire, an oppositional gaze. By courageously looking, we defiantly declared: 'Not only will I stare. I want my look to change reality'. Even in the worse circumstances of domination, the ability to manipulate one's gaze in the face of structures of domination that would contain it, opens up the possibility of agency. (Hooks, 1992, p. 160)

In 2017, Jones made a series of works titled *The Grand Tour* as part of a new artist residency program at Western Australia's Parliament House. This series explicitly addresses the power of monuments, statues, ritual, pomp and public art collections displayed in collective sites of statehood and nation making. The name 'Grand Tour' refers to a practice popular from the seventeenth to nineteenth century of sending the young men of aristocratic families around Europe as a rite of passage to gain an education in culture and study the classics of western civilisation. The heart of the Tour were cities such as Rome, where a reverence for marble statues, classical antiquities and sculpture influenced ideas of monuments, art and architecture across the British Empire and colonies.

Jones's *Grand Tour* draws on performance, embodiment and humour to point out the disparate and historically oppressive aspects of the commemorative and memorial objects that the public walk past in the official tour of Western Australia's Parliament House. Jones appears in the works dressed in a suit styled as a contemporary male parliamentarian, touring the sites where portraits and busts of figures are placed prominently honouring of key past members of the government. In one work, Jones stands next to a painting portraying the so-called *founders* of the state. The painting is titled *An Early Meeting of the Legislative Council*, and while it has the appearance of a historical oil painting, the artist, Owen Garde, was commissioned in 1981 as part of a celebration of 150 years of Western Australia's government. The painting shows the first governor of Western Australia, Sir James Stirling. At the table are four men he appointed to administer the Swan River Colony. Their names are listed as His Excellency Hon. Capt. James Stirling, Hon. Peter Broun, Hon. William Henry Mackie, Hon. Capt. Frederick Chidley Irwin, Hon. John Septimus Roe, along with the council clerk. Cm. Mark. John. Currie. At Parliament House, the didactic text to the side of the painting speaks to the commission of Garde, showing some early pencil sketches and the context of the work as commemorative. There is no mention that the majority of men honoured at this table are implicated in the murder of First Peoples (Fig. 7.5).

Jones' work responds to calls to recognise the violence committed by figures elevated as heroes in Western Australia that have been mounting for years. In 2019, there was a campaign to change the name of the Stirling Highway to an Aboriginal name, in recognition of Stirling's role in the massacres of Aboriginal people. The campaign did not succeed. In 2020, Stirling's statue in Perth was amended with red paint and the commemorative plaque transformed into an Aboriginal flag by protestors. Greens Senator Jordon Steele-John not long after caused a media sensation with his tweet 'Time to stop celebrating these men and hold them accountable for the roles they played in WA's history of First Nations Genecide [sic]' (cited in Hondros, 2020).

**Fig. 7.5** Dianne Jones, *The Great Clock* (2017) from *The Grand Tour* series. Ink jet print on paper 53.0 × 80.0 cm. State Art Collection, The Art Gallery of Western Australia. Image courtesy of the artist

In 2020, an art collective called The Statue Review ensured the violence such figures committed was publicly exposed in an action where new, unofficial plaques were placed under the statues of Stirling and Roe, telling of their role in the Pinjarra massacre. The plaques read:

ON 28 OCTOBER 1834 CAPTAIN STIRLING LED THE PINJARRA MASSACRE, AN ATTACK ON THE BINDJAREB NOONGAR CAMP THAT KILLED UP TO 80 NOONGAR MEN, WOMEN AND CHILDREN.

**HE BELONGS IN A MUSEUM, NOT ON OUR STREETS**

THE STATUE REVIEW. (cited in Conaghan, 2020)

In a video by The Statue Review documenting the engraving of these plaques and their unsanctioned installation at the feet of these statutes, a voice over from the collective observes that: '… in the future people will look back and be astonished that we ever tolerated living under the shadow of statues of men who were slave traders or colonialists' (Juanola, 2020).

Research from the 'Western Australian Legacies of British Slave Ownership Project' is proving critical in exposing and providing compelling evidence of the details in these connections with slavery (Arnott et al., 2022). The emerging recognition of the entanglement between colonisation and slavery has led to revelations that Stirling was a figure with direct connections to the Atlantic slave trade. As Georgia Arnott notes in her article arguing for the need to update history books, Stirling's rise to captaincy was connected with this status. He came from a Glaswegian family whose immense wealth was earned through British slavery. Stirling lobbied for the founding of the colony in Western Australia, with his campaign:

… driven by his father-in-law, James Mangles, a wealthy Atlantic ocean slaver whose ships were transporting convicts to New South Wales by the 1820s… In his proposals for the Western Australia settlement, Governor James Stirling worked with the pro-slavery advocate Thomas Moody to recommend to the Colonial office a three-tiered, racially segregated society. (Arnott, 2021)

Chief investigator on the Western Australia Legacies project, Jane Lydon, reveals in the article 'From Slavery to Settler Colonisation' how:

In 1834 the 21st Regiment of Foot led the most intense phase of violence between colonists and Binjareb Nyungar, climaxing in the infamous 1834 Pinjarra Massacre. A decade earlier in 1823, soldiers in the 21st Regiment of Foot played a prominent role in quelling the landmark Demerara slave rebellion, in what is now Guyana. The common use of legal violence reveals continuities between British slave and settler colonies. (Lydon, 2023)

The links are literal and embodied with the same soldiers experienced in enforcing slavery being organised by Stirling in his massacre of First Peoples at Pinjarra. In the painting of the legislative council, Stirling is represented as the leader of the 'founding fathers', the only one standing up at the table. As well as Stirling and Roes, others seated have also been subject to interrogation for their role in massacres. For the Perth Festival in 2021, a walking performance took place at a site of colonial killings, entitled *Galup*. This piece was created by Noongar theatre maker Ian Wilkes with oral history from Elder Doolann Leisha Eatts and a team of Noongar Elders. Official records report that on 3 May 1830, British forces murdered Noongar people at Galup. Irwin and Mackie were involved in these violent attacks. On 18 May 1830, Captain Irwin wrote a letter to Governor Stirling describing the objective of the attack he led as 'impressing a salutary dread of our superiority and arms' (cited in Owen & Bracknel, 2021).

Jones stands beside the stately commissioned painting of these colonists looking directly back at the camera rather than at the image. She titles this work *The Great Clock* (2017). Greatness here is bestowed on the random clock that happens to be hung on the wall above the painting. This shift in expectation of the central focus, plays on the honorific titles given to such portraits of the many apparently *great* white men and their *grand* histories. Jones highlights the fact that it is a matter of intention and attention. The choice of who is remembered and how the language of memorialisation can be manipulated to convey heroics, rather than the facts of violence, reflects colonial and contemporary power relations. The public is kept at bay from the work, which is cordoned off with red rope. Anything one chooses can be called *great*, elevated and partitioned off with official props. In making the unassuming clock *great*, Jones points to the ridiculous nature of pomp and ceremony, the reliance of these representations on performance and staging, and ultimately the artificial and contrived nature of memory laundering.

In other works in *The Grand Tour* series, Jones plays a range of subversive roles. She highlights the absence of First Peoples from the parliament spaces, and also the way in which the celebration of men contrasts with the few portraits and busts of women, and the choice of sites. One wall of women's portraits is placed opposite the women's toilets. After pointing to the erasures and comparative gaps, Jones then makes a work that turns this silencing around. She clones herself multiple times to take over the entire legislative chamber. She positions herself in all of the minister's seats and embodies their forms, performing the various poses that she watched them adopt during question time. In one chair, she is sleeping, in another she is chewing gum, or rubbing her temples or laughing. She is the minister speaking passionately on the floor, surrounded by more images of herself in various stages of attentiveness or boredom. Jones is the speaker. She also sits in front of the speaker wearing robes and wigs, listening to the arguments of parliamentarians. In one pose she has her hands over her mouth, another over her eyes and the third, over her ears to symbolically speak no evil, hear no evil, see no evil. This work is titled *The Great Echo Chamber* (2017) (Fig. 7.6). In a sense, this is counter memorial making in action. The laws that were made in that very room were not made by First Peoples but were inflicted on them. The laws and policies born in that site, shaped the innumerable forms of cruelty, exclusion and oppression that entrenched legacies of inequality and injustice since colonisation when men like so-called *His Excellency* Captain Stirling and those seated at that table, invaded Western Australia. As Jones asks:

> What if there were Aboriginal bodies in this place? Would my family have been sent onto a reserve? What decisions would be made if Aboriginal people would have been able to make the decisions? What would have changed? Whose bodies are in this frame and why? In every seat in parliament house, they were making decisions for Aboriginal people. My

**Fig. 7.6** Dianne Jones, *The Great Echo Chamber* (2017) from the Grand Tour series. Ink jet print on paper 120 × 180 cm. State Art Collection, Art Gallery of Western Australia. Image courtesy of the artist

people. Always the same questions—why are we so controlled and why are decisions made for us by people not invested in our culture?

A lot of people will put an Aboriginal person in a traditional outfit or try to put colonised ideas into those spaces but not know what it is like to be who we are. We haven't been able to grow up on our land. We've lost so much of how to be on our land but I can't put what we have lost into an artwork. I can only talk about how we have been forced into the dominant culture. We are forced off our lands. These were concentration camps. So I sat in the back row at parliament house while question time was on, while they were in session. There are people on their phone—there is a lot happening in that space—some talking heatedly, others walking in and out. Decisions are being made that are really important for the whole state. What if they were all Aboriginal bodies? Aboriginal people in parliament house in every seat. It's never been seen. (Personal communication, 10 June 2022)

Jones continues the truth-telling with work taking on the legend of the ANZAC hero, bringing attention to the treatment of Aboriginal soldiers on returning from war. Jones created a public billboard that would list the laws and restrictions her own grandfather faced on coming back *home*. This work titled *Lest We Forget* (2007) shows the army photo of Murry Jones. On one side of his image is the list:

He was not a citizen

Did not have the right to vote

Refused entry into hotels

6.00pm street curfew.

**Fig. 7.7** Dianne Jones, *Lest We Forget* (2007). Unrealised design for a public billboard. Image courtesy of the artist

On the left side of the image is the text, 'australian hero' (Fig. 7.7).

This billboard was entered into a competition to create a public work. It was not chosen and has not had the opportunity yet to appear in any public space. This speaks to the many resistant artworks made that do not ever get seen. Those that are rejected because of the very nature of refusing dominant memory making and pointing instead to the ironies and hypocrisy of a country willing for Aboriginal men to give their lives and still not give them freedom or citizenship.

Bodies that matter, those of the coloniser, are worthy of memory. Other bodies, such as those of Aboriginal warriors and soldiers, are disappeared. The hope of the dominant culture is that they will be forgotten. Their fight, strength and resistance will have no traces. The way that murder is remembered is critical to the narratives of war, and in the Australian context, there is denial that there was even any Frontier War at all. A story that speaks to the stakes of retrospective commemoration is one that Jones explores in her series *What Lies Buried Rises* (2013). This series came about following an invitation to make art for an exhibition on the first courthouse of the colony. The court case Jones explored was the trial for the murder of the first white woman Sarah Cook by two Aboriginal men, Burrabong and Doodjeep. This case happened in York, Western Australia where Jones was born. Upon investigating the historical documents, Jones realised that there was no legally sound evidence for the hanging of these Aboriginal men for this crime. As Ann Hunter writes in her thesis on colonial law and the legality of this case:

> …the question of whether the accused had an understanding of British law and the court process was not considered, and in fact this ignorance was relied on in order to ensure a conviction. (2007, p.141)

Whilst Jones recalls talk of building a memorial for Sarah Cook in York, there appeared to be no talk of any memorial for the many Noongar peoples killed in the vigilante violence that occurred in retaliation for Cook's death. These were some of the worst massacres in Western Australia's history (Jones, 2015). Jones' art reflects on the challenges of delving into the past and finding out truth when archives prove unreliable and subject to interference, possibly buried with secrets and lies. As Jones says:

> In order to get the truth, you have to go through this traumatising experience, reading offensive racist language, trying to find out what happened, the stories that are told, what is left out. You can bury the past but it rises up. I literally dug into the earth around York finding pieces

of crockery, glass, spear shards. Searching for something with my hands in the ground. Being on your own land, trying to find bits of human existence. You want the earth to tell you what happened. Everything was broken. (Personal communication, 10 June 2022)

Jones created installations from found objects in York, displayed like pieces of evidence, incomplete and fractured. Some of her works inspired by this court case also played with repetition of an image that constantly changes clarity across the canvas, blurring pixels in the style of the Harvard Implicit Bias Test. In this test developed by social psychologists, subjects are primed with images of black or white faces and then shown repeated frames of a picture that slowly becomes clearer. Depending on the response to the racial priming, they see either a gun or a hairdryer first. This is the kind of testing to determine police racial bias, how quick they pull the trigger in deciding a person is holding a weapon or an innocuous object. It has also been used to determine racial bias in the legal system, effecting whether someone is found guilty or innocent (Scott, 2015). In the works inspired by this testing of doubt and bias, the eye is unsettled by the blurring of multiple miniature frames. Viewing the works can produce a physical affect, a sensation of imbalance or vertigo. For Jones, this destabilising is akin to the feeling of trying to unearth past stories. A history of distortion, omission and prejudice obscures truths and provokes more questions.

## 7.3 Conclusion

While writing this chapter, the council responsible for the inner north Melbourne local government area we live in declared they were changing its name of Moreland to the local Wurundjeri Woi Wurrung word of Merri-Bek (meaning 'rocky country') in recognition that the Moreland family was complicit in slavery. There are changes happening in response to the growing recognition of slave history and the movements to remove statues that are unlike anything that has occurred in the past. Exposure by artists of historical crimes and ongoing violences takes a particular form of intensive creative labour contributing to this activist momentum. As author Kelada has argued elsewhere with Genevieve Grieves, 'Artists are "hijacking" official archives to carve strategic interventions into the body of the nation state and ideas of hegemonic "truth" and "history"' (Kelada & Grieves, 2017). Through artworks the public has the opportunity to learn truths that continue to be denied in mainstream educational institutions. The fact that terms such as 'slavery', 'invasion' and 'war' are seen by some people in Australia, including the former Prime Minister, as having happened *elsewhere* and are too confronting to acknowledge, speak to the urgent need for increasing racial literacy and ensuring proper recognition, respect, platforms, autonomy and renumeration for artists, writers, activists and practitioners who continue to rupture the 'Great Australian Silence' (Stanner, 1968). In relation to the new research connecting imperial slavery networks with British colonisation of this country, as Arnott states:

> ... Plenty of questions remain. How did these former slave-owners and children of slave-owners shape the burgeoning Australian colonies, especially on matters of race and labour? How were relations between colonists and First Nations people influenced by the mass enslavement of Africans that some colonists had perpetuated and benefited from? (2021)

Artists are ensuring such questions are unable to be ignored as they expose the power that evasive rhetoric insists on reifying through national pride and celebrating peaceful 'settlement' over understanding and acknowledging realities of empirical domination, colonisation, extractive economies and labour exploitation.

While this chapter has focused on the work of Jones, so many other First Peoples artists have dedicated their practices to deep interrogation and truth-telling about these unacknowledged and denied pasts. Artists are indeed bending 'the world into fractals of truth and justice to help us see ourselves' (Maree Brown, 2019). It is critical to recognise how long artistic activism has been happening, as well as the resistance of the public and institutions that artists have endured given that their work compels non-Indigenous audiences to confront unpalatable truths. To mention just a few of the art works engaged in mass-exposure over the years, that exemplify the stories and truths vital to understanding the past and how it shapes inequality and racism today:

r e a in their artwork *Look Who's Calling the Kettle Black* (1993) incorporated with permission, photographs of young Aboriginal women into computer-generated images of kitchen appliances. These women were taken from family to be trained at Cootamundra mission to be servants and slaves in the 1930s. One of these women is the artist's grandmother. Across ten works, each of the depicted women's faces are represented as literally trapped inside domestic appliances, including a kettle, an electric frypan and an electric iron. Each of the works included printed dictionary definitions of words connecting the tropes and offensive labelling of Aboriginal women with labour abuse and enslavement: 'Lubra', 'Servant', 'Domestic', 'Slave'.

Fiona Foley's *Stud Gins* (2003) stamped words 'Aboriginal', 'Woman', 'Property', 'Defiled', 'Ravished, 'Shared', 'Discarded' onto grey blankets, pinned to the gallery walls. With the interplay of language and basic bedding (as these type of blankets were rationed out along with flour, tea and sugar as a form of welfare), Foley speaks to the state sanctioned abuse of Aboriginal women in a stark example of how artistic truth-telling reveals the legacies of brutality and trauma continuing from colonial times to the present day.

In *Florey and Fanny* (2011), Yhonnie Scarce hung white aprons on hooks with black glass yams creeping out of holes in the pockets, unable to be contained. The names of her grandmother and great grandmother were stitched on these pockets. The black growing roots of the yams extended like spectral fingers through holes in these aprons. This work exposed the exploitation of Aboriginal women in domestic servitude and their desire to escape.

In protesting the treatment of Aboriginal soldiers returning from war, as with Jones' work on her grandfather discussed above, in *Stand* (2001) Darren Siwes used a photographic technique of long exposure to capture himself as an apparition standing in front of statues commemorating the non-Indigenous Anzacs. His transparent ghostly body appeared to haunt memorials to war, a spectral unsettling of heroic narratives and white nationalism.

In *Bittersweet* (2022) South Sea Islander artist Jasmine Togo-Brisby carved a mound of 100 skulls made of sugar and resin to expose the practice of blackbirding. From 1847 to 1901, thousands of South Sea Islanders, including her own family, were kidnapped and forced to work on sugar plantations and for other industries to generate national wealth. These skulls represent the unmarked mass graves of the labourers.

There are many more works deserving of proper recognition and to be shared with future generations as part of a racial literacy education that teaches about truth-telling, and the power of art and representation to shape racial imaginaries. Julie Gough (2001) uses the term 'artistic archivists' to describe the approach and practice of artists unearthing historical records to create these powerful interventions (2001, p. 89). In this country, a legion of artists including Gough, Foley, Brenda Croft, Destiny Deacon, Richard Bell, Tracey Moffatt, and Vernon Ah Kee, have led the way in bringing to light the secret shames and lies hidden from public sight/sites. The work to uncover buried stories and voices is the fruition of incredible artistic skill, courage and vision since invasion. While we are in a period of mass exposure and mass disruption, with the rolling of statues into the sea and figures sprayed red for the blood on their hands, the appreciation and acknowledgement of this committed artistic counter memory activity has been a long time coming and is way overdue. Recognition of this work cannot be confined to any contemporary moment of social rupture. This art is alive, driven by survival and passed through generations. It is ongoing, accumulative and unable to be supressed. For those challenged by the revolution in the streets and the artists countering the laundering of memory to create new futures, Kuku Yalandji, Waanji, Yidinji and Gugu Yimithirr artist Vernon Ah Kee's signature black and white text work provides an eloquent response: *What you inherit is what you have to reckon with* (2009).

# References

Albert, T. (2020). *You Wreck Me* [Video Artwork]. Sullivan + Strumpf. https://vimeo.com/428 332201. Accessed 15 June 2023.

Arnott, G., Laidlaw, Z., & Lydon, J. (2022). Writing slavery into biography: Australian legacies of British slavery. *Australian Journal of Biography and History, 6*, 3–19. https://doi.org/10.22459/ AJBH.06.2022.01

Arnott, G. (2020). Australia's deep connection with enslavement. *The Age.* https://www.theage. com.au/national/victoria/australia-s-deep-connection-with-enslavement-20200616-p55355. html. Accessed 15 June 2023.

Arnott, G. (2021). Lachlan Macquarie was a slave owner and he wasn't the only one. It's time to update the history books. *ABC Radio National.* https://www.abc.net.au/news/2021-12-15/lac hlan-macquarie-was-slave-owner-time-to-update-history-books/100573218. Accessed 16 June 2023.

Australian Associated Press. (2022). A small step to reconciliation: Hobart Council to remove statue of William Crowther who stole aboriginal skull from Morgue. *The Guardian.* https://www.theguardian.com/australia-news/2022/aug/15/a-small-step-to-reconciliation-hobart-council-to-remove-statue-of-william-crowther-who-stole-aboriginal-skull-from-morgue. Accessed 15 June 2023.

Borys, S. (2020). Prime Minister criticised after suggesting 'no slavery' in Australia's history. *ABC News.* https://www.abc.net.au/radio/programs/pm/prime-minister-criticised-after-sugges ting-no-slavery/12346388. Accessed 15 June 2023.

Brown, L., Kelada, O., & Jones, D. (2021). 'While I knew I was raced, I didn't think much of it': The need for racial literacy in decolonising classrooms. *Postcolonial Studies, 24*(1), 82–103. https://doi.org/10.1080/13688790.2020.1759755

Hooks, B. (1992). *Black looks.* South End Press.

Buchanan, K. (2020). Scott Morrison's 'no slavery' comment prompts descendants to invite him to sugar cane regions. *ABC News.* https://www.abc.net.au/news/2020-06-12/call-for-scott-mor rison-visit-bundaberg-to-learn-about-slavery/12347686. Accessed 15 June 2023.

Carey, A., Prytz, A., & Visentin, L. (2021). New curriculum teaches cultural diversity dumps Christian Heritage. *The Age.* https://www.theage.com.au/national/victoria/new-curriculum-teaches-cultural-diversity-dumps-christian-heritage-20210429-p57nh9.html. Accessed 15 June 2023.

Churchill, W. (1943a). Speech in the house of commons, October 28, 1943. *Oxford Reference.* https://doi.org/10.1093/acref/9780191843730.001.0001/q-oro-ed5-00002969. Accessed 15 June 2023.

Churchill, W. (1943b) Speech at Harvard University, September 6, 1943. *Oxford Reference.* https://doi.org/10.1093/acref/9780191843730.001.0001/q-oro-ed5-00002969. Accessed 15 June 2023.

Churchill, W. (1948). Speech in the house of commons, January 23, 1948. *Oxford Reference.* https://doi.org/10.1093/acref/9780191843730.001.0001/q-oro-ed5-00002969. Accessed 15 June 2023.

Conaghan, R. (2020). Statues of two men linked to an aboriginal Massacre have been given new plaques by activists. *Junkee.* https://junkee.com/perth-statue-review/271145. Accessed 16 June 2023

Gough, J. (2001) *Transforming histories: The visual disclosure of contentious pasts.* PhD Thesis. University of Tasmania. https://doi.org/10.25959/23210888.v1

Guinier, L. (2004). From racial liberalism to racial literacy: Brown v. board of education and the interest-divergence dilemma. *The Journal of American History, 91*(1), 92–118.

Hunter, A. (2007). *A different kind of 'subject': Aboriginal legal status and colonial law in Western Australia, 1829–1861.* PhD Thesis. *Murdoch University.*

Hondros, N. (2020). WA Greens senator silent on tweets calling for the destruction of historical statues. *WAtoday.* https://www.watoday.com.au/politics/western-australia/wa-greens-senator-silent-on-tweets-calling-for-the-the-destruction-of-historical-statues-20200609-p550xo.html. Accessed 16 June 2023.

Johnson, M. (2009). *Race(Ing) around in rhetoric and composition circles: Racial literacy as the way out.* PhD Thesis. *University of North Carolina.*

Jones, D. (2015). *What lies buried will rise: Exploring a story of violent crime, retribution and colonial memory.* PhD Thesis. University of Melbourne. https://rest.neptune-prod.its.unimelb.edu.au/server/api/core/bitstreams/029dc07b-aa49-56ba-b5cf-c4ad89a6ba92/content. Accessed 28 June 2023.

Juanola, M. (2020). Perth artist group replaces plaques of historical CBD statues in bid to 'rewrite history'. *WAtoday.* https://www.watoday.com.au/perth-news/perth-artist-group-replaces-pla ques-of-historical-cbd-statues-in-bid-to-rewrite-history-20200915-p55vxa.html. Accessed 16 June 2023.

Kelada, O., & Grieves, G. (2017). Bleeding the archive, transforming the mythscape. In I. McLean & D. Jorgensen (Eds.), *Indigenous archives: The making and unmaking of aboriginal art* (pp. 321–341). UWA Press.

Legacies of British Slavery (LBS) Database. (2024). University College London. https://www.ucl.ac.uk/lbs/. Accessed 29 January 2024.

Lydon, J. (2023). *From slavery to settler colonisation*. Australian Academy of Humanities. https://humanities.org.au/power-of-the-humanities/from-slavery-to-settler-colonisation/. Accessed 29 January 2024.

Maree Brown, A. (2019). *'Build as we fight': Remarks from the 2019 American Studies Association Annual Meeting*. https://adriennemareebrown.net/2019/11/10/build-as-we-fight-remarks-from-the-2019-american-studies-association-annual-meeting/. Accessed 15 June 2023.

Owen, C., & Bracknell, C. (2021). A buried history. *Same Drum*. https://www.samedrum.com/research. Accessed 16 June 2023.

Pol, G. (2021). Truth-telling. *Common Ground*. https://www.commonground.org.au/learn/truth-telling. Accessed 15 June 2023.

Riley, S. (Director). (2000). *Confessions of a Headhunter* [Film]. Scarlett Pictures.

Rogers, R., & Mosley, M. (2006). Racial literacy in a second-grade classroom: Critical race theory, whiteness studies, and literacy research. *Reading Research Quarterly, 41*(4), 462–495.

Scott, S. (2015). A hard look at how we see race. *Stanford Magazine*. https://stanfordmag.org/contents/a-hard-look-at-how-we-see-race. Accessed 24 July 2023.

Sky News. (2021). New crime bill makes protecting statues more important than punishing rape. *Sky News*. https://news.sky.com/story/new-crime-bill-makes-protecting-statues-more-important-than-punishing-rape-says-labour-12248534. Accessed 15 June 2023.

Sprunt, B. (2020). Trump threatens prison for attempts to topple statues. *NPR*. https://www.npr.org/2020/06/23/882020026/trump-threatens-prison-for-attempts-to-topple-statues-heres-the-law-he-cites. Accessed 15 June 2023.

Stanner, W. E. H. (1968). *After the dreaming: Black and white Australians—An anthropologist's view. Boyer Lectures*. Australian Broadcasting Commission.

Twine, F. (2004). A white side of Black Britain: The concept of racial literacy. *Ethnic and Racial Studies, 27*(6), 878–907.

Visentin, L., & Baker, J. (2021). Tudge 'concerned' about colonisation emphasis in proposed curriculum changes. *Sydney Morning Herald*. https://www.smh.com.au/politics/federal/tudge-concerned-about-colonisation-emphasis-in-proposed-curriculum-changes-20210430-p57nsb.html. Accessed 15 June 2023.

Woolley, S. (2022). Lake Macquarie High School's Year 9 slave trade assignment under investigation. *7 News*. https://7news.com.au/news/education/lake-macquarie-high-schools-year-9-slave-trade-assignment-under-investigation-c-6156644. Accessed 15 June 2023.

Western Australian Legacies of British Slavery. (2021). University of Western Australia. https://australian-legacies-slavery.org/. Accessed 29 January 2024.

**Odette Kelada** is a senior lecturer in the School of Culture and Communication at the University of Melbourne. Kelada researches on race, sexuality and gender in Australian writing and the arts. She is interested in the constructions of nation, body and identity in creative representations and the teaching of Racial Literacy. Kelada has Anglo and Egyptian heritage and her writing has appeared in numerous publications including the Australian Cultural History Journal, Outskirts: Feminisms on the Edge, the Australian Critical Race and Whiteness Journal, Postcolonial Studies and the Journal of the Association for Australian Literature.

**Dianne Jones** is a Nyoongar artist whose photo-media work deals with Indigenous identity and cultural history. Dianne completed a Masters of Visual Arts at the Victorian College of the Arts and is currently undertaking a PhD. Her work has been exhibited in numerous exhibitions in Australia and overseas, and is included in the collections of National Gallery of Victoria, Art Gallery of Western Australia, Monash University Museum of Art and the National Gallery of Australia.

# Chapter 8
# This Full Agency, This Decolonised Spirit: Talking Blak to Cooks' Cottage

**Paola Balla, Kate Golding, and Clare Land**

**Abstract** This chapter discusses a project to counter the colonial fantasy presented by Cooks' Cottage, a large monument to white colonial nation-building located in a central Melbourne park. In 2018, Paola Balla, Clare Land, and Kate Golding came together to respond collaboratively to an approach from the City of Melbourne to assist the City in 'incorporating Indigenous perspectives' into the historical displays at Cooks' Cottage. They renegotiated the brief from the City of Melbourne and produced an image-rich monograph, *Blak Cook Book* (2021), a set of provocations that platforms sharp critique of Cook and his memorialisation by First Nations and other artists, activists and scholars. Balla, Land and Golding worked from the starting point that the Cottage itself is irredeemably colonial; they also came up with several propositions that could counter the Cottage more substantively than any gestures towards incorporating Indigenous perspectives into its existing displays.

## 8.1 Introduction

This chapter discusses a recent attempt to counter the narrative offered by Cooks' Cottage, an English cottage built in 1755 originating in Yorkshire and now located on Wurundjeri Country in Melbourne's Fitzroy Gardens, that operates as a monument to the life and voyages of British navigator Captain James Cook. The chapter takes as a given that in so-called Australia there are two main competing views of Captain Cook and what he symbolises. Key themes of the white social memory of Cook are:

---

P. Balla · C. Land (✉)
Moondani Balluk Indigenous Academic Unit, Victoria University, Naarm/Melbourne, Australia
e-mail: clare.land@vu.edu.au

P. Balla
e-mail: paola.balla@vu.edu.au

K. Golding
Naarm/Melbourne, Australia
e-mail: kate@kategolding.com.au

© The Author(s), under exclusive license to Springer Nature Singapore Pte Ltd. 2024    123
G. Grieves and A. Spiers (eds.), *Art and Memorialisation*, Indigenous-Settler Relations in Australia and the World 6, https://doi.org/10.1007/978-981-97-6289-7_8

a religious (sacred) figure, a nation-builder, and an example of the promise of capitalism (he is a man who rose from humble beginnings on his own merit) (Healy, 1997; Thomas, 2006). By contrast, the Aboriginal social memory of Cook is that he was 'the original invader' (Foley, 2019a) and a harbinger of death to First Nations peoples and culture (Healy, 1997).[1] As Gweagal community member and researcher Dr. Shayne Williams says, 'Cook's landing…is symbolic because it portended the end of our cultural dominion over our lands. Not surprisingly, discussion of Cook's landing sparks a sadness among my peoples—a sadness that laments Cook's voyage, precipitating some 18 years later, the landing of the First Fleet (1788)' (n.d.). Amongst Aboriginal and Torres Strait Islander peoples, this sense of Cook bringing in an unwelcome new era is expressed by the term 'Before Cook'—rebuffing the white Australian idolisation of Cook and the Christian dating system, Before Christ (BC) and Anno Domini (AD). In 2018, an officer within the City of Melbourne Tourism and Events branch initiated work to bring First Nations perspectives on Captain Cook into greater prominence in the interpretation offered at Cooks' Cottage. Our sense is that this officer's suggestions tapped into management's anxiety about how to better deal with the Cottage given its original purpose to celebrate and consolidate white colonial nation-building. The City's response included commissioning work by this chapter's authors—researchers Clare Land, Paola Balla and Kate Golding. This chapter presents our reflection on our involvement in this project as an example of counter-monument practice. It describes the site as it was when we were commissioned to address it,[2] our approach to the project, and a proposition for an intervention at the Cottage.

The resulting *Blak Cook Book: New Cultural Perspectives. A set of provocations*, published by the City of Melbourne in 2021, centres Māori, Kānaka Maoli and First Nations perspectives, artworks and protest actions in response to Cook. The booklet and accompanying double-sided fold-out poster combine granular historical detail and imagery to encourage debate and critical thinking. One side of the poster features Biripi artist, Jason Wing's sculptural artwork, *Captain James Crook* (2013) (Fig. 8.1). The non-linear timeline featured on the reverse side of the poster offers a visual representation of First Nations perspectives on Cook's place in history.[3]

---

[1] Healy's take is included in the 1993 Conservation Management Plan for the Cottage; while significant to the Anglo majority in expressing a link with cultural origins, to Aboriginal people it represents 'the veritable end of an uninterrupted culture... and the beginning of a long period of repression' (cited in Young, 2008).

[2] Certain features of the site have been changed quietly by the City of Melbourne and loudly by anonymous citizens since the conclusion of our work. A statue of Cook in the curtilage was found sawn off at the ankles in late February 2024 and has since been stored by the City of Melbourne, which has not addressed the question of reinstatement. The City of Melbourne has removed the Union Jack and the period costumes which visitors used to be encouraged to dress up in. Visitor Services Guides continue to wear period costumes though.

[3] See Appendix for a full list of all artworks and images featured in *Blak Cook Book*.

**Fig. 8.1** Jason Wing, *Captain James Crook* (2013). Bronze sculpture 70 × 50 × 30 cm. Collection of the Art Gallery of New South Wales. Image courtesy of the artist

## 8.2 Cooks' Cottage

Cooks' Cottage is a diminutive cottage with a neatly laid-out display garden in which a life-sized statue of Captain Cook and a flagpole with the Union Jack stand. Initially brought from Yorkshire, in the United Kingdom (UK), to Melbourne in 1934 as a gift from a local philanthropist to the State of Victoria in celebration of the 100th anniversary of colonisation of the area, the Cottage is maintained by the City of Melbourne's Tourism and Events branch as a tourist attraction and a site for excursions for school children. Its listing, first inscribed in 1978 (Young, 2008), on Victoria's heritage database claims that it: 'stands today as a monument to Captain Cook and to Sir Russell Grimwade who purchased the cottage and arranged for its [transport to Australia]. It provides Australians with a unique historic link to England' (Heritage Council Victoria, n.d.). The Cottage is titled in the listing as 'Cook's Cottage'—which perpetuates the inaccurate notion that the Cottage was James Cook's. Around 1993, the City of Melbourne quietly moved the apostrophe and began referring to the Cottage as Cooks' Cottage, so that in name if not in narrative the City can claim that it realises the Cottage never belonged to and nor was it frequented by James Cook but rather his parents.[4]

The situation of the Cottage suggests several untruths. It would be natural to assume that the 'Cook' in Cooks' Cottage refers to James Cook not to his parents; and further, that James Cook built the Cottage in Melbourne and lived in it; and that he was involved in the founding of Melbourne. The chief credible contribution the Cottage makes to the historical understanding of its predominant, somewhat captive, audience of international tourists and school children, who are bussed to the site as part of organised tours, is to provide an insight to English home life around the time James Cook lived.[5] This is achieved by visitors being allowed to enter and move around the inside of the Cottage and see the kinds of furnishings and objects English people used at that time. Audio recordings are played throughout the Cottage to support the narrative of daily life in 1700s Yorkshire. Outside the Cottage there are traditional English costumes that visitors can put on to augment their experience.[6] Presumably, the Cottage is valuable from a tourism point of view due to Melbourne lacking spectacular attractions such as Sydney's Harbour, Harbour Bridge and Opera House. It is a place where visitors can be directed, and is included in bus tours and the like. Guides tell visitors about 'the history of Cooks' Cottage and how it came to be in Melbourne… what life was like in the eighteenth century, and … the incredible voyages and life of Captain James Cook' (City of Melbourne, n.d.a). Visitors can extend their experience by seeing the nearby Fairies Tree, model Tudor village and 'majestic avenues of English elms' (City of Melbourne, n.d.a). To be fair, the City of Melbourne website includes oblique references to the Cottage's contested presence by describing the Cottage as an 'historical oddity' (n.d.b) and mentioning that 'native wildlife' (n.d.a) may be encountered in the Fitzroy Gardens, but the narrative remains overwhelmingly that of *terra nullius* in the most twee form possible. Aligning with the *terra nullius* legal doctrine, the Cottage and its Europeanised surrounds pretend that First Nations peoples and laws do not exist and that colonisation was a peaceful and benign process.

Indications of First Nations' cultural dominion of the land and present day realities—such as a culturally-modified tree near the Cottage, and the survival and resurgence of First Nations communities within Melbourne—are not embraced nor amplified through prominent signage nor any other cue. To the rear of the Cottage, for example, there is a built-in stable where visitors can see a multimedia interpretation, added in 2007 and updated in 2018, of the significance of Cook's journeys to enhancing British knowledge of the Pacific. There is a cursory mention of First Nations peoples, and of protests situated at the Cottage, in this audiovisual display.

---

[4] Linda Young argues that the present approach is unsatisfactory due to 'the bad faith of simultaneously denying and not-denying an authentic connection to the hero' (2008).

[5] The English home life presented is that of a more respectable class of family than the Cooks, due to changes made to the Cottage both before it was bought by philanthropist Russell Grimwade and when it was reconstructed in Melbourne and the way it was then furnished (see Young, 2008).

[6] Like the Union Jack formerly displayed on the flagpole within the Cottage Garden, these costumes—only introduced in 2007 (Young, 2008)—have also been quietly put away recently by management since the publication of *Blak Cook Book*.

The City of Melbourne's promotional website seems to be referring to this display when it claims that 'modern interpretations of Captain Cook's adventures' are available at the Cottage (n.d.c). At the Cottage, we did not detect *modern interpretations* that could be considered sufficient to counter the white social memory of Cook. The cursory mention of First Nations peoples in the audiovisual display suggests that the City of Melbourne has for some time been aware of the Aboriginal social memory of Cook and is at some level anxious to avoid the even more acute criticism that would be inevitable if the display made zero mention of this set of truths. Historian and heritage consultant Linda Young has analysed the three management regimes of the Cottage since 1934 and their accompanying logics. In 1993, in what could have been a pivotal point, a Conservation Management Plan (CMP) was developed for the Cottage. Incorporating the work of non-Aboriginal cultural studies scholar Chris Healy, the CMP's Statement of Significance identified the competing social memories of Cook and highlighted the opportunity to present juxtaposing interpretations at the Cottage (Young, 2008). It seems the City of Melbourne did not try to pursue this opportunity in a substantive way until the project that produced *Blak Cook Book*.

Cooks' Cottage in no way provides visitors and passers-by with substantive cues nor encouragement to consider the wide-ranging negative associations of Cook's legacy for Indigenous peoples (see Healy, 1990; Howell, 2008; McBride & Smith, 2019) nor to consider Indigenous peoples at all, really. The Cottage is, however, covered by ivy which was grown from a cutting from the Cottage's original garden in Yorkshire, UK. We would argue that this ivy, as an invasive weed, is the most eloquent feature of the Cottage for those who are searching for anything which refers to the association between Cook and the colonisation of Australia.

## 8.3 A Project to Incorporate Indigenous Perspectives

The huge scope for improvement in the narrative offered by Cooks' Cottage was both a reason to engage and a reason to question any engagement when an officer from the City of Melbourne Tourism and Events team approached Clare Land about a project to incorporate 'perspectives of First Australians' into a redesign of the Cottage exhibition space. This indicated that there was recognition within parts of the City of Melbourne that change had to happen at the site.

The genesis of the project can be attributed to questioning by an incoming employee within the City of Melbourne who noticed the misalignment between the historical interpretation offered at the Cottage and the City's goal of becoming a 'city with an Aboriginal focus'.[7] As a result of this internal questioning, the City of Melbourne approached a number of Indigenous scholars with historical and counter-memorial expertise to assist in a re-interpretation of the Cottage. Having been unable to interest anyone in the consultancy, eventually the City of Melbourne approached

---

[7] Strategic Goal 9 in City of Melbourne, Future Melbourne 2026 Plan (2016).

non-Indigenous scholar Clare Land who had previously worked with the Aboriginal Melbourne branch of the City of Melbourne on a counter-monument project.[8]

Around the time of the initial approach in late 2017, and discussions about the intent and aims of the project in early 2018, the Australian Government announced it would commit $50 million to additional commemorations of Cook's landing site at Kurnell, Sydney in the lead up to the 250th anniversary of Cook's 1770 journey along Australia's eastern coastline. Clare foresaw strategic merit in engaging in the project given the platform it might provide in offering space for counter narratives in the lead up to the 250th anniversary, an anniversary that promised to promote nationalistic celebrations of colonial exploration and conquest rather than criticisms. However, she remained uncertain about whether to take it on.

Clare had a couple of conversations with First Nations colleagues about the appropriateness of accepting the consultancy; one of these conversations was with Paola Balla who decided to work with Clare on the project. As a Blak community member, and curator, artist and educator this was not a straightforward decision for Paola; she wondered, 'why would I want to work on anything to do with Cooks' Cottage—a life-size memento mori to a white colonial mythic figure?' A sense of obligation to engage with this as a vehicle to educate a new audience persuaded Paola to get involved. Paola brought in non-Indigenous artist and theorist, Kate Golding because of her Masters research which examined Cook monuments across the globe.

Paola also considered the extent with which she could contribute to a collaboration as the only Aboriginal academic with two white colleagues: would Paola's voice be heard? Would the 'colonial load' (Weenthunga, 2023) of inevitably needing to challenge and educate these colleagues be worth it?[9] Would this additional burden be taken into account when negotiating the workload across the team? Would the personal costs to Paola be compensated by real outcomes for Community? What was the project's actual potential for subverting the huge national investment in reiterating the white social memory of Cook? How could incorporating Indigenous perspectives within the Cottage counter the hero status attributed to Cook and to this colonial and colonising building? What was Paola's responsibility here in disrupting the public white supremacist narratives and carefully constructed colonial educational dialogues, literature and lies that have been told about Cook, and the little-Australian-dream cottage on Kulin Country that wasn't actually his and that he never actually lived in? Could the project undermine the ways white colonial institutions and staff facilitate colonial projects like the Cottage?

As potential project collaborators, collectively we discussed the limitations and challenges in speaking back into the white colonising institutions and discourses that are at stake in the Cottage. What could our speaking back make happen in the spaces of tourism, colonial educational approaches and broader white storytelling

---

[8] Research project as part of City of Melbourne's steps towards memorialising Tasmanian Aboriginal men, Tunnerminnerwait and Maulboyheener (see City of Melbourne n.d.d; Land 2014a).

[9] 'Colonial load' is the invisible workload 'placed knowingly and unknowingly on First Nations people by Settlers and institutions' (Weenthunga, 2023), eg providing Indigenous knowledge, education and support (see Sivertsen et al., 2023). Importantly, Weenthunga teases out 'cultural load' into 'cultural responsibility' and 'colonial load'.

# 8 This Full Agency, This Decolonised Spirit: Talking Blak to Cooks' Cottage

and mythologising? What sort of speaking back would work to counter the near-complete erasures of the truth, Blak history and First Peoples' lived experiences of genocide, invasion, displacement, trauma and survival we were invited to contend with? We also as a group considered the limited scope of the initial brief, which was to merely provide material that could supplement the existing textual or video displays within the Cottage and augment visitors' experience with a more acceptably 'modern interpretation' and cross-cultural perspective on Cook's legacy.

We decided that trying to improve the interpretation within the Cottage was insufficient and not something we felt comfortable doing. We came to the conclusion that we could not significantly improve, critique or subvert the interpretive displays radically enough within the project parameters for the Cottage to be transformed in ways that approached anything that was remotely *culturally safe* for Community. In other words, the Cottage can never be a place that feels comfortable for a First Nations person to enter. The Cottage is just too much itself: no matter what signage or interpretative panels or videos might be installed in the Cottage to explain its real owners, place of construction and even the Aboriginal social meaning of Cook and the After Cook era, the Cottage will still declare *Viva Captain Cook!* and *Always Was Always Will be a White Nation!* It is a site *for white people* to connect with their culture of origin and to celebrate Captain Cook and the invasion of Australia (see Young, 2008). We resisted the project's conservative aims and ambitions by declaring the Cottage *irredeemable.* Instead, we formulated a counterproposal which aimed to provoke people to question how much they really know about Cook and his voyages and by extension to question the narrative provided by and at the Cottage. We wanted our work to be as much a resource for the City and the tour guides ('Visitor Services Guides') who help visitors to interpret the Cottage, as for the visitors themselves. Given our team's strengths in activism, art and history, we wanted our response to Cooks' Cottage to be informed by activists' and artists' responses to Cook and Cooks' Cottage. Hence, *Blak Cook Book* was born.

Our research began with the creation of two databases—one listing what we called 'citizen actions,'[10] and one listing artworks. Our research into citizen actions started with a broad focus including *corrections*[11] to Cook monuments through to the full-scale renaissance of worldwide navigation and seafaring by the Polynesian Voyaging Society led by artist and historian, the late Herb Kawainui Kāne. The databases served as a way for us to categorise the ways in which various people across the globe have responded to Cook. Categorising the actions in this way enabled us to determine which actions and artworks to eventually focus on more deeply. The theorising that citizens and activists articulated in their actions powerfully shaped *Blak Cook Book.* We understood First Nations mediations of and resistance against Cook's journeys as

---

[10] Here we used the term 'citizen' to describe activities and/or activisms that were driven by people in the general population operating outside any major institution. These were responses that would not be interpreted as formal artworks. Many citizen actions remain anonymous, with no author to credit.

[11] Corrections, as we defined them, were any writing, painting or damaging of a regressive or historically incorrect monument or memorial that undermined the narrative presented by the monument or memorial.

**Fig. 8.2** Tupaia, *Māori trading a crayfish with Joseph Banks* (1769). Drawing by Tupaia, from 'Drawings illustrative of Captain Cook's First Voyage, 1768–1771'. Watercolour, on paper, 26.8 × 20.5 cm. British Library, London, UK. © British Library Board. Add. MS 15,508, fol. 12

starting in 1770 and read primary and secondary accounts of First Nations responses to colonisation through this lens and up to the present day.[12]

Our art research identified 99 key artworks by both Indigenous and non-Indigenous artists that responded to Cook. These ranged from the 1700s including formal portraits by European painters, to works made by Tupaia—a Ra'iataen navigator who acted as a guide onboard Cook's ship (Fig. 8.2), the *Endeavour*, through to works by contemporary artists. Of the 99 key artworks that informed our analysis, we selected 16 works to be included in *Blak Cook Book*.

---

[12] The scholarship of the late Tracey Banivanua Mar was key here. A renowned historian and Melburnian of Fijian (Lauan), Chinese and British descent, she authored *Decolonisation and the Pacific: Indigenous globalisation and the ends of empire*. Cambridge University Press (2016).

## 8.4 How Have Cook Monuments and Cooks' Cottage Been Countered by Activists?

Cooks' Cottage has frequently been the site of protests by First Nations people and supporters; likewise Cook monuments all over the Pacific have been subjected to contest by often anonymous citizens. Contestations range from paint being thrown on statues; dissenting words spray painted on monuments; inverted commas applied in gold-leaf around the word *discovered* that correct the monument plinth of a colonial explorer; and weather and erosion causing a colonial memorial to fall into the sea.

Actions specific to Cooks' Cottage show a distinct and sustained politics of frustration at the persistent national denialism about Australia's Blak History and the unresolved issues of land rights and Treaty. Examples by anonymous actors include the side of the Cottage being spray painted with *26th January Australia's Shame!!!* and *Fuck Aus Day* on the stable door in 2014, and a tombstone-shaped sign placed near the statue of Cook on the grounds of the Cottage saying *Rest in Piss Australia Day* in 2019. Examples by protest groups over decades include a 1000-strong Black Moratorium for Land Rights rallying at the Cottage in July 1972, that went on to march to City Square and stage sit-downs at two city intersections (see Ningla A-Na, 1972; Mansell, 2020).

During the *Stolenwealth Games* protests on the occasion of the 2006 Commonwealth Games in Melbourne, members and supporters of the Black GST Collective (Genocide, Sovereignty, Treaty) wrapped the Cottage in crime scene tape. This transcendent act of survival, resistance and contestation was devised by Gunai and Gunditjmara campaigner and community radio broadcaster, Robbie Thorpe. The action declared *Australia is a crime scene*, and speakers made particular reference to Cook claiming possession without the *Consent of the Natives*, thereby disobeying the Secret Instructions the explorer had been issued by the British Admiralty. Photographer, broadcaster, performer, poet, and artist, the late, great Lisa Bellear, documented this action at the Cottage. One of Bellear's photographs depicting a smoking ceremony performed for the Black GST protest assembled outside of Cooks' Cottage, is given prominence in *Blak Cook Book* along with poems by Robbie Thorpe.

Thorpe's poem, *Ruling the waves, Waiving the rules*, characterises the unlawfulness of Cook's acts of possession, and evokes the genocidal implications of the expansion of British sovereignty overseen by successive colonial leaders that came in Cook's wake:

Ruling the waves, Waiving the rules

It's incredible, Australia's history

And the narrative of colonialism in this country

It's only 250 years ago that they were

Cooking the books

Banking on Banks

Ruling the waves

Waiving the rules

A pre-emptive strike

On innocent people

Weapons of mass destruction, namely

Smallpox

Vile potions

Vial potions

Genocide notions

It's the beginning of your history here

If it wasn't for the acts of terror

And the policies of genocide

Australia wouldn't exist

It's a Crown, naval, corporation-backed war

Undeclared

Secret

Come on folks!

You're in denial

It was important to us to give prominence to Thorpe's voice, as a legendary Gunai and Gunditjmara protestor of colonial Cook myths, but also because while Cooks' Cottage is located upon Kulin lands—meaning the City of Melbourne consults only with traditional owner bodies representing the Kulin nation about what they want to happen at the Cottage—we felt that the First Nations stakeholders of this story should extend more widely within Victoria to include the perspective of the Gunai/Kurnai peoples whose oral record includes the first sighting of Cook's ship, the *Endeavour*, at 90 Mile Beach in the eastern reaches of Gunai/Kurnai territory as the ship voyaged up the east coast of the continent. Following the sighting, the Gunai/Kurnai peoples set off smoke signals of warning up the coast in the direction of the ship's travel. We asked for this to be brought into the City of Melbourne's frame of reference concerning the Cottage but we were told that this did not align with the City's First Nations stakeholder engagement priorities for the site.

Re-enactments of Cook's landing have been popular with governments at all levels and have also been contested by Aboriginal protestors. In 1970, the Australian Government officially celebrated the bicentenary of Cook's 1770 arrival on Gweagal lands at Botany Bay NSW, by staging a re-enactment by actors, in the presence of Queen Elizabeth II.[13] Aboriginal community members from the local La Perouse mission and beyond, with supporters, boycotted the re-enactment. Addressed by Frank Roberts, Bert Groves, Oodgeroo Noonuccal (then known as Kath Walker), Trudy Longbottom, Faith Bandler, Paul Coe and John Newfong, a crowd of community members and supporters staged a vigil of mourning and cast wreaths into the water, ensuring that the prevailing tides would carry them into view of the Queen. It was an assertion of the right to mourn, and an attempt to wake up 'white Australia… out of their apathetic attitudes' (see Foley, 2019b).

---

[13] On another contested re-enactment in 1901, see Schlunke (2015).

# 8 This Full Agency, This Decolonised Spirit: Talking Blak to Cooks' Cottage

On Invasion Day 2003, Robbie Thorpe with Aboriginal Black Power activist (now academic historian and Professor) Gary Foley reworked the colonial re-enactment phenomenon with their own performance on St Kilda Beach, Melbourne, presenting a version that indicated 'what should have happened when the First Fleet arrived' (see Foley, 2011). Thorpe tells the incoming soldiers and convicts, 'If you are prepared to abide by our law, go through our customs and pay the rent, you're welcome to stay' (see Foley, 2011). The soldiers and convicts duly sign up to *Pay The Rent* while Foley and Thorpe address gratified members of the press. Political actions sited at the Cottage or Cook monuments have not always sought to engage directly with the narrative around Cook but have utilised white Australian public attachment to Cook to gain media attention for whatever was necessary at the time. Gary Foley explains: 'Whenever we felt like getting a little bit of public attention, you could always be guaranteed to get a headline if you brought a can of paint down here to Hyde Park in Sydney and chucked it over Captain Cook' (2019a).

Non-Aboriginal comedian Shaun Micallef gave his satirical view of the protest tradition at the Cottage when he wrote this list of 'Reasons Why People Shouldn't Vandalise Cooks' Cottage' (2016):

1. It isn't Captain Cook's cottage; it belonged to his parents.
2. It was built 10 years after Cook joined the navy, so he never lived there.
3. There is no proof he even visited.
4. It isn't even really the house that Captain Cook's parents lived in. Having been extensively renovated in the 1800s, the original house (built in 1755) barely resembles the one that was disassembled, shipped to Australia and which now stands in Fitzroy Gardens.
5. It contains no furniture, fixtures or fittings from the original house.
6. It contains nothing at all that was owned, used or even touched by Captain Cook. (There is a hide-covered 'Diddy Box' bearing the initials 'JC' but this is not the famous coffin-shaped one carved by his crew and containing a lock of his hair that was presented to his wife after his death (and now in the State Library of New South Wales). Nor is it the box they made and later threw overboard on their way home from Hawaii containing Cook's head.)
7. The real house Captain Cook was born and raised in no longer exists but is now the site of the Captain Cook Birthplace Museum. It is in Marton, Middlesbrough
8. Captain Cook never set foot in Victoria, Australia. Only Victoria, Canada.
9. Captain Cook was asleep when Australia was first sighted.
10. The first European to have seen Australia was, in fact, the *Endeavour's* Lieutenant, Zachary Hickes—although it is probable that what he saw was, in fact, just a cloud bank.

In this list Micallef is usefully highlighting the many aspects in which the Cottage and its narrative is inauthentic. He reveals the Cottage as a fabricated white colonial construction, and construct, that has tenuous links to Cook's life and legacy.[14]

In contrast with Cooks' Cottage, the coffin shaped ditty box Micallef mentions is intimately, personally and authentically connected to Cook but has nothing of

---

[14] In this light, the ivy covering the Cottage is again interesting—it is one of the most authentic aspects of the Cottage as it now stands.

**Fig. 8.3** Kirsten Lyttle, *Death in Hawaii* (2009–2011). Hand-painted and home-sewn Hawaiian shirt. Cotton, cotton thread, paint, ink and transfers. Image courtesy of the artist

the profile of the Cottage as a tourist attraction. The small box, which would fit in an adult's hand, is held in the collection of the State Library of New South Wales. Crew members carved the ditty box from the oak of the *Resolution*—the ship Cook made his final voyage in—after their Captain's death at the hands of Kānaka Maoli (Native Hawaiians) at Kealakekua, Hawai'i in 1779 (Fig. 8.3). The ditty box was presented to Mrs Cook upon the *Resolution's* return to London and contains a small watercolour depicting Cook's death and a lock of the Captain's hair. This almost unknown memento mori reminds us that Cook, despite the mythology surrounding him, is dead. Monuments to Cook such as Cooks' Cottage in Melbourne suggest the opposite: that he is somehow *still alive*—a life-sized statue of him stands in the back garden of the Cottage (see footnote 2). These monuments work to keep him at the forefront of our contemporary consciousness.

As Mudburra man Hobbles Danayarri from the Wave Hill/Victoria River district of the Northern Territory explained to anthropologist Deborah Bird Rose, 'Aboriginal people all know that Captain Cook is dead. It's the white people, European people, who don't know that he's dead, or who don't accept that he's dead, or who refuse to allow him to die because they still "follow his law"' (cited in Rose, 1993, pp. 43–4). Rose goes on to explain that 'Australian Aboriginal people have accurately grasped the importance of Captain Cook as a white Australian culture hero' (1993, p. 47). While Vic River people do not 'demonise' Cook, they offer a critique linked to their view that Europeans in Australia have some confused foundational ideas and dispositions. Rose continues:

> Europeans, many Aboriginal people say, are unable to understand how to evaluate the quality of events and thus are unable to discern the difference between that which it is important to remember and that which it is important to forget. This failure of discernment enables

8  This Full Agency, This Decolonised Spirit: Talking Blak to Cooks' Cottage          135

Europeans to make heroes out of those who bring destruction and to destroy those who make peace (1993, p. 47).

From the deepest cultural point of view, Europeans, symbolised by Cook, are child-like, clown-like, lawless and dangerous (Nugent, 2009, p. 60; Redmond, 2008, p. 262). This softening of colonisers was exhibited at the Cottage where Visitor Services Guides dress in period costumes and formerly encouraged visitors to take part in dressing-up as colonisers too.

Many of the protest actions against the Cottage and other Cook monuments and re-enactments that we surveyed engage the fundamental questions of law and legitimacy that attend Cook's actions and legacy. These questions remain unfinished business and drive continued struggles for justice. A major impediment to these struggles is the immature understanding the majority of Australians have of their own history and legal status—as Danayarri argues. Cooks' Cottage, due to its contribution to sugar-coated narratives of the colonial process and its persistence in centring a white Australian culture hero will remain a target of protests.

## 8.5  How the Cottage Has Been Countered by Artists

The inauthenticity of Cooks' Cottage is the subject of a 1999 artwork by non-Indigenous artist Callum Morton. *Cottage Industry: Bawdy Nights* is a scale model of Cooks' Cottage, situated on top of a packing crate. A raucous soundtrack animates the Cottage, suggesting there is more going on with the Cottage and its situation in the Fitzroy Gardens than its homely appearance suggests. Morton's work provokes the audience to picture what is happening within; the raucous noises verge on the dangerous rather than the inviting.

Bellear's work depicting a smoking ceremony outside the Cottage as part of a 2006 Stolenwealth Games protest also disrupts the predominant narrative: the ceremony offers cleansing to those who have gathered on the unsettling site while crime scene tape condemns it and debars entry. We reproduced these Cottage-specific works in *Blak Cook Book* along with a number of sharp and eloquent works that counter the Cook narrative more broadly (see Appendix for full list of works).

As we described at the beginning of this chapter, Cook is regarded across the First Nations of the Pacific as *the original invader*. Indigenous artists and intellectuals have expressed a sense of invasion as *everywhen*—still happening today—through sharp and creative artworks, protests and performances.[15] For instance, Vincent Namatjira's *Captain Cook with the Queen and Me* collapses 250 years of history into one moment. In the work, Namatjira stands as if posing for a photograph, smiling with full agency between Cook and Queen Elizabeth II, two Britons who were the catalyst for, and

---

[15] We adapt this from the anthropological explanation of The Dreaming: while conjuring up the past colonisation is still a part of the present (Stanner, 1970).

perpetuators of, the ongoing colonial project. The work points to a direct correlation between Cook's three Pacific voyages and the late monarch of the United Kingdom.[16]

In our research we found that First Nations artists who choose to respond to Cook are actively reinterpreting, reframing and remaking Eurocentric perspectives on Cook. They are part of First Nations community processes of resistance, survivance, and celebration; strengthening themselves and others (Vizenor, 2008). In a Pacific still dominated by colonial powers, the space of autonomy within Indigenous minds and bodies is strengthened and sustained by creativity and political resistance.

A recent, community-led monument to their encounter with Cook is neither an idealisation of, nor a protest against, Cook, but rather a reflection by the Guugu Yimithirr people that Cook was important but not foundational to their history. Taking its name from the Guugu Yimithirr word for story, the *Milbi Wall* (1998) affirms that most of First Nations peoples' history existed BC (Before Cook) and life goes on in the immediate and longer-term aftermath of colonisation (see Thomas, 2006, pp. 149–151). The 12m wall is divided into three sections, decorated with hand-painted tiles, telling the story of the region and its people. The first section depicts the creation of the area, the second section traces from the Guugu Yimithirr encounter with Cook through to World War Two, and the final section features the 1967 Referendum and discusses the survivance of First Nations despite colonisation and dispossession. Cook features as merely a part of the overall story. This is a firm and gentle rebuttal of the dominant historical narrative.[17]

As the late historian of Pacific decolonisation Tracy Banivanua Mar has written, colonial dynamics are ongoing, but so are Indigenous practices of independence. Provocative critiques by First Nations artists and communities are an expression of independence and sovereignty. The decolonial space inside Indigenous people can't be quashed (Mar, 2016). Nunga (Kaurna), Māori (Te Arawa) and European artist, James Tylor, has coined the term 'DeCookolisation', subverting English to speak back to Cook's legacy.[18] This process of DeCookolisation of selves, national memories and laws continues, propelled by First Nations resistance. It is this full agency, this decolonised spirit, that comes across so forcefully in Indigenous perspectives on Captain Cook, whether settlers in so-called Australia and beyond are ready and willing to countenance it or not.

---

[16] See also Redmond (2008) who writes of the Ngarinyin *Captain Cook jurnba* (critique/song/dance) which collapses the historical figures of Captain Cook and General Macarthur in time and meaning.

[17] On the discursive importance of this strategy, see Mar and Edmonds (2010).

[18] James Tylor's *DeCookolisation* (2015) is a photographic series comprised of 12 Becquerel Daguerreotypes. View on James Tylor's website: https://www.jamestylor.com/decookolisation.html.

# 8.6 Time Spiral

In our process for *Blak Cook Book* we took the brief to heart to some degree in that we considered numerous written, performed and visual sources, enabling us to collate First Nations perspectives on a range of important cross-cultural encounters related to Cook's Pacific voyages. However, we centred First Nations peoples by seeking in particular to find traces of encounters between different First Nations individuals and communities; not just encounters between Cook and the *natives*.

We were sensitive to the work of academic theorists and historians Irene Watson, Linda Tuhiwai Smith and Tracey Banivanua Mar in our approach to interpreting the historical and visual sources we drew on. We applied Watson's (2015) lens of Law to the sources we had about encounters: we wanted to highlight ways in which First Nations peoples expressed sovereignty and practiced diplomacy in encounters with Cook's journeys. With reference to Smith (2012), we sought to present both stability and change in our presentation of First Nations survivance in the spaces traversed by the journeys. Finally, following Mar (2016) and incorporating key events recounted in her highly original book *Decolonisation and the Pacific*, we identified additional examples of age-old practices of networking between First Nations of the Pacific, including Australia, from BC to the present.

To encapsulate much of this in *Blak Cook Book* we created a poster with a time spiral—a non-linear visual representation of significant events from the 1500s through to 2021, titled, 'Negotiating Captain Cook's Voyages' (Fig. 8.4). This offers a visual representation of First Nations perspectives on Cook's place in history; it brings both stability and change into view in a way that aligns with First Nations critical scholarship and philosophies. A recent collaborative film work, 'We are still here' (2022) interweaves eight short films by Pacific directors (including Australia, of course) responding collectively to the 250-year legacy of Cook: as in our time spiral the narratives resonate across time and place. The reverse of the *Blak Cook Book* poster featured Biripi artist, Jason Wing's *Captain James Crook*, an artwork comprised of a bronze bust of Cook with a balaclava obscuring his face (see Fig. 8.1). This is a visually striking work and speaks directly to the correction of a monument to give a fuller picture of Cook's role in illegal invasion and stolen land.

# 8.7 Propositions

Throughout the research and analysis for *Blak Cook Book* we remained convinced that the Cottage is irredeemable; that the City of Melbourne's plan for a counter-interpretative response was not sufficient, nor was it grounded in an ethos of putting First Nations first or a genuine investment in truth-telling. Rather than updating the Cottage displays with new text or video content to add some rudimentary balance to the dominant narrative at the site we spent some time speculating about what a completely different approach to countering the Cottage could entail. We imagined

**Fig. 8.4** Clare Land, Paola Balla, and Kate Golding, *Negotiating Captain Cook's Voyages* (2021). Time spiral from *Blak Cook Book*, reproduced with the blessing of Stephen Banham & Letterbox typographic design studio. Image courtesy of the authors

8 This Full Agency, This Decolonised Spirit: Talking Blak to Cooks' Cottage

Fig. 8.4 (continued)

something in the realm of a counter-monument of the same scale to negate the Cottage, such as a gathering place or fire pit near the Cottage that was dedicated to truth-telling. The hope that one day someone will get away with just blowing up the monument—as per Horst Hoheisel's proposition to blow up Berlin's Brandenberg Gate (Brandenburger Tor) as a memorial to Nazi genocide[19]—or burning the Cottage down as in Wotjobaluk and Ngarrindjeri writer/director Tracey Rigney's narrative within the film, *We are still here* (2022), crossed our minds.[20]

We hypothesised a scenario where First Nations people led a takeover, moved in and lived in the Cooks' dwelling, or ran Blak history classes from it, or smoked the fuck out of it.[21] It was conceivable to us that the City of Melbourne could take further steps such as raise an Aboriginal Flag nearby to counter the Union Jack or re-contextualise the whole of the Fitzroy Gardens, including abolishing the twee Tudor Village and Fairies Tree, and bringing the nearby culturally modified tree, whose scarred bark holds a living connection to First Nations cultural practices, and related narratives into much more prominence.

We also loved collaborator Kate Golding's proposition to create a camera obscura in the Cottage which would project Country into the Cottage.[22] A camera obscura is a naturally occurring optical phenomenon by which the exterior scene is projected onto the walls of a darkened room via a small aperture or hole. Standing inside the darkened space we see the outside world projected in a way we perceive as upside down. In Kate's proposal the ephemeral exterior live view would be projected onto the interior walls of the Cottage. The scene viewed inside the camera obscura is First Nations land, wherever the camera points is First Nations land. Notably, due to its present state, the Country that would be projected into the Cottage is in large part Europeanised: manicured lawns and introduced vegetation. This points to the complexities and impossibilities of the project of decolonisation and of the unfinishable nature of any process of DeCookolisation (Fig. 8.5).

---

[19] Horst Hoheisel's 1994 proposal for a Holocaust Memorial in Berlin was presented in a photographic diptych with the text on one image stating: 'The Brandenburg Tor is going to be ground to dust. The dust will be spread on the area of the memorial. The area will be covered with granit [sic] plates. As the memorial two blank voids are created, its double voids—and this is the actual memorial—are hard to stand. But it almost shows the impossibility of expressing the Holocaust by means of art'. This text is then repeated in German (Jewish Museum, n.d.).

[20] In *We Are Still Here* (2022), two contemporary warriors of the Aboriginal resistance Michael (Meyne Wyatt) and Janet (Leonie Whyman) fulfill Janet's mum's dream to burn down Cooks' Cottage.

[21] A Robert E. Lee confederate statue in Richmond, Virginia became a site of anti-racist and decolonial protest action, where reading groups, art, performances, speeches and screenings were held during the 2020 Black Lives Matter protests (McCammon, 2020; Colarossi, 2020).

[22] Kate Golding first developed this proposition in 2017. In 2021, she had the opportunity to participate in the City of Melbourne's Test Sites program where she proposed building a camera obscura inside Cooks' Cottage. Test Sites is a professional development program for artists who wish to expand their practice into the realm of public art. Unfortunately, Melbourne was placed in a lockdown for the duration of the Test Sites program so Kate wasn't able to physically test the proposition within the Cottage.

# 8 This Full Agency, This Decolonised Spirit: Talking Blak to Cooks' Cottage

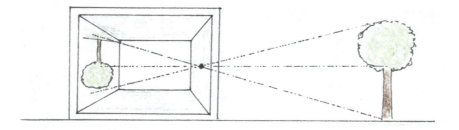

**Fig. 8.5** Kate Golding, Camera obscura illustration (2023). Image courtesy of the artist

Kate's proposition was conceived in response to observations and theories by First Nations thinkers. Worimi artist and curator Genevieve Grieves and historian and novelist Tony Birch, for example, have discussed together the city's 'lack of opportunities to remember, mourn and heal'.[23] Grieves has argued powerfully of the amnesia that occurs when the history that is reflected back to society through public commemorations is predominantly white, citing that of the approximately 525 monuments that exist in the City of Melbourne, 510 commemorate white men (Grieves & Birch, 2017). For Birch, monolithic, permanent monuments ask little of their audience, compared to the provocative potential of temporary monuments we are starting to see. These ask, for instance: how do we carry their message of remembrance with us? Both Grieves and Birch express the need to transform the memorial space, to find alternate ways to remember and to create opportunities for feeling and healing where both the colonised and settler colonisers can engage in the process. The camera obscura transforms the Cottage into a space for contemplation and provocation while providing a means to question 'the idea of monumentality and its implied corollary, permanence' (Young, 1992, p. 278) (Figs. 8.6 and 8.7).

An image in a camera obscura can only be seen from inside it, as any attempt to view the projection from the outside interferes with the light that creates the projected image, vanquishing it. A projected image in the Cottage would be interrupted by the opening of a door to enter it. Would the proposition involve visitors going inside the Cottage to see the projection of Country filling the space? Or better, would the Cottage be shut up, and visitors know Country is in there? Country is only inside the Cottage when it is shut up. In this proposition, the Cottage would be reclaimed by Country and would no longer function as a gubbah (white) only space. Would this be enough?

---

[23] Grieves and Birch (2017) in one of three talks which coincided with an exhibition entitled *The Violence of Denial*, curated by Grieves for Yirramboi festival and presented at Arts House, North Melbourne (see Part I, Chap. 4 of this edited volume).

**Fig. 8.6** Kate Golding, *Camera obscura (VCA), Boon Wurrung and Wurundjeri* (2016) installation detail. Site-specific installation, dimensions variable. Image courtesy of the artist

**Fig. 8.7** Kate Golding, *Camera obscura (Ballarat Observatory) Wadawurrung* (2017) installation detail. Site-specific installation, dimensions variable. Image courtesy of the artist

## 8.8 Conclusion

*Blak Cook Book* (2021) is available for downloading from the City of Melbourne's website, and in hard copy from the Visitor Centre adjacent to Cooks' Cottage. However, on our request it will not be available within the Cottage. Again, this aligns with our conviction that the Cottage is not a space that can ever be redeemed or made 'culturally safe' for Aboriginal and Torres Strait Islander people. We cannot

8  This Full Agency, This Decolonised Spirit: Talking Blak to Cooks' Cottage    143

see any reason for anyone to visit the Cottage at all in its current form and in the current social and political context—except if it were to be dismantled and returned to Yorkshire. When viewed side-by-side, *Blak Cook Book* and Cooks' Cottage present a stark mismatch, a cognitive dissonance. *Blak Cook Book* is grounded in reality while the Cottage, and all it represents, is a shallow colonial fantasy.

While *Blak Cook Book* serves as provocation for visitors, the process of creating and realising it also created ripples within the City of Melbourne. At certain points in the process there was a long gap between us providing material and hearing back from the City of Melbourne that the project would progress to printing, and then launching. We took this to mean that there was some degree of internal angst about the value and meaning of *Blak Book Book*. That we, particularly Paola, were shielded from having to weigh into these internal battles, which were nevertheless overcome, was a rare and welcome experience and points to the smarts and dedication of the project's sponsors within the City of Melbourne. It contrasts with past experiences of navigating projects through large institutions, during which Aboriginal consultants tend to be called on to troubleshoot resistance internal to the institution. This showed that the sponsors were cognisant of these dynamics and able to take responsibility for dealing with their own people and evolving the culture within the institution. The project has in this sense been part of the City of Melbourne's DeCookolisation. As it transpired, Yoorrook Truth-Telling Royal Commission—the first formal truth-telling process into injustices experienced by First Peoples in the state of Victoria—was announced during the duration of the project, so *Blak Cook Book* was launched as a 'truth telling conversation'.

We hope that in *Blak Cook Book* we have done justice to the many amazing artists, activists and cultural workers whose work has contributed to DeCookolisation across many spaces, and has inspired and informed our approach.

**Acknowledgements**  We would like to thank all the artists who allowed us to reproduce their work in *Blak Cook Book*. Thank you to Ciaran McCormack for proofreading this chapter. Thank you to the City of Melbourne for their understanding of our timelines as we worked on this project. We pay tribute to Sophia Hanover for her exemplary work within the City of Melbourne and with us. Special thanks to Jeanette Vaha'akolo for her support of Sophia during the project. *Blak Cook Book* was shortlisted in the 2021 Victorian Local History Awards. We entered the book in The Local History—Small Publication category and the judges saw fit to move it to the Community Diversity category. The City of Melbourne printed 2000 copies of *Blak Cook Book*. Copies are available free of charge at Fitzroy Gardens Visitor Centre. A PDF of *Blak Cook Book* can be accessed via: https://mvga-prod-files.s3.ap-southeast-4.amazonaws.com/public/2024-05/blak-cook-book.pdf.

# Appendix

**Artworks and Images Featured in *Blak Cook Book:***

Walter Hobbs, *Cook's Cottage, Fitzroy Gardens, Melbourne*, 1940, State Library Victoria, Accession no: H2010.56/59.

Lisa Bellear (Minjungbul/Noonuccal/ Kanak), *Black GST protestors including Wayne Thorpe and Robbie Corowa, Captain Cook's Cottage, Fitzroy Gardens, Melbourne*, 2006. Digitised colour photograph. Lisa Bellear Collection. Gift of John Stewart, 2012. Koorie Heritage Trust, ph 05529.

Callum Morton, *Cottage Industry: Bawdy Nights*, 1999. Wood, epoxy, Perspex, acrylic, lights, sound, 80 × 50 × 50 cm. © Callum Morton. Courtesy the artist and Anna Schwartz Gallery. Photo: McClelland Gallery. Collection of McClelland Sculpture Park and Gallery.

Christian Thompson, *Othering the Explorer, James Cook* from the series *Museum of Others*, 2016. C-type print, 120 × 120 cm. Courtesy the artist and Sarah Scout Presents, Melbourne.

Photograph of Gary Foley at the Captain Cook statue, Hyde Park, Sydney. Photo: Haydn Keenan, 2009.

Cannon from HMB *Endeavour* 1725–50. Photography by George Serras, National Museum of Australia.

Secret instructions issued to James Cook by the British Admiralty (1768), *Cook's voyage 1768–71: copies of correspondence,* etc. National Library of Australia, Canberra.

Jason Wing, *Captain James Crook*, 2013. Bronze, 60 × 60 x 30 cm. Edition of 5. Image courtesy of the artist and Artereal Gallery. Photograph by Garrie Maguire, Red Gate Gallery Artist in Residence programme.

Polynesian Voyaging Society's recreated traditional voyaging canoe *Hōkūle'a*. Photo: Polynesian Voyaging Society/'Ōiwi TV. Photographer: Jason Patterson.

Attributed to James Cook (1728–79), *Chart of the Society Islands, with Otaheite [Tahiti] in the centre*, from 'Charts and Maps made during the Voyage of Discovery in the South Pacific Ocean, by Captain James Cook, commander of the *Endeavour*, in 1769 and 1770', 1769. Ink on paper. British Library, London, UK. Add. MS 21593 C. © British Library Board. All Rights Reserved. Bridgeman Images.

Tupaia (c. 1725–70), *Māori trading a crayfish with Joseph Banks, drawing by Tupaia*, from 'Drawings illustrative of Captain Cook's First Voyage, 1768–1771', 1769. Watercolour, on paper, 26.8 × 20.5 cm. British Library, London, UK. Add. MS 15,508, fol. 12. © British Library Board. All Rights Reserved. Bridgeman Images.

## 8 This Full Agency, This Decolonised Spirit: Talking Blak to Cooks' Cottage

Tupaia (c. 1725–70), *Indigenous Australians in bark canoes, drawing by Tupaia*, from 'Drawings illustrative of Captain Cook's First Voyage, 1768–1771', 1770. Pencil and watercolour, on paper, 26.4 × 36 cm. British Library, London, UK. Add. MS 15,508, fol. 10. © British Library Board. All Rights Reserved. Bridgeman Images.

Tommy McRae, Kwatkwat people, (c. 1833/1837–1901), *Victorian Blacks— Melbourne tribe holding corroboree after seeing ships for the first time*, c.1890s, Wahgunyah, Victoria. Drawing in pen and iron-gall ink, cream wove paper, 23.8 × 36.0 cm. Purchased by the National Gallery of Australia, Canberra 1994. nga94.1232.2.

Lisa Reihana, detail *in Pursuit of Venus [infected]*, 2015–17, Ultra hd video, colour, 7.1 sound, 64 min. Image courtesy of the artist, New Zealand at Venice and Artprojects. © Lisa Reihana/Copyright Agency, 2021.

Herbert Kawainui Kāne, *The Death of Cook, February 14, 1779*, 1983. Oil painting, 91.4 × 53.3 cm. Copyright Herbert K. Kane, LLC.

Dr. Kirsten Lyttle, *Kuki Bones*, 2011, from the *Killing Kuki* series, 2009–2011. Hand-printed silk screen print on home- sewn Hawaiian shirt, cotton, cotton thread, screen print ink. © Dr. Kirsten Lyttle.

Dr. Kirsten Lyttle, *Death in Hawai'i*, 2009–2011, from the *Killing Kuki* series, 2009–2011. Hand-painted and home-sewn Hawaiian shirt, cotton, cotton thread, paint, ink and transfers. © Dr. Kirsten Lyttle.

Dr. Kirsten Lyttle, *Killing Kuki*, 2011, from the *Killing Kuki* series, 2009–2011. Hand-printed silk screen print on home-sewn Hawaiian shirt, cotton, cotton thread, screen print ink. © Dr. Kirsten Lyttle.

Lin Onus, *Kaptn Koori*, 1985. © Lin Onus Estate/Copyright Agency, 2021.

Gordon Bennett, *Home décor (Algebra) Daddy's little girl (1998)*. Acrylic on linen, 182.5 × 182.5 cm. Collection: Private, Melbourne. © The Estate of Gordon Bennett.

Vincent Namatjira, Western Arrernte people, Northern Territory, born 1983, Alice Springs, Northern Territory. *Close Contact* 2018, Indulkana, South Australia, synthetic polymer paint on plywood, 188.0 × 62.0 × 3.5 cm. Gift of the James and Diana Ramsay Foundation for the Ramsay Art Prize 2019. Art Gallery of South Australia, Adelaide, photography Grant Hancock 20193S2 © Vincent Namatjira / Copyright Agency, 2020. Courtesy of Iwantja Arts and this is no fantasy.

Kate Golding. *The Milbi Wall, Gan-gaarr (Cooktown), Guugu Yimithirr Nation*, 2015. Courtesy of the artist and the Gungarde Community Centre Aboriginal Corporation and community members who created the Milbi Wall.

Karla Dickens, *I'd better go and get something' harder*, 2014. Mixed media, polyptych (28 components), dimensions variable. Collection: Australian National Maritime Museum. Photograph: Mick Richards. Photograph courtesy of the artist and Andrew Baker Art Dealer, Brisbane.

# References

Bird Rose, D. (1993). Worshipping captain Cook. *Social Analysis: THe International Journal of Social and Cultural Practice, 34*, 43–49.

City of Melbourne. (n.d.a). Booking a visit to Cooks' Cottage. *What's On*. https://whatson.melbourne.vic.gov.au/book-cooks-cottage. Accessed 12 July 2023.

City of Melbourne. (n.d.b). Cooks' cottage. *What's On*. https://whatson.melbourne.vic.gov.au/things-to-do/cooks-cottage. Accessed 12 July 2023.

City of Melbourne. (n.d.c). Cooks' cottage. https://www.melbourne.vic.gov.au/fitzroy-gardens/CooksCottage/Pages/CooksCottageHome.aspx. Accessed 12 July 2023.

City of Melbourne. (n.d.d). Tunnerminnerwait and Maulboyheenner. https://www.melbourne.vic.gov.au/about-melbourne/melbourne-profile/aboriginal-culture/Pages/tunnerminnerwait-and-maulboyheener.aspx. Accessed 9 August 2023.

City of Melbourne. (2016). Future Melbourne 2026. https://www.melbourne.vic.gov.au/SiteCollectionDocuments/future-melbourne-2026-plan.pdf. Accessed 9 August 2023.

Colarossi, N. (2020). Photos show how the Robert E. Lee statue in Virginia has been reclaimed to support the Black Lives Matter movement. *Insider*. https://www.insider.com/robert-e-lee-statue-repurposed-black-lives-matter-images-2020-7. Accessed 11 January 2023.

Foley, G. [goori2]. (2019a). On captain Cook [video]. YouTube. https://youtu.be/f2CKlgeUXMo. Accessed 8 August 2023.

Foley, G. [goori2]. (2019b). 1970 anti-Captain Cook Protest [video]. https://youtu.be/B6WqGDhn7XU. Accessed 8 August 2023.

Foley, G. [goori2]. (2011). Invasion Day 2003 St Kilda Beach [video]. http://youtu.be/Yr0yUOwcWgE. Accessed 23 June, 2022.

Grieves, G., & Birch, T. (2017) The violence of Denial. *Yirramboi First Nations Art Festival*. Arts House, 11 May 2017.

Healy, C. (1990). We know your mob now': Histories and their cultures. *Meanjin, 49*(3), 512–523.

Healy, C. (1997). *From the ruins of colonialism: History as social memory*. Cambridge University Press.

Heritage Council Victoria. (n.d.). Cook's cottage Fitzroy Gardens, EAST MELBOURNE VIC 3002—Property No B1264. https://vhd.heritagecouncil.vic.gov.au/places/64909. Accessed 9 August 2023.

Howell, E. (2008). It's captain Cook all over again. *Australian Critical Race and Whiteness Studies, 4*(2), 1–7.

Jewish Museum. (n.d.). Collection highlights: The crushed Brandenburg Gate, proposed memorial for the murdered Jews of Europe. https://thejewishmuseum.org/collection/27605-the-crushed-brandenburg-gate-proposed-memorial-for-the-murdered-jews-of-europe. Accessed 12 May 2022.

Land, C. (2014a). Tunnerminnerwait and Maulboyheenner: The involvement of Aboriginal people from Tasmania in key events of early Melbourne. *City of Melbourne*. https://www.melbourne.vic.gov.au/SiteCollectionDocuments/tunnerminnerwait-and-maulboyheenner.pdf. Accessed 9 August 2023.

Land, C. (2014b). Forms for monuments to complex histories. *City of Melbourne*. https://www.melbourne.vic.gov.au/SiteCollectionDocuments/forms-for-monuments-complex-histories.pdf. Accessed 13 July 2021.

Land, C. Balla, P. and Golding, K. (2021). *Blak Cook Book*. New Cultural Perspectives on Cooks' Cottage. A set of provocations. Melbourne: City of Melbourne. https://mvga-prod-files.s3.ap-southeast-4.amazonaws.com/public/2024-05/blak-cook–book.pdf. Accessed 10 October 2024.

Mansell, K. (2020). 'Taking to the streets against the Vietnam War': A timeline history of Australian protest 1962–1972. Labour History Melbourne. https://labourhistorymelbourne.org/taking-to-the-streets-against-the-vietnam-war-a-timeline-history-of-australian-protest-1962-1972-introd uction/taking-to-the-streets-against-the-vietnam-war-a-timeline-history-of-australian-protest-1962-1972-1972/. Accessed 23 June 2022.

Mar, T. B. (2016). *Decolonisation and the Pacific: Indigenous globalisation and the ends of empire.* Cambridge University Press.

Mar, T. B., & Edmonds, P. (Eds.). (2010). *Making settler colonial space: Perspectives on race, place and identity.* Palgrave Macmillan.

McBride, L., & Smith, M. (2019). The 2020 project: First Nations community consultation report. *Australian Museum.* https://media.australian.museum/media/dd/documents/2020_report_web_version_spreads_lr.abef674.pdf. Accessed 5 September 2019.

McCammon, S. (2020). In V. Richmond (Ed.), Protesters transform a confederate statue. *NPR.* https://www.npr.org/2020/06/12/876124924/in-richmond-va-protestors-transform-a-con federate-statue. Accessed 9 August 2023.

Micallef, S. (2016). Shaun Micallef on the duplicity of Cooks' cottage. *Sydney Morning Herald.* https://www.smh.com.au/entertainment/shaun-micallef-on-the-duplicity-of-cooks-cot tage-20161012-gs0kjo.html. Accessed 18 January 2019.

Nugent, M. (2009). *Captain Cook was here.* Cambridge University Press.

Redmond, A. (2008). Captain Cook meets General Macarthur in the Northern Kimberley: Humour and ritual in an Indigenous Australian life-world. *Anthropological Forum, 18*(3), 255–270. https://doi.org/10.1080/00664670802429370

Schlunke, K. (2015). Entertaining possession: re-enacting Cook's Arrival for the Queen. In K. Darian-Smith & P. Edmonds (Eds.), *Conciliation on colonial frontiers: Conflict, performance, and commemoration in Australia and the Pacific Rim* (pp. 227–242). Routledge.

Sivertsen, N., Ryder, C., & Johnson, T. (2023). First Nations people often take on the 'cultural load' in their workplaces. Employers need to ease this burden. *The Conversation.* https://theconversation.com/first-nations-people-often-take-on-the-cultural-load-in-their-workplaces-employers-need-to-ease-this-burden-193858. Accessed 21 March 2023.

Smith, L. T. (2012). *Decolonizing methodologies: Research and indigenous peoples* (2nd ed.). Zed Books.

Stanner, W. E. H. (1970). The dreaming. In T. J. Harding & B. J. Wallace (Eds.), *Cultures of the Pacific* (pp. 304–315). Free Press.

Thomas, N. (2006). The uses of Captain Cook: Early exploration in the public history of Aotearoa New Zealand and Australia. In A. Coombes (Ed.), *Rethinking settler colonialism: History and memory in Australia, Canada, Aotearoa New Zealand and South Africa.* Manchester University Press.

Vizenor, G. (Ed.). (2008). *Survivance: Narratives of native presence.* University of Nebraska Press.

Watson, I. (2015). *Aboriginal peoples, colonialism and international law: Raw law.* Routledge.

Weenthunga Health Network (2023). Reframing "cultural load" [Instagram]. 16 November. Available at: https://www.instagram.com/p/Czsq_vDLn0h/?utm_source=ig_web_copy_link&igsh= MzRlODBiNWFlZA==. Accessed 1 December 2023.

Williams, S. (n.d.). An indigenous Australian perspective on Cook's arrival. The voyages of Captain James Cook. *British Library.* https://www.bl.uk/the-voyages-of-captain-james-cook/articles/an-indigenous-australian-perspective-on-cooks-arrival. Accessed 2 March 2019.

Young, J. E. (1992). The counter-monument: Memory against Itself in Germany today. *Critical Inquiry, 18*(2), 267–296.

Young, L. (2008). The contagious magic of James Cook in Captain-Cook's cottage. *Recollections: Journal of the National Museum of Australia, 3*(2), 123–142. https://recollections.nma.gov.au/issues/vol_3_no_2/papers/the_contagious_magic_of_james_cook. Accessed 17 February 2023.

## Archives

Ningla, A.-Na. (1972). *Hungry for our land [poster]*. A00003056 Aboriginal History Archive (VAHS Collection).

**Paola Balla** is a Wemba-Wemba and Gunditjmara woman. She works as an artist, curator, writer, educator and public speaker. Her practice-led research focuses on Aboriginal women's stories and resistance, centring Aboriginal women's voices and activism, sovereignty, matriarchy and First Nations ways of being, knowing and doing. Her visual practice engages with the impacts of racism and traumas in colony australia on Blak women's bodies and encapsulates identity and narrative realms in photography and installation through practice-led research. She works at Moondani Balluk Indigenous Academic Unit, Victoria University lecturing in Indigenous Education and Indigenous Art and collaborative research projects with local community in the Western Suburbs Koorie communities. She completed her PhD. Doctorate at Victoria University through practice-led research. She was proudly an inaugural Lisa Bellear Indigenous Research Scholar during the PhD.

**Kate Golding** is a settler Australian of English ancestry based on unceded Wurundjeri Country. As an artist she utilises a variety of photographic processes to examine colonisation and the representation of people and place through long-term projects. For many years her focus has been on Indigenous sovereignty and critiquing the memorialisation of Captain Cook.

**Clare Land** is an Academic/Researcher at Moondani Balluk Indigenous Academic Unit, Victoria University, where she serves as Director of Research, which includes advancing the research agenda of the Aboriginal History Archive alongside Professor Gary Foley and his team. Clare is an Anglo-identified non-Aboriginal person. She has a long-standing commitment to supporting land justice and Indigenous-led struggles and is known in particular for the book, *Decolonizing Solidarity: Dilemmas and Directions for Supporters of Indigenous Struggles* (Zed Books, 2015).

# Chapter 9
# What Should the City of Melbourne Do with the Inaccurate and Offensive John Batman Memorial Obelisk?

**Amy Spiers**

**Abstract** In this chapter, settler artist and researcher Amy Spiers speculates about forms of imaginative visual and spatial justice that could be enacted to address contentious monuments and truth-tell the past in public spaces permeated with colonial place-making. The chapter focuses on a critical examination of the bluestone memorial obelisk to John Batman, located at the Queen Victoria Market, Naarm (Melbourne), that inaccurately describes Batman as founder of Melbourne on a site that was in 1835 'then unoccupied'. Drawing on lessons from previous creative (counter-)monuments addressing traumatic histories in Naarm (Melbourne); Nipaluna, Lutruwita (Hobart, Tasmania) and Berlin, Germany, Spiers argues that the City of Melbourne to date has failed to provide substantive remembrances to the victims of Batman's horrific deeds that includes mass murder, deception and land theft. Addressing speculation that the Batman obelisk will quietly disappear due to a forthcoming multi-million-dollar renewal of the market, Spiers' chapter argues that the redevelopment provides a significant opportunity for the City of Melbourne to fulfil its declared commitment to truth-tell the impact of the colonial past by meaningfully atoning for Batman's memorial and legacy, and acknowledging the anguish caused to First Peoples, by fostering a culture of remembrance through creative commemorations.

## 9.1 Don't Miss This Opportunity for Truth-Telling: Removing Batman's Obelisk in Naarm

My regular walk to my office at work is a veritable passage through colonising placemaking. Disembarking from the 58 tram at the Queen Victoria Market, I make my way to the Royal Melbourne Institute of Technology's (RMIT) city campus walking by J. W. Brown's bluestone obelisk to John Batman: an obdurate memorial erected in 1881 to the 'founding' land-grabber of Melbourne. Batman's remains

A. Spiers (✉)
RMIT University, Naarm/Melbourne, Australia
e-mail: amy.spiers@rmit.edu.au

© The Author(s), under exclusive license to Springer Nature Singapore Pte Ltd. 2024    149
G. Grieves and A. Spiers (eds.), *Art and Memorialisation*, Indigenous-Settler Relations in Australia and the World 6, https://doi.org/10.1007/978-981-97-6289-7_9

were originally interred here in the colony's first cemetery but were relocated to Fawkner Cemetery in 1922 when the graveyard was de-registered so the market could expand over it. Today in the early months of 2024, the memorial is easily overlooked, awkwardly 'marginalised' (Edensor & Sumartojo, 2023, p. 562) between the entrance to the market's carpark and 'Testing Grounds', a temporary, open-air space dedicated to artistic experimentation in the public realm. Routinely passing the monument serves as an antagonising reminder that commemorations naturalising and legitimising white invasion and possession insidiously persist in our public spaces (Carlson & Farrelly, 2023a; Mar, 2012). Surrounded by a sea of concrete, parked cars, bustling marketgoers, and the provisional creative infrastructure of experimental public artists, the memorial appears—to me at least—like an anachronistic 'nail house' resisting the urban development and societal changes around it.[1] For many passers-by, however, it is easy to ignore and tacitly tolerate this symbol celebrating the 'opening up' of First Peoples' lands in this region for white occupation.

Although statues, plaques and memorials commemorating racists and imperialists have recently been reappraised, recontextualised and removed in many cities across the globe in response to anti-colonial and anti-racism social movements, this valorisation of Batman endures. While the memorial resides in the jurisdiction of the City of Melbourne—a council that has formally recognised 'that Aboriginal peoples were the first inhabitants of this land' and who have a declared commitment to 'truth-telling about the impact of colonisation' (City of Melbourne, 2021, n.p.)—this commemoration of Batman still stands denying the Kulin Nation's sovereign presence: its inscription pronouncing Batman the founder of a settlement in 1835 'on this site of Melbourne then unoccupied'. Even as activism and scholarship in recent years has led to the re-evaluation of Batman as a 'mass murderer' (Quilty cited in Hinchliffe, 2017, n.p.; Clements, 2011), his name stripped from an inner Melbourne electoral division and a nearby Northcote park (Barolsky et al., 2023; Carlson & Farrelly, 2023a), Batman's obelisk inexorably remains despite appeals for its removal (Hinchliffe, 2017; Holsworth, 2020; James, 2018; Perkins, 2017): a violent, inaccurate, offensively celebratory reminder to First Peoples that this area of Kulin Country was stolen by an opportunistic and deceitful squatter.

Historians attest that Batman played a key role in the Black War in Lutruwita (Tasmania): he was a bounty hunter actively participating in the capture, slaughter and dispossession of Palawa, Lutruwita's First Peoples, including leading a massacre of 17 Palawa at Ben Lomond in 1829 (Clements, 2011; Lyndall et al., 2022). Batman's thirst for profiting from stolen lands also drove him to extend his land-grabbing unlawfully into Kulin Country and act duplicitously towards First Peoples, foisting a dubious treaty on Kulin leaders on his arrival in 1835 (Attwood, 2009; Boyce, 2013; Pascoe, 2007; Stephens & Stewart-Muir, 2023). Having learnt in Lutruwita that First Peoples 'posed the gravest risks to stock and profit' (Boyce, 2013, p. 53), Batman's motivation in forging an agreement with the Kulin was not benign. Instead, he sought the *appearance* of a legal and ethical claim to land that would smooth the

---

[1] A 'nail house' is a term derived from the Chinese word 'dingzihu' which refers to a building owners refuse to vacate to make way for property development.

way for acquisition of vast portions of Kulin Country without contestation from First Peoples or colonial authorities (Attwood, 2009; Boyce, 2013). The treaty, however, was short lived and declared invalid by the colonial government who deemed the land was the possession of the Crown, not the Kulin Nation. Despite this, Batman's arrival to this region ushered in colonial violence and land theft in the Southeast, the scale of which had not been seen before in the colony. As historian James Boyce has noted, Batman's brazen and unsanctioned squatter camp that illegitimately spawned Melbourne, provoked an unfettered land rush with squatters seizing 'nearly twenty million hectares of the most productive and best-watered Aboriginal homelands', and occupying more land in the Southeast in the years between 1835 to 1838 than in the proceeding fifty (Boyce, 2013, p. xiii). As Wurundjeri Elder Uncle Andrew Gardiner has elaborated about the enduring consequences of this frenzied land grab of Country:

> We live in the unspoken shadow of catastrophic dispossession [...] This destroyed our civilisation that had been in harmony with this Country for tens of thousands of years. With our culture and community shattered, echoes of this devastation still reverberate today (cited in Merri-Bek City Council, 2024, n.p.)

There is no mention of Batman's participation in the slaughter of Palawa people in Lutruwita on the bluestone obelisk, nor his unlawful land-grab as 'founder' of Melbourne. Batman's landing was calamitous for Southeastern First Peoples, provoking disastrous dispossession and upheaval of their way of life, yet the monument is silent on this too. The monument is, however, inscribed with the word 'Circumspice', a Latin term that suggests if you want to see Batman's legacy, you must 'look around'. If passers-by were to look around in the early months of 2024, they would observe a 'dramatically altered', 'highly urbanised environment' that includes the grubby carpark and some introduced London plane trees that shed trichomes causing coughing and eye watering each spring: stark legacies of colonisers' disruption to what was once lush plains of biodiverse grassland (Lendlease, 2023, p. 38). Additionally, they might notice signs of a redevelopment instigated by the City of Melbourne that aims to upgrade the tired site of the Queen Victoria Markets to capitalise on this major tourist destination, raising questions about the future of the contentious Batman memorial.

In a document entitled *Queen Victoria Market Southern Precinct Development Plan Volume 1*, the City of Melbourne's chosen development partner, Lendlease, outlines a proposal for a new precinct named 'Gurrowa Place'—named after a Woi Wurrung word, the language of the Wurundjeri people of the Kulin Nation, meaning 'a place for exchange' (2023, p. 19). As part of the vision for this ambitious new retail, commercial and residential precinct, it is proposed that the current dingy market carpark will be replaced with a 'drawcard destination', 'global exemplar' 1.8 hectare landscaped public open space (Lendlease, 2023, p. 8). The plan acknowledges the Aboriginal cultural heritage value of the development area—noting 'reverence' will be displayed for the former colonial burial ground that once shared the market site and includes significant First Peoples' remains (p. 47). Yet intriguingly, in all the developer's talk of heritage-sensitive urban enhancement, there is no mention of the

Batman memorial or plans for its fate. Indeed, it has already been speculated that it will be the demands of urban development that will finally compel the memorial's removal—as also transpired with the contentious John Batman statue formerly located on Collins Street until 2018—rather than any moral or truth-telling impulse from City of Melbourne (Carlson & Farrelly, 2023a). Can we take silence on the Batman obelisk in the proposal as a sign that the memorial will not survive the renewal?

In a plan avowedly 'informed by conversations and collaboration with the Wurundjeri Woi-wurrung People', and underpinned by visions to 'contribute to Melbourne being recognised as an Aboriginal City' (Lendlease, 2023, p. 42), Lendlease claims to ultimately offer a development proposal that delivers 'a legacy that Melbourne deserves' (p. 8). But if the plan is indeed an intention to quietly subtract the memorial to make way for a 'drawcard destination', is this not a lost opportunity to address the city's 'deserved shame' (Grand, 2018; Veracini, 2023) regarding the monument's prolonged existence and Batman's colonial legacy? This bold, collaborative, Aboriginal-centred urban renewal begs the question: will the development substantively respond to calls for the monument's removal, advance the City's declared commitment to truth-telling and generate an occasion for public acknowledgement of Batman's wrongdoing, settler education and First Peoples' healing?

I contend in this chapter that we deserve a city that tells the truth of its founding in public spaces and atones for it through forms of public commemorative art. What is at stake is a chance to enact visual and spatial justice (Andron & Lata, 2024): to not just remove the monument inconspicuously but instead to provide an important public opportunity to collectively reflect upon the remembrances and iconography that appear—and do not appear—in our public spaces, and the social values and shared sense of place and identity commemorations strongly shape. In what follows I will reflect on lessons we can learn from previous creative (counter-)monument efforts addressing difficult histories in Naarm (Melbourne); Nipaluna, Lutruwita (Hobart, Tasmania) and Berlin, Germany to inspire more imaginative vision and truth-telling action from the City of Melbourne regarding the Batman obelisk.

## 9.2 Truth-Telling Monuments Deserve Central Permanency: Creative Contestations to Batman's Obelisk and Legacy in Naarm

To date, City of Melbourne authorities have made minor, unsatisfactory efforts to render the crude, colonial obelisk more palatable. In 1992, for example, the Council responded to changing sentiment about the memorial by adding a plaque inscribed with an acknowledgement that stated:

> When the monument was erected in 1881, the colony considered that the Aboriginal people did not occupy land. It is now clear that prior to the colonisation of Victoria, the land was inhabited and used by Aboriginal people.

# 9 What Should the City of Melbourne Do with the Inaccurate ...

After this plaque was deemed 'too feeble' and insufficiently apologetic by the Council's Aboriginal Consultative Group (Edensor & Sumartojo, 2023, p. 5), the plaque was replaced with an alternate statement in 2004 explaining:

> The City of Melbourne acknowledges that the historical events and perceptions referred to by this memorial are inaccurate. An apology is made to indigenous people and to the traditional owners of this land for the wrong beliefs of the past and the personal upset caused.

As local critic Mark Holsworth has noted, the slightness of this apology containing 'vague weasel words' (2020, n.p.), the weathered and vandalised condition of the plaque, and the smallness of the font compared with the gold gilded letters of the original inscription and the unblemished monument—with 'acts of vandalism' reportedly regularly removed by the City's Rapid Response Clean Team (City of Melbourne, 2023, p. 141)—are grossly unsatisfactory, failing to acknowledge Batman's theft of land and participation in attempted genocide. Yorta Yorta writer and advocate, Daniel James, has described the plaque as 'symptomatic of Australia's approach to true history' that renders First People's experiences 'as nothing more than a footnote, an obscure reference' (2018, n.p.).

Amidst these plaque amendments in 1995, attempts were made by a collaborative creative team consisting of Gunnai artist Ray Thomas, non-Indigenous artist Megan Evans and Woorabinda and Berigaba researcher and writer Robert Mate Mate to install a brass map displaying sites of massacre of First Peoples in the state of Victoria close to the Batman obelisk. The proposed map was part of a now decommissioned public artwork by Thomas, Evans and Mate called *Another View Walking Trail* (1995) that intended to disclose overlooked First Peoples' histories, and sites of contact and conflict with settlers, through a self-guided walk leading viewers past a series of small mosaics and artworks placed in conversation with various colonial commemorations and sites across the city. The trail was originally commissioned by the City of Melbourne as part of wider national reconciliation initiatives and received funding from the Council for Aboriginal Reconciliation (Morgan, 2016; Pinto, 2021). As noted by historian Sarah Pinto, however, these government-led processes of reconciliation were often more concerned with settler nation-building and 'unifying Indigenous and non-Indigenous peoples', than exposing troubling histories that challenged the legitimacy of the settler state (Pinto, 2021, pp. 25–26). Consequently, many proposed components of *Another View*, including the brass massacre map, were subjected to censorship and withdrawn (Morgan, 2016). Described by one City of Melbourne public art officer as 'extremely confrontational' (Morgan, 2016, p. 72), the unrealised pieces were ultimately 'regarded by the council as too inflammatory, and inimical to the spirit of reconciliation' (Edensor & Sumartojo, 2023, p. 12). Evidently, what these settler government authorities did not take into consideration was how the Batman memorial's continued presence is confrontational for First Peoples, and runs counter to truth-telling, relations, and justice on their terms.

Also created within the remit of reconciliation, and raising questions about Batman's legacy, is Batjala artist Fiona Foley's *Lie of the Land* (1997), an artwork commissioned by the City of Melbourne to coincide with the inaugural Australian Reconciliation Convention held in Melbourne in 1997. The convention notably launched the *Bringing Them Home* report (1997) that exposed Australia's history of forcibly removing First Nations' children from their families, in what is known as the Stolen Generations. Artist Foley has been working boldly to produce timely commemorations that expose colonial atrocities on this continent for several decades. *Lie of the Land* is a powerful example of these efforts. It consists of monumental, three meter high headstone-like, sandstone pillars etched with the items Batman claimed he traded with Kulin Elders in 1835—'knives', 'beads', 'tomahawks', 'looking glasses', 'blankets', 'flour', 'scissors'—in exchange for 600,000 acres of their Country to form the settlement that would become 'Melbourne'. Accompanying the artwork is a sound installation by Chris Knowles that translates the account of the trade from Batman's diary into languages spoken in the region at the time of colonisation: Chinese, Portuguese, Dutch, French, Indonesian, English and Woi Wurrung. These spoken accounts are overlaid with the sounds of the Kulin Nation's creator, Bunjil the Eagle, and protector, Waa the Crow (Fig. 9.1).

Coinciding with the convention, *Lie of the Land* was installed on Swanston Street outside Melbourne Town Hall from 19 March to 13 July 1997. The work's presence and power were enhanced by the fact it stood defiantly right outside the coloniser's administrative seat of Melbourne, displaying the flimsy and pernicious deal the city was founded on. Foley noted at the time: 'As the history was written by the victors it is only now that the silent history of the Indigenous populations is given a voice' (cited in Carmody, 2007, p. 98). Senior Wurundjeri Elder Aunty Joy Murphy Wandin, who acted as advisor during the work's creation, asserted on the installation's launch that the work should serve as a strong reminder of the cost of Batman's land grab:

> In this position outside the Town Hall, many of the broader community can take the opportunity to be informed about the history, and the pain, and heartache suffered by the Aboriginal people of this area. Hopefully this history will motivate people to be more understanding in their awareness of the social issues facing Aboriginal people. The past must be dealt with before we move on to the future. (Murphy, 1997, pp. 8–9)

**Fig. 9.1** Fiona Foley, *Lie of the Land* (1997). Sandstone, 7 pillars, 300 × 100 cm. Accompanying sound component by artist Chris Knowles. The work is shown here in its temporary location in front of the Melbourne Town Hall, Swanston Street in 1997. City of Melbourne public art collection. Image courtesy of the artist, City of Melbourne and Andrew Baker Art Dealer

# 9 What Should the City of Melbourne Do with the Inaccurate … 155

While reactionary uproar accompanies any suggestion of a colonial monument being relocated, First Peoples' commemorations are largely tolerated as temporary public artworks. Despite calls for the monument to remain in its powerfully informing position, when City of Melbourne permanently acquired *Lie of the Land* it was relocated to the below-ground forecourt of Melbourne Museum (Pinto, 2021). In the move, it lost its central location and 24-hour public visibility on a street with high foot-traffic where it conspicuously commemorated—as monuments do—significant, painful events in the city's history. Contained as a museum object, it has been described as 'more exhibit than experience' (Carmody, 2007, p. 98). The work's unflinching reminder of the city's foundation on stolen land and the understanding and awareness the piece promotes—no longer in plain sight—is today 'hidden' (Stephens, 2023).

In more recent years, the City of Melbourne have supported other less confrontational public art challenges to Batman's memorial and legacy by non-Indigenous artists. In 2016, for example, experimental creatives from the architectural practice Sibling produced a critical, temporary architectural folly to surround the Batman obelisk. Installed for just one week as part of City of Melbourne's inaugural Public Art Melbourne Biennial Lab, *Over Obelisk* (2016) stimulated dialogue about the contentious nature of the monument. Comprised of mobile stepped seating and signage that asked, 'Do you acknowledge that the historical events referred to by this monument are inaccurate?' in both English and Woi Wurrung, the structure encouraged the public to sit with and examine the obelisk from a range of angles. A public talks program featuring Koori historian and writer Tony Birch and Wailwan/Gamillaraay architect Jefa Greenaway promoted First Peoples' perspectives and a critical re-view of the colonial object (Melbourne Biennial Lab, 2016).

In 2021, the City of Melbourne, in collaboration with the Australian Centre for Contemporary Art (ACCA), also commissioned non-Indigenous artist Tom Nicholson to produce the public artwork, *Chimney in store (Towards a monument to Batman's Treaty)*. Developed out of extensive research and extended conversations with Kulin Elders, First Nations scholars and artists—including Aunty Joy Murphy Wandin, Tony Birch and Jonathan Jones—Nicholson installed an understated mound comprised of 3520 buried bricks planted over with native grasses in the city's unfortunately-named Batman Park. The bricks recall the city's first European chimney built in 1836 for John Batman by bricklayer William Buckley, who remarkably escaped as a convict from the failed 1803 settlement of Port Phillip Bay and lived with Wathaurung people of the Kulin Nation for 32 years before returning to work as a labourer and interpreter for Batman and the newly established colony. Comprised of enough bricks to build a chimney, the store imagines and anticipates a future monument to Batman's Treaty involving 'a brick form poised between a free-standing chimney and an obelisk', covered in thousands of words inscribed on plaques. An accompanying artist's book that can be accessed online presents the texts for a variety of plaques that would inscribe this speculative chimney (Nicholson, 2022). Drawing on multiple historical references and discourse on the memorialisation of complex histories, Nicholson describes the work as:

an attempt to modestly enact an alternative monumental language. It mobilises the way a monument can speak to the place and scale of our collective life as a society, but also repudiates the false certainties of the monuments we have inherited. (cited in ACCA, 2022, n.p.)

These more recent conceptual and discreet gestures cleverly question forms for monuments and anti-monuments, making knowing reference to the history of art, architecture and memorialisation, and resist the didacticism of traditional colonial monuments. Their challenges to the city's colonial origin myths, however, lack the unambiguous repudiation of Batman's legacy—that put in plain sight obscured histories and give forceful expression to First Peoples pain—that *Another View* and *Lie of the Land* attempted. Where *Over Obelisk* was mobile and *Chimney in store* is avowedly modest, both works comfortable with no stable, assertive footprint, *Lie of the Land* and *Another View* challenged denial through direct confrontations with the truth rendered enduring and monumental in materials of sandstone and brass—but their ambitions for public permanence were thwarted.

The twenty-first century settler city, as Pinto observes, 'does not give up its commemorative landscapes easily', with First Peoples' remembrances kept modest, short-lived or on the margins (2012, p. 116). After decades of denial since invasion—where colonial violence has been disregarded, minimised, ceaselessly debated and evoked as an afterthought on a plaque—why cannot First Peoples' accounts of

**Fig. 9.2** Fiona Foley, *Lie of the Land* (1997). Sandstone, 7 pillars, 300 × 100 cm. Accompanying sound component by artist Chris Knowles. The work is shown here in its present location in the foyer of the Melbourne Museum. City of Melbourne public art collection. Photograph by Collin Bogaars. Image courtesy of the artist, City of Melbourne and Andrew Baker Art Dealer

this history be granted definitive monumental expression and central positioning in a city that has a declared commitment to truth-telling? It begs the question: what if the Gurrowa Place development could provide such an opportunity? The city's new 'place for exchange' could offer a new prominent, permanent site for Foley's memorial, *Lie of the Land*, to prompt traders, shoppers and visitors to consider Batman's original trade and dishonest exchange with Kulin leaders. Imagine the lasting truth-telling legacy such a monumental re-centring of this work would promote (Fig. 9.2).

## 9.3 Re-storying Offensive Monuments: *Crowther Reinterpreted* in Nipaluna, Lutruwita

In their recent analysis of debates surrounding colonial commemorations in so-called Australia, Carlson and Farrelly assert that history isn't always written by the supposed victors, and that protests and challenges to offensive colonial commemorations are re-writing and changing the meaning of problematic monuments (2023a). Wiradjuri librarian and museum educator, Nathan 'mudyi' Sentance, similarly has observed that creative protest and other acts of 're-storying' have had the effect of transforming the colonial monument 'from celebratory to a site of truth-telling', presenting powerful opportunities for the 'reclaiming of history by First Nations peoples' (2021, p. 826). Re-storying's power, Sentance asserts, can 'force people to question what they think they know of the foundations of the society we live in, and the figures often used to symbolise these foundations' (2021, p. 827). By bringing the public into critical encounters with Australia's colonial monuments, artists are strongly engaged in these efforts to critically transform meaning, re-story, and shift tolerance for controversial commemorations in public spaces.

One of the most effective recent examples of this re-storying has occurred in Nipaluna, Lutruwita (Hobart, Tasmania), where temporary, creative installations by Aboriginal artists from Lutruwita have contributed to the reappraisal of a prominent statue to a vile grave robber and mutilator. In one corner of Franklin Square, a busy, central park and public transport hub in Nipaluna, a statue celebrating the public service of medical practitioner, politician and former Premier of Tasmania, William Crowther, has stood since 1889. The statue's tribute omits the sickening detail that in 1869 Crowther surreptitiously gained possession of Palawa leader William Lanne's deceased remains, which Crowther then mutilated to steal Lanne's skull for donation to the Royal College of Surgeons in London. It was an act that was derided even in Crowther's own time and saw him suspended from practice as honorary medical officer at the Hobart General Hospital (Carlson & Farrelly, 2023b).

The statue has long been a source of distress for First Peoples in Lutruwita, with Trawulwuy historian, curator and scholar, Greg Lehman, describing the statue in 2017 as 'probably the most confronting to Tasmanian Aboriginal people' and many 'would love to see the thing just torn down' (cited in Shine, 2017, n.p.). In 2021, responding to community concerns, local council authorities at the City of Hobart initiated *Crowther Reinterpreted*, a project which oversaw the commissioning of four temporary public artworks by Palawa artists, who were each given a $5000 budget to creatively respond to the Crowther statue for a duration of two months and provoke public discussion about the problematic monument's future.

The first commission by Allan Mansell, entitled *Truth Telling* (2021), tackled the monument bluntly and directly, covering the statue's head and hands with blood red rubberised paint and flexible vinyl, and giving Crowther an Aboriginal flag and a surgical saw to brandish. Obscuring the plinth's original inscription with a plaque labelling Crowther a criminal and Lanne a leader, the artwork re-storied the offensive statue into a memorial to Lanne, 'our King Billy' (City of Hobart, 2024, n.p.).

For the second commission, *The Lanney Pillar* (2021), Greg Lehman, quoted above, collaborated with filmmaker Roger Scholes to exhibit a multi-media installation nearby to the statue and an accompanying 12 minute video, *The Whaler's Tale*, accessible by a QR code and viewable online, which tells the little-told story of Lanne's life. Featuring images of the stunning landscapes of Lanne's 'precious' Country in North-East Lutruwita, the video presents Lanne affectingly as a man whose people were brutally dispossessed by invading colonisers, and who experienced incomprehensible losses and changes in his lifetime as 'one of the last Tasmanian Aboriginal children born on the traditional Country of their ancestors' (Scholes & Lehman, 2021). The work re-stories Lanne's life by describing his deep connection to and yearning for Country, his skills as a whaler, the advocacy he undertook for his people, and the fortitude with which he endured devastating, cataclysmic circumstances that included witnessing many of his people die. These details render Lanne a vivid human who experienced too much injustice in his lifetime, with the work deliberately refusing the trend of the many historical and contemporary accounts that remember him merely and incorrectly as the last *full-blooded* Tasmanian Aboriginal man who was mutilated by Crowther (City of Hobart, 2024).

In the third commission, *Breathing Space* (2021), Trawlwoolway artist Julie Gough enclosed the Crowther statue in a practical black plywood crate. During a radio interview discussing the launch of her work, Gough jokingly admitted, 'I think mine might be the least art-like. I've just made the crate to get rid of the guy [...] The [commission] fee was very small, so it could pay for a crate' (ABC Hobart, 2021, n.p.). In the interview, Gough is explicit that Crowther was evil and the statue's presence causes significant mental anguish to Lutruwita's Aboriginal community, with the artist admitting she has avoided walking near that central part of the city for decades. With Gough's straightforward gesture the work both affectively and pragmatically reveals the monument's unbearability and demonstrates one of the simplest, cost-effective means to remove its offending presence. An accompanying digital poster, available for free download, directly responds to commentary that removal of the statue from public space is an erasure of history, overlaying a rubbing of the statue's celebratory inscription with words rendered in shaded red letters: 'We don't have to look into the face of evil to know that it is there' (Gough, 2021). Speaking about the work to *The Guardian*, Gough asserted:

> I decided to encase Crowther, to give everyone literally 'breathing space' from his presence. To be able to literally see a way forward, a world without it, by physically demonstrating that the sky doesn't fall down, the world doesn't end, when a statue is removed [...] Crowther's presence in statue form has for 132 years offended, openly disrespected and disregarded the feelings of Aboriginal people, while asserting the power and might of ongoing Anglo-British rule of this island as it overrides First People's distress. (cited in Aitken, 2021)

The final commission, *Something Missing* (2021) by photographer and emerging filmmaker Jillian Mundy, in collaboration with Troy Melville, was comprised of a video installation erected by the statue. The video presents a series of vox pop interviews Mundy captured during Gough's installation, where she approached 100 or so passers-by and asked if they knew what was under the crate. The majority of people interviewed, settler locals young and old, shake their heads in the video admitting they don't have any idea who he is, and neither do they appear to care. 'Some colonial bureaucrat?', one interviewee offers. 'I don't know, some old white man?', another wonders. Eventually Mundy interviewed a man who is very aware of who he was, commenting 'Yeah, William Crowther, he's a dog, [censored] him off'. Over the course of the 10-minute video only two elderly white men believe this veneration of Crowther should stay in Franklin Square, while the rest of the interviewees, once learning who Crowther was, support the statue's removal (City of Hobart, 2024).

Collectively, the works in the *Crowther Reinterpreted* project decisively moved the threshold of tolerability for the statue, re-storying the Crowther monument as an unwanted marker of colonial domination that glorifies a repellent figure who represents a shameful history of 'racial science' and the stealing of Palawa remains for study (Kelly, 2023, n.p.): a vile icon that First Peoples cannot bear. Meanwhile, Mundy's video attests that many in the settler community—even after a months of critical art commissions and media attention—remain blithely ignorant of the monument, Crowther's dreadful deeds and the pain it causes. Indeed, the City of Hobart staff that instigated the project noted: 'Often when we went to talk about Crowther, non-Aboriginal people had little or no knowledge about him or his story' (cited in Carlson et al., 2023, p. 572). This reflects what visual culture theorist Nicholas Mirzoeff has observed, that while a racist colonial monument 'may be invisible to those to whom it reinforces their sense of presence', it is 'extremely visible' to those it does not (Mirzoeff & Samudzi, 2020, n.p.). Though the Crowther monument recalls to settler minds very little, the temporary installations by local Aboriginal artists demonstrate that it is unquestionably a hurtful, violent symbol for First Peoples and representative of how their trauma remains unrecognised by the broader community. As one Tasmanian Aboriginal woman, Michelle Maynard, commented in response to the project: 'It's hard to live in a city where genocide has been committed and to walk on this country everyday feeling like it's all forgotten' (cited in Carlson et al., 2023, p. 563).

While arguments for removing the statue were already strong prior to the reinterpretation project, based on the plentiful historical evidence of Crowther's interest in the discredited racial science of phrenology and participation in the unethical theft and trade of First Peoples' human remains, these objections were given affective force and visibility through the four public art projects. As noted by members of the Tasmanian Aboriginal Centre on behalf of Lutruwita's Aboriginal community, however, the reinterpretation project came at no small cost, with artists having to use a symbol of racism to make visible their grievances against it, while the commissioning process prolonged the anguish of the Aboriginal community—making them targets of racism and re-traumatisation—when a motion to just immediately remove it would have been far more moral and culturally safe (City of Hobart, 2022a, Appendix 4; Carlson & Farrelly, 2023b; Carlson et al., 2023). Staff overseeing the *Crowther Reinterpreted* project have also expressed regret that the project was 'such a difficult/painful process for the artists and for the members of the Tasmanian Aboriginal community' (Carlson et al., 2023, p. 571). In August 2022, councillors at the Hobart City Council did finally vote in favour of removing the bronze component of the Crowther statue from Franklin Square to the City's Valuables Collection until an appropriate permanent location for recontextualising the statue is determined, and to leave the plinth in place for reinterpretation (Carlson et al., 2023). It is reportedly the first local government in settler colonial Australia to heed First Peoples' calls and act—albeit much belated—to remove a distressing colonial monument from public space (MacDonald, 2023).

The range of reasons City of Hobart outlined regarding 'Why should the City make a change to this statue now?' should be heeded by City of Melbourne when reflecting on what to do with Batman's memorial. All points specified below are applicable to the Batman Memorial and the context of the City of Melbourne:

*Showing leadership*—this is an opportunity to demonstrate leadership and confront the difficult history of an asset owned by Council, and set an example for the other Australian cities keenly observing the progress of the project to gain insight into how they might deal with their own difficult historic monuments.

*Visibility and truth-telling*—the City has made a clear commitment to visibility and truth-telling, and this requires physical changes to public spaces to tell these difficult stories where they can be seen by all.

*Historical validity*—considering the statue of Crowther raises questions regarding the significance and relevance of Crowther to contemporary Hobart.

*Connection to current values of the City of Hobart*—is Crowther's presence right for our city now and into the future?

*Equitable representation*—within the one formal, civic park in Hobart stand three statues, all of Caucasian males.

*Cultural safety*—the City has many processes in place to ensure physical safety of its residents, but there are few to ensure cultural safety. The palawa community have made it clear that the continued presence of the Crowther statue in Franklin Square is a culturally unsafe element.

> *The life of an asset*—this project raises the question of just how long any one monument should stay in place (Carlson et al., 2023, pp. 569–570; City of Hobart, 2022b)[2]

What is made plain by the *Crowther Reinterpreted* project is that like the Crowther statue, there exists no good justification for the Batman memorial to remain as it stands, but it should not just vanish from public space without truth-telling either. As in the case of Crowther, there is abundant historical evidence and First Peoples' testimony on record that has decisively re-storied Batman from a celebrated founder to horrific figure that needs to be acknowledged by City of Melbourne. Batman's massacre of Palawa people has already merited actions of redress and withdrawal of his name, which must now also compel the swift amends of his culturally unsafe memorial obelisk. It is apparent too that to avert further hurt to First Peoples, City of Melbourne must show leadership by assuming full responsibility for the inaccuracy of their 'asset' and the disturbing history of the coloniser it honours. Council, I contend, must instigate public truth-telling of Batman's memorial aimed at healing and redress, a process that at inception is undertaken in full solidarity with First Peoples and openly recognises that the City's *John Batman Memorial* (1881) no longer represents the city's values.

Lessons from the *Crowther Reinterpreted* project equally suggests that a culturally safe procedure that reappraises and decides the future of a racist memorial should not be left to the Council's settler authorities to publicly prevaricate and debate over but must be handed over and led by First Peoples—a group that could include Kulin people on whose Country the memorial resides, as well as the descendants of Palawa and other Southeastern First Peoples harmed by Batman's destructive crimes—all communities who are fully acquainted with the damage such an object causes. As the Professional Historians Association (Victoria and Tasmania) (PHA) formally recommended to City of Hobart, a reinterpretation process led by First Peoples could make amends for the harms of the past. Likewise for Batman's memorial:

> PHA (Vic & Tas) strongly believe that the reinterpretation of the statue, whether that be through its removal, replacement or alteration, should be led by palawa voices. Throughout Australia white elites have used statues in an attempt to re-image an Aboriginal landscape as European. Being led by palawa voices would allow for a redress in the way that history, which has glorified white male power and privilege, has been told and memorialised in the past. (cited in City of Hobart, 2022a, appendix 7).

Such a First Nations-led process instigated as part of the new Gurrowa Place precinct development would present meaningful opportunities for self-determination and enacting sovereign justice on Country: granting First Peoples a restorative opportunity to lead truth-telling on Batman's offensive memorial, but also, drive decision-making on the public programs of re-storying, heritage interpretation and creative commemoration that are needed to sensitively address his legacy. A city that avowedly has a vision to foster an 'Aboriginal focus' and declared commitment to truth-telling (City of Melbourne, 2016, p. 24, 2021), must take these steps to

---

[2] In regard to *equitable representation*, Genevieve Grieves undertook research and noted in 2017 that of the 520 + memorials, statues and monuments in central Melbourne only a dozen were not 'dead, white, men' (cited in Perkins, 2017, n.p.).

promote cultural safety, foment public understanding of a shared traumatic history and to mitigate further harm. As Worimi memorial researcher, Genevieve Grieves, has noted when questioned about what should be done about Batman commemorations in Naarm (Melbourne):

> If people have committed atrocious crimes against humanity, we have to consider if they should be commemorated. But we absolutely don't want to just cover up what has happened and pretend it didn't occur. Many Australians are ready for the truth [...] I'm surprised a city that's so forward-thinking, diverse and progressive hasn't done the work to better reflect who we are. (cited in Perkins, 2017, n.p.)

## 9.4 Cultivating a Culture of Remembrance: Learning from the Counter-Monuments and Memory Politics of Berlin

Artist and researchers grappling with settler-colonial Australia's memorialscape of denial have frequently looked to Germany's capital Berlin, and its much-celebrated Holocaust culture of remembrance (*Erinnerungskultur* in German), to learn from the numerous, bold memorial examples that acknowledge the tragedy of Nazi genocide while confronting the German nation with its crimes. Celebrated contemporary artist Yhonnie Scarce, a descendant of the Kokatha and Nukunu people, for example, calls Berlin 'memorial city' after the numerous monuments she encountered that were 'all over the place there' (Browning & Scarce, 2021, n.p.). As part of her artistic research, Scarce has visited places including Berlin, Chernobyl, Hiroshima, Wounded Knee and Auschwitz to understand how state-sponsored atrocities and mass murder are commemorated elsewhere (Perkins & Scarce, 2021). Those trips have consequently made Scare reflect upon the lack of memorials in Australia to First Peoples victims of colonisation, and particularly the lack of acknowledgement 'regarding Frontier Wars and the bigger picture of genocide' (Browning & Scarce, 2021, n.p.). Scarce describes that what attracted her to Berlin particularly was how:

> open it is to acknowledging the Holocaust through memorials in many different forms. I decided to create memorials when I came back to Australia because there weren't enough in the public realm. (cited in Perkins & Scarce, 2021, n.p.)

Scarce is among other artists, writers and scholars from so-called 'Australia', such as Brook Andrew and Clare Land, who have researched the remembrance cultures of other places that have experienced traumatic histories to draw lessons in ways to address Australia's monumental silences (Andrew, 2017; Land, 2014). Artist, curator and researcher Brook Andrew (Wiradjuri/Ngunnawal), for example, was chief investigator of the research project *Representation, Remembrance and the Memorial* from 2016 to 2019 that addressed the absence of memorials commemorating the wars fought over the possession of Australia (referred to as Frontier or Homeland Wars), and explored 'how to give visibility to the magnitude of Aboriginal loss and survival' through a national memorial (Andrew, 2017, p. 63). In observing

# 9 What Should the City of Melbourne Do with the Inaccurate …

a notable lack of memorials to Homeland Wars at the Australian War Memorial and in the nation's public spaces, Andrew noted that this deficiency:

> […] reverberates when the international scene is considered and the plethora of national memorials to genocide, to fascism and to state violence that have been created in the last twenty years. The Jewish Museum in Berlin, the Judenplatz Holocaust Memorial in Vienna, the Monument to the Victims of State Terrorism in Buenos Aires and the District Six Museum in Cape Town are just some examples that have introduced new visual forms to address the complexities of representing traumatic histories and account for the disappeared. (Andrew, 2017, p. 63)

Berlin's Holocaust memorials are exemplary of this global shift in remembrance activity that Andrew observes. Precipitated by twentieth century social movements and upheaval, this shift in public memorial practice is marked by a turn away from the nationalistic veneration of heroic subjects to focus instead on the acknowledgement of painful events, state crimes, trauma and genocide, and commemorate marginalised subjects and victims of violence (Strakosch, 2010; Atkinson-Phillips, 2021; Stevens et al., 2018; Cento Bull & Clarke, 2021). Germany's Holocaust public commemorative art was notably theorised by historian and Holocaust memory scholar James E. Young, who coined the term 'counter-monument' to describe the critical mode of memorial practice that emerged in the 1980s as Germany's artists contended with the unrepresentable nature of the horrors of the Holocaust (Young, 1992). Counter-monuments, Young identified, rejected the triumphant subjects, singular meanings and glorifying forms of traditional monuments, refusing closure and redemption through conceptual, abstract and non-representational creative strategies that hold interpretation open and implicate the viewer in the activation of memory (Stevens et al., 2018; Young, 1992, 2000).

Berlin memorials such as Misha Ullman's *Empty Library* (1995) and Christian Boltanski's *Missing House* (1990) exemplify German counter-monuments. In both these works there are no positive forms for the viewer to look at, but instead voids and absences in the street for the viewer to locate, marked with plaques noting the missing content of a library in Ullman's case and stolen Jewish homes in Boltanski's. Describing Ullman's memorial, for example, Young notes the plaza where *Empty Library* is located:

> […] is still empty of all forms except for the figures of visitors who stand there and peer down through a window in the ground plane into the ghostly white, underground room of empty shelves Ullman has installed. A steel tablet set into the stones simply recalls that this was the site of some of the most notorious book burnings and quotes Heinrich Heine's famously prescient words: 'Where books are burned, so one day will people be burned as well'. But the shelves are still empty, unreplenished, and it is the absence of both people and books that is marked here in yet one more empty memorial pocket. (Young, 1999, n.p)

Representative too of this searching, innovating and at times audacious counter-monument culture are the unrealised submissions to the 1994–95 design competition for Berlin's *Memorial for the Murdered Jews of Europe*. Young, in examining the German artist Horst Hoheisel's counter-monument output, has analysed the artist's 'provocative anti-solution' to the memorial competition where Hoheisel proposed to blow up the Brandenburg Gate, a prominent landmark in

Berlin (Young, 1999, n.p.). Young observed of the conceptual work: 'How better to remember a destroyed people, than by a destroyed monument? [...] Rather than concretising and thereby displacing the memory of Europe's murdered Jews, the artist would open a place in the landscape to be filled with the memory of those who come to remember Europe's murdered Jews' (1999, n.p.). Artists Renata Stih and Frieder Schnock's proposition for the competition, meanwhile, was *Bus Stop— a non-monument* (1994–95); a 'social sculpture' that sought to activate memory quite literally by establishing a bus terminal that would commute people all over Europe in dedicated buses to concentration camps and sites of Nazi terror (Stih & Schnock, 2005). Young has described the proposal as, 'a kind of memorial travel office that would extol history and memory over the usual forgetfulness, the attempt at amnesia, that drives most leisure vacations' (Young, 1999). As the German artists have elaborated on their proposal, they sought:

> a formative experience. You take your time and you give it to the dead. Going to a former concentration camp is no simple day trip: it requires preparation in order to be able to stand the shock of comprehension. The way back offers the opportunity to talk about things seen and experienced. (Stih and Schnock, 2005)

What perhaps is most compelling about Berlin's Holocaust remembrance culture then for artists and researchers attentive to settler colonial Australia's structural silence on colonial violence, is the persistent, inventive way (counter-)monuments work to resist amnesia and provoke memory of the city's complicity in genocide. The sheer variety and ingenuity invested in Holocaust public commemorative art in Berlin is striking, representative of an extraordinary city-wide memory-effort that dedicates considerable municipal space, time and resources to the victims of Nazi violence. As writer Masha Gessen has recently noted, 'Berlin never stops reminding you of what happened there' (2023). While the larger state monuments are impressive, such as architect Peter Eisenman's immersive and disorienting *Memorial to the Murdered Jews of Europe* (2005) that occupies an entire city block, Gessen identifies it is the memorials that 'sneak up on you' which 'reveal the pervasiveness of the evils once committed in this place' (2023, n.p.). Gessen lists as examples Ullman's *Empty Library*; the engraved brass *Stolpersteine* (stumbling stones) embedded in city streets that recall missing residents taken by the Nazi regime; as well as the *Führerbunker* site where the Nazi's leader, Adolf Hitler, spent the final months of his life.

This last site is not the counter-monument handiwork of an artist but instead the City of Berlin, with the remains of the *Führerbunker* today covered over by a deliberately unremarkable, easily overlooked, weed strewn carpark not far from the *Memorial to the Murdered Jews of Europe*. A denazifying act, the site was intentionally unmarked until 2006 to discourage the site becoming a shrine for Neo-Nazis, but now has an information stand, which Gessen notes, has the innocuous appearance of a 'neighbourhood bulletin board, but tells the story of the Führer's final days' (2023). Reminders of colonial evils committed against First Peoples in the City of Melbourne meanwhile are far from pervasive, tenacious and quotidian. Instead, Batman's memorial is preserved within a carpark, and in 2024 goes on celebrating a landgrabber who participated in genocide while the city's public spaces, heritage interpretation and monuments remain largely mute about colonisers' violence and mass murder.

As a result, Berlin has been celebrated as a city 'doing what most cultures cannot: looking at its own crimes, its own worst self' (Gessen, 2023). It would be remiss, however, to overly idealise Germany's Holocaust remembrance culture. As noted by settler Australian scholar, Elizabeth Strakosch, German commemorations confronting the nation's Nazi crimes and persecutions arose from the unique political situation Germany faced postwar, with international pressure forcing it to denazify and emphasise a radical break with its fascist past (2009). German historians have observed that atoning for the Holocaust subsequently became reunified Germany's 'moral fundament' (Gruner & Schüler-Springorum, 2023, n.p.). But while it was once 'exhilarating to watch [Berlin's] memory culture take shape', as Gessen has reflected, good intentions have hardened into a sort of dogma over time, with political instrumentalisation of a notion that the Holocaust is a uniquely singular, incomparable atrocity that Germany has a special responsibility to remember operating to stifle historical debate and obscure German complicity in other instances of mass violence, including Germany's genocide of Herero and Nama as a coloniser in Southwest Africa (Gessen, 2023; Gruner & Schüler-Springorum, 2023). Most acutely in recent months, Germany's unwavering support for Israel as a form of post-Holocaust remorse and responsibility has led to the suppression and silencing of criticism of the Israeli state, and its genocidal collective punishment of the citizens of Gaza for Hamas' attacks on 7 October 2023 (Gessen, 2023). This has led commentators to ask, why doesn't Germany's Holocaust tenet of *Never again* apply to Gaza? (Al-Najjar, 2024; Oltermann, 2023).

In the context of settler colonial Australia, however, First Peoples have a long, established history of expressing solidarity with other victims of genocide and mass violence while seeking a greater share of recognition and visibility for their losses and traumas caused by British colonisation (Foley, 1997; Gory, 2018). Yorta Yorta Elder and activist William Cooper notably led a delegation of the Australian Aborigines' League, following the Nazi 'Kristallnacht' pogrom in 1938, to deliver a formal petition to the German Consulate in Naarm (Melbourne) condemning the 'cruel persecution of the Jewish people by the Nazi government of Germany' (cited in Gory, 2018, n.p.; Attwood, 2021). Cooper saw parallels between the Nazi's crimes against the Jewish people and settler colonial maltreatment of First Peoples, remarking in a separate letter to the federal government: 'We feel that while we are all indignant over Hitler's treatment of the Jews, we are getting the same treatment here and we would like that fact duly considered' (cited in Attwood, 2021, p. 111; Foley, 1997).[3] More recently, activist group Blackfullas for Palestine have amplified an ongoing history of Blak and Palestinian solidarity, foregrounding their shared struggle against settler colonial regimes (Blackfullas for Palestine, 2024). As Munanjahli and South Sea Islander scholar and writer Chelsea Watego asserted at an Invasion Day protest rally

---

[3] In a satisfying reversal, in 2019 campaigners were successful in prompting the renaming of the inner-north Melbourne electoral division of Batman to Cooper, after the Yorta Yorta leader and activist, due to Batman's involvement in massacres of First Peoples.

in 2024: 'When we say "no pride in genocide", we mean here and everywhere—from West Papua to Palestine' (2024).[4] Any culture of memory that inculcates collective remembrance and settler responsibility for colonial crimes in Australia should similarly activate a tenet of *No pride in genocide*, and promote an enlarged historical awareness connecting the ways racialised and colonial oppression has been employed in Australia and elsewhere, historically and in ongoing forms.

To draw inspiration from Berlin's commemorative culture requires us to stay mindful then of these specific complexities and shortcomings in Germany's memory politics. Nontheless, truth-telling iniatives aimed at countering entrenched ignorance and structural silences about Australia's foundations in racialised violence might still retrieve lessons from the widespread culture of counter-monuments and creative remembrances that took shape in Germany from the 1980s. As I write, Jacinta Allan, the current Premier of Victoria has in the last fortnight fronted a hearing of the Yoorrook Justice Commission in Naarm (Melbourne), becoming Australia's first state leader to provide evidence at a formal truth-telling inquiry aimed at putting on record a fuller account of Victoria's history (Ore, 2024). In her testimony Allan admitted the state has for too long overlooked the 'bloody stains of colonisation', noting that during research for the hearing she learnt of historical massacres of First Peoples that occurred near her home (Yoorrook Justice Commission, 2024, p. 9). Allan elaborated:

> And I was sitting there in my backyard, reading through the materials, and just felt so distressed that these were massacres that occurred not far from where I was sitting and I didn't know about them [...] It brings me a sense of shame and distress personally that I did not know that, and it brings me a sense of shame and distress that this was done - all in the pursuit of taking land off First Peoples [...] it is not that before my appearance today I was not aware of the dispossession and disadvantage and the wrongs that occurred [when] the state was colonised. My learning was deepened by and expanded in terms of the brutality [...] that was the area that was particularly concerning to me that I hadn't learnt about the depth and the extent of the brutality. (Yoorrook Justice Commission, 2024, pp. 28, 40)

It's clear that many settlers in Australia, like Allan, frequently possess just a detached, abstract sense that First Peoples were dispossessed by colonisers, with a culture of denial ensuring collective understanding and remorse for the full scale and brutality of colonial violence is limited and needs to be radically deepened.

Writer Andreas Pohl, a German migrant living in Australia for over 35 years has recently reflected on how Germany's culture of remembrance—*Erinnerungskultur*—might have resonances for his adopted home as it reckons with its own shameful national history of genocide (2023). Pohl notes, *Erinnerungskultur* is primarily an inward-looking process of self-reflection for descendants of the perpetrators of mass violence, with dedicated days of remembrance, memorials and museums serving as 'symbolic manifestations of the willingness not just to acknowledge but to confront those unpalatable aspects of a country's past' (2023, n.p.). As First Peoples repeatedly call upon settler Australia to engage in truth-telling and Treaty processes, Pohl

---

[4] Australians celebrate an annual national day (known as 'Australia Day') on 26 January marking the arrival of the First Fleet and commencement of the first British colonial outpost in 1788. For First Peoples and their supporters, however, it is known as Invasion Day, a day of protest and mourning.

argues settler Australians might reciprocate by inculcating meaningful forms of *Erinnerungskultur* that sees the true history 'woven into the fabric of everyday culture' (2023, n.p.).

Surely the time is well overdue for City of Melbourne authorities who preside over a leading city of art and culture to show leadership, and commit to confronting the city's memorialscape of denial by fostering a visionary culture of truth-telling remembrances embedded across the city fabric of Naarm (Melbourne). The Gurrowa Place open public space development provides an opportunity to begin a bold program of commissioning enabling a proliferation of public commemorative artworks of many different forms that provoke memory of colonial atrocities at local sites of violence. The proposed area for a 1.8 hectare landscaped open public space is fittingly a central city block encompassing the city's first burial ground where significant First Peoples remains are interred, including those of Tunnerminnerwait and Maulboyheenner, two freedom fighters from Lutruwita that were the first prisoners executed by public hanging in the early Melbourne colony for the crime of resisting colonisation and killing two whalers (City of Melbourne, 2024). In 2016, City of Melbourne erected a public marker, *Standing by Tunnerminnerwait and Maulboyheenner*, by artists Brook Andrew and Trent Walter at the Old Melbourne Goal—just a few blocks away from Queen Victoria Market—commemorating the two warriors at the site where they were executed (City of Melbourne, 2024). It is one of the very few official memorials in Naarm (Melbourne) recognising homeland violence, its establishment coming after a decade of campaigning by the Tunnerminnerwait and Maulboyheenner Commemoration Committee, convened by non-Indigenous broadcaster and anarchist Joseph Toscano (Carlson & Farrelly, 2023a). The committee continue to hold an annual public ceremony on 20 January honouring the Aboriginal heros, followed by a silent walk from Tunnerminnerwait and Maulboyheenner's execution site to their final resting place at the market (Carlson & Farrelly, 2023a). This remembrance ceremony held on the day of the warriors' execution, bringing First Peoples and settlers together to solemnly reflect on a shared past, represents an important grassroots culture of truth-telling already firmly established in Naarm (Melbourne), which City authorities could support at the new public space by promoting further commemorative activity to complex colonial pasts.

Truth-telling, recontextualising and removing the inaccurate and offensive Batman memorial, in a process led by First Nations communities affected by Batman's deeds, would be a welcome act in overturning this City's celebration of genocide but it will by no means be adequate on its own to reverse entrenched silences on colonisation's grievous impact on First Peoples. The city needs a unique, brave culture of truth-telling and public commemorative art: one that makes a concerted break with denial, stimulates collective memory of our foundations in colonial theft and violence, and foregrounds the perspective of survivors. As I have suggested, one meaningful move would be to recentre another City of Melbourne asset, Foley's monumental *Lie of the Land*, to a prominent, permanent place in the new Gurrowa Place development. My other more subversive proposition is inspired by Berlin's *Führerbunker* anti-memorial and Stih and Schnock's Holocaust remembrance 'social sculpture': remove the Batman memorial and replace it with free of charge car parking spaces specially reserved for First Peoples. This would be an inventive way for City of Melbourne to enact visual and spatial justice upon a heinous mass murder commemorated for too long in the city, and to manifest a public gesture underscoring that all First Peoples survivors of colonisation are a central, honoured presence in Naarm (Melbourne) who will help us activate memory, make sense of our shared traumatic past and lead us to a more just future.

# References

ABC Hobart. (2021). *Tasmanian Aboriginal artist covers William Crowther statue in a wooden crate*. Tasmania Afternoons. https://www.abc.net.au/listen/programs/hobart-your-afternoon/julie-gough-reimagines-william-crowther/13522508. Accessed 7 May 2024.

ACCA. (2022). *Past exhibition: Tom Nicholson: Chimney in store (Towards a monument to Batman's Treaty) 26 Mar–31 Dec 2022*. https://acca.melbourne/exhibition/tom-nicholson-chimney-in-store/. Accessed 7 May 2024.

Aitken, S. (2021). A statue of a Tasmanian colonist has been covered up. Should it ever return? *The Guardian*. https://www.theguardian.com/culture/2021/sep/16/a-statue-of-a-tasmanian-colonist-has-been-covered-up-should-it-ever-return. Accessed 7 May 2024.

Al-Najjar, A. (2024). Where is the 'never again' for Gaza?. *Aljazeera*. https://www.aljazeera.com/opinions/2024/1/21/where-is-the-never-again-for-gaza. Accessed 10 May 2024.

Andrew, B. (2017). Remembrance, representation and the memorial. In B. French & A. Loxley (Eds.), *Civic actions: Artists' practices beyond the museum* (pp. 62–69). The Rocks: Museum of Contemporary Art Australia.

Andron, S., & Lata, L. N. (2024). Images shape cities, but who decides which ones survive? It's a matter of visual justice. *The Conversation*. https://theconversation.com/images-shape-cities-but-who-decides-which-ones-survive-its-a-matter-of-visual-justice-216003. Accessed 1 May 2024.

Atkinson-Philiips, A. (2021). Interpreting difficult knowledge: What difference do artists make? In A. Spiers, C. Day, & C. Morton (Eds.), *Let's go outside: Art in public* (pp. 70–97). Monash University Publishing.

Attwood, B. (2009). *Possession: Batman's treaty and the matter of history*. Melbourne University Publishing.

Attwood, B. (2021). *William Cooper: An aboriginal life story*. Melbourne University Publishing.

Barolsky, V., Berger, K., & Close, K. (2023) Recognising community truth-telling: An exploration of local truth-telling in Australia. *Reconciliation Australia*. https://www.reconciliation.org.au/wp-content/uploads/2023/09/Recognising-community-truth-telling-report.pdf. Accessed 30 April 2024.

Blackfullas for Palestine. (2024). https://www.blackfullasforpalestine.com/. Accessed 4 May 2024.

Boyce, J. (2013). *1835: The founding of Melbourne & the Conquest of Australia*. Black Inc.

Browning, D., & Scarce, Y. (2021). Yhonnie Scarce: 'Australia is very good at forgetting the past'. *Ocula*. https://ocula.com/magazine/conversations/yhonnie-scarce-at-acca-melbourne/. Accessed 10 May 2024.

Carlson, B., & Farrelly, T. (2023a). *Monumental disruptions: Aboriginal people and colonial commemorations in so-called Australia*. Aboriginal Studies Press.

Carlson, B., & Farrelly, T. (2023b). You can handle the truth: Aboriginal peoples, colonial commemorations and the unfinished business of truth-telling. In B. Carlson & T. Farrelly (Eds.), *The Palgrave handbook on rethinking colonial commemorations* (pp. 573–596). Springer International Publishing.

Carlson, B., Farrelly, T., Abell, J., & Castle, J. (2023). The 'crowther reinterpreted' project. In B. Carlson & T. Farrelly (Eds.), *The Palgrave handbook on rethinking colonial commemorations* (pp. 557–572). Springer International Publishing.

Carmody, S. (2007). John Batman's place in the village. *The LaTrobe Journal, 80*(Spring), 80–101.

Cento Bull, A., & Clarke, D. (2021). Agonistic interventions into public commemorative art: An innovative form of counter-memorial practice? *Constellations, 28*(2), 192–206.

City of Hobart. (2022a). *Community engagement summary report: Crowther reinterpreted*. City of Hobart. https://hobart.infocouncil.biz/Open/2022/08/CCEC_04082022_AGN_1607_AT_files/CCEC_04082022_AGN_1607_AT_Attachment_9915_2.PDF. Accessed 1 May 2024.

City of Hobart. (2022b). *Agenda community, culture and events committee meeting: Open portion, Thursday, 4 August 2022 at 5.30pm Council Chamber, Town Hall*. https://hobart.infocouncil.biz/Open/2022/08/CCEC_04082022_AGN_1607_AT.htm. Accessed 4 May 2024.

City of Hobart. (2024). *Crowther reinterpreted*. https://www.hobartcity.com.au/Community/Creative-Hobart/Creative-Hobart-projects/Crowther-Reinterpreted. Accessed 7 May 2024.

City of Melbourne. (2016). *Future Melbourne 2026*. https://www.melbourne.vic.gov.au/SiteCollectionDocuments/future-melbourne-2026-plan.pdf. Accessed 1 May 2024.

City of Melbourne. (2021). Declaration of recognition and commitment aboriginal peoples. https://www.melbourne.vic.gov.au/sitecollectiondocuments/aboriginal-melbourne-declaration.pdf. Accessed 1 May 2024.

City of Melbourne. (2023). *City of Melbourne annual report 2022–23*. https://www.melbourne.vic.gov.au/SiteCollectionDocuments/annual-report-2022-23.pdf. Accessed 1 May 2024.

City of Melbourne. (2024). Tunnerminnerwait and Maulboyheenner. https://www.melbourne.vic.gov.au/about-melbourne/melbourne-profile/aboriginal-culture/Pages/tunnerminnerwait-and-maulboyheener.aspx. Accessed 13 May 2024.

Clements, N. (2011). The truth about John Batman: Melbourne's founder and 'murderer of the blacks'. *The Conversation*. https://theconversation.com/the-truth-about-john-batman-melbournes-founder-and-murderer-of-the-blacks-1025. Accessed 4 May 2024.

Edensor, T., & Sumartojo, S. (2023). Reified monuments, counter memorials and anti-memorials: Contested colonial heritage in Melbourne—Commemorating John Batman. *Postcolonial Studies, 26*(4), 557–580.

Foley, G. (1997). Australia and the holocaust: A Koori perspective. *KooriWeb*. https://www.kooriweb.org/foley/essays/pdf_essays/australia%20and%20the%20holocaust.pdf. Accessed 4 May 2024.

Gessen, M. (2023). In the shadow of the holocaust. *The New Yorker*. https://www.newyorker.com/news/the-weekend-essay/in-the-shadow-of-the-holocaust. Accessed 10 May 2024.

Gory, S. (2018). William Cooper, Kristallnacht, and a Radical Act of empathy. *Meanjin*. https://meanjin.com.au/latest/william-cooper-kristallnacht-and-a-radical-act-of-empathy/. Accessed 4 May 2024.

Gough, J. (2021). *Breathing space*. City of Hobart. https://www.hobartcity.com.au/Community/Creative-Hobart/Creative-Hobart-projects/Crowther-Reinterpreted/BREATHING-SPACE. Accessed 7 May 2024.

Grand, S. (2018). The other within: White shame, native-American genocide. *Contemporary Psychoanalysis, 54*(1), 84–102.

Gruner, W., & Schüler-Springorum, S. (2023). Two German perspectives on a German discussion. *Central European History, 56*(2), 278–282.

Hinchliffe, J. (2017). Call to remove statue of John Batman, 'founder of Melbourne', over role in Indigenous killings. *The Age*. https://www.theage.com.au/national/victoria/call-to-remove-statue-of-john-batman-founder-of-melbourne-over-role-in-indigenous-killings-20170826-gy4snc.html. Accessed 1 may 2024.

Holsworth, M. (2020). The John Batman Memorial. *Black Mark Melbourne Art and Culture Critic*. https://melbourneartcritic.wordpress.com/2020/10/17/the-john-batman-memorial/. Accessed 1 May 2024.

James, D. (2018). Then unoccupied. *IndigenousX*. https://indigenousx.com.au/daniel-james-then-unoccupied/. 1 May 2024.

Kelly, C. (2023). William Crowther: Statue of Tasmanian premier who beheaded body of Aboriginal man to be taken down. *The Guardian*. https://www.theguardian.com/australia-news/2023/aug/24/william-crowther-statue-franklin-square-hobart-taken-down-beheaded-aboriginal-man. Accessed 8 May 2024.

Land, C. (2014). Forms for monuments to complex histories. *City of Melbourne*. https://www.melbourne.vic.gov.au/SiteCollectionDocuments/forms-for-monuments-complex-histories.pdf. Accessed 10 May 2024.

Lendlease. (2023). *Queen Victoria market southern precinct development plan volume 1*. City of Melbourne. https://www.melbourne.vic.gov.au/about-council/committees-meetings/meeting-archive/meetingagendaitemattachments/1048/18543/feb24%20fmc2%20agenda%20item%206.1%20part%201%20of%202.pdf. Accessed 7 May 2024.

Lyndall, R., et al. (2022). *East of Ben Lomond. Colonial frontier Massacres in Australia 1788–1930*. University of Newcastle. https://c21ch.newcastle.edu.au/colonialmassacres/detail.php?r=482. Accessed 7 May 2024.

MacDonald, L. (2023). Colonial-era William Crowther statue to be removed from Hobart's Franklin Square, in an Australian first. *ABC News*. https://www.abc.net.au/news/2023-08-24/william-crowther-statue-to-be-removed-from-display/102737854. Accessed 1 May 2024.

Mar, T. B. (2012). Settler-colonial landscapes and narratives of possession. *Arena Journal, 37/38*, 176–198.

Melbourne Biennial Lab. (2016). Over Obelisk. https://www.bienniallab.com/over-obelisk. Accessed 7 May 2024.

Merri-bek City Council. (2024). *Local Wurundjeri History*. https://conversations.merri-bek.vic.gov.au/renaming/local-history. Accessed 2 February 2024.

Mirzoeff, N., & Samudzi, Z. (2020). *The Forum//Zoé Samudzi and Nicholas Mirzoeff*. The Lab. YouTube. https://youtu.be/kJ1MPRjy4LU?si=ijLZ7nlUWAc9JZQP. Accessed 7 May 2024.

Morgan, F. (2016). What lies beneath: Reading Melbourne's CBD through 'The Another View Walking Trail.' *PAN: Philosophy Activism, Nature, 12*, 69–80.

Murphy, J. (1997). The lie of the land. *Artlink, 17*(3), 8–9.

National Inquiry into the Separation of Aboriginal and Torres Strait Islander Children from Their Families (1997). Bringing them home: report of the National Inquiry into the Separation of Aboriginal and Torres Strait Islander Children from their Families. Sydney: Human Rights and Equal Opportunity Commission.

Nicholson, T. (2022). *Chimney in store. ACCA*. https://chimney-in-store.acca.melbourne/. Accessed 1 May 2024.

Oltermann, P. (2023). Israel-Hamas war opens up German debate over meaning of 'Never again'. *The Guardian*. https://www.theguardian.com/world/2023/nov/22/israel-hamas-war-opens-up-german-debate-over-meaning-of-never-again. Accessed 10 May 2024.

Ore, A. (2024). Victorian premier confronts 'bloody stains of colonisation' at historic Indigenous truth-telling inquiry. *The Guardian*. https://www.theguardian.com/australia-news/2024/apr/30/victorian-premier-confronts-bloody-stains-of-colonisation-at-historic-indigenous-truth-telling-inquiry. Accessed 13 May 2024.

Pascoe, B. (2007). *Convincing ground: Learning to fall in love with your country*. Aboriginal Studies Press.

Perkins, M. (2017). Historic statues: Where Indigenous people and women go missing. *The Age*. https://www.theage.com.au/national/victoria/historic-statues-where-women-and-indigenous-people-go-missing-20170831-gy8ev2.html. Accessed 1 May 2024.

Perkins, H., & Scarce, Y. (2021). Cloud chamber—Yhonnie Scarce in conversation with Hetti Perkins. *Nets Victoria*. https://netsvictoria.org.au/essay/cloud-chamber/. Accessed 10 May 2024.

Pinto, S. W. (2021). *Places of reconciliation: commemorating indigenous history in the heart of Melbourne*. Melbourne University Press.

Pohl, A. (2023). Can Australia learn from Germany's notion of *Erinnerungskultur* to confront our genocidal past? *Arena Quarterly, 15*. https://arena.org.au/a-culture-of-remembrance/. Accessed 4 May 2024.

Scholes, R., & Lehman, G. (2021). *The Whaler's tale*. City of Hobart. https://www.hobartcity.com.au/Community/Creative-Hobart/Creative-Hobart-projects/Crowther-Reinterpreted/The-Whalers-Tale. Accessed 7 May 2024.

Sentance, N. (2021). Remembering, re-storying, returning. *History Australia, 18*(4), 823–829.

Shine, R. (2017). Tasmania's difficult history: Monuments leave out dark side to colonial past. *ABC News*. https://www.abc.net.au/news/2017-08-31/monuments-to-tasmanias-colonial-past-have-dark-side/8851554. Accessed 1 May 2014.

Stephens, A. (2023). These 10 extraordinary Victorian stories have been hidden for too long. *The Age*. https://www.theage.com.au/culture/art-and-design/larded-guinea-fowl-anyone-old-menus-and-medical-scandals-reveal-our-hidden-history-20221216-p5c6xk.html. Accessed 1 May 2024.

Stephens, M., & Stewart-Muir, F. (2023). *Banbu-deen: The years of terror*. Australian Scholarly Publishing.

Stevens, Q., Franck, K. A., & Fazakerley, R. (2018). Counter-monuments: The anti-monumental and the dialogic. *The Journal of Architecture, 23*(5), 718–739.

Stih, R., & Schnock, F. (2005). *Bus stop*. Stih & Schnock. https://www.stih-schnock.de/bus-stop.html. Accessed 10 May 2024.

Strakosch, E. (2010). Counter-monuments and nation-building in Australia. *Peace Review, 22*(3), 268–275.

Strakosch, E. (2009). Abstraction and figuration in monuments and counter-monuments. In *When the soldiers return: November 2007 conference proceedings* (pp. 270–276). University of Queensland, School of History, Philosophy, Religion and Classics.

Veracini, L. (2023). *Recognition beyond recognition! Interventions* (pp. 1–15).

Watego, C. (2024). *Blackfullas for Palestine*. https://www.blackfullasforpalestine.com/thewords/prof-chelsea-watego. Accessed 13 May 2024.

Yoorrook Justice Commission. (2024). Transcript of Day 12—public hearing. https://yoorrookjusticecommission.org.au/wp-content/uploads/2024/05/WUR.HB06.0012.0001.pdf. Accessed 13 May 2024.

Young, J. E. (1992). The counter-monument: Memory against itself in Germany today. *Critical Inquiry, 18*(2), 267–296.

Young, J. E. (1999). Memory and counter-memory. *Harvard Design Magazine* 9(Fall). https://www.harvarddesignmagazine.org/articles/memory-and-counter-memory/. Accessed 1 May 2024.

Young, J. E. (2000). *At memory's edge: After-images of the Holocaust in contemporary art and architecture*. Yale University Press.

**Amy Spiers** is an artist and researcher of settler descent, and currently a Vice Chancellor's Postdoctoral Fellow at RMIT School of Art. She has presented art projects across Australia and internationally, including at Australian Centre for Contemporary Art (ACCA), Monash University Museum of Art (Melbourne) and the 2015 Vienna Biennale. Spiers has also published widely, including co-editing *Let's Go Outside: Art in Public* with Charlotte Day and Callum Morton for Monash University Museum of Art (Monash University Publishing 2022) and co-authoring the book, *Art/Work: Social Enterprise, Young Creatives & the Forces of Marginalisation*, with Grace McQuilten, Kim Humphery and Peter Kelly (Palgrave Pivot, 2022). Most recently, she was awarded a 2024 Australian Research Council Discovery Early Career Researcher Award (DECRA) to examine non-Indigenous artists' engagements with truth-telling Australia's colonial past through creative practice.

# Chapter 10
# Exposure Therapy: Spectacles, Monuments and the Question of Care

**Arlie Alizzi and Neika Lehman**

**Abstract** This text is part of an ongoing critical conversation between the authors that began in 2015 about who public monuments are for. It is informed by the authors' double positions as descendant relatives of Aboriginal historical figures represented by public monuments as well as observers of an emerging cultural obsession with public monuments that commemorate traumatic colonial events. In this dialogical text Alizzi and Lehman discuss their shared relationship to monuments through a series of examples in cultural practice and public art, across Australia and Turtle Island (North America). In particular, the authors consider the public work, *Standing by Tunnerminnerwait and Maulboyheenner*, a permanently installed commemorative marker, commissioned by the City of Melbourne and produced by Wiradjuri artist Brook Andrew and settler artist and designer Trent Walter in late 2016. In the chapter that follows, the authors reflect upon Christina Sharpe's notion of *wake work* and through it identify a need for a deeper ethical relationship of care between the living and those who have passed when engaging in acts of memorialisation.

This chapter, that unfolds dialogically between us, is part of an ongoing critical conversation that began in 2015 about who public monuments are for. It is informed by our experiences of grief, of trauma and of physical and mental illness. It is informed by our being on, and travelling through, Country and speaking from peculiar, double positions as descendant relatives of Aboriginal historical figures represented by public monuments, as well as observers of an emerging cultural obsession with public monuments that commemorate and educate the (settler) public about traumatic colonial pasts. In this conversation we discuss our shared relationship to monuments through a series of examples in cultural practice and public art, across

A. Alizzi (✉)
University of Melbourne, Naarm, Melbourne, Australia
e-mail: arlie.alizzi@unimelb.edu.au

N. Lehman
RMIT University, Naarm, Melbourne, Australia
e-mail: neika.lehman@rmit.edu.au

© The Author(s), under exclusive license to Springer Nature Singapore Pte Ltd. 2024
G. Grieves and A. Spiers (eds.), *Art and Memorialisation*, Indigenous-Settler Relations in Australia and the World 6, https://doi.org/10.1007/978-981-97-6289-7_10

Australia and Turtle Island (North America), with particular focus on the commemorative marker commissioned by City of Melbourne, *Standing by Tunnerminnerwait and Maulboyheenner* (2016).

*Standing by Tunnerminnerwait and Maulboyheenner* by Wiradjuri artist Brook Andrew and settler artist and designer Trent Walter memorialises the 1841–1842 trial and hanging of Tunnerminnerwait and Maulboyheenner, two young First Nations men from Lutruwita, who became the first people publicly executed by the Port Phillip colony's judicial system in 1842.[1] The monument was erected in 2016 at the approximate site of the men's execution, which sits just outside of the Old Melbourne Goal museum and RMIT University in the present day central business district of Naarm (Melbourne). Described by Brook Andrew as more in line with contemporary art than traditional war memorial design, the artwork's focal point is a monumental, oversized children's swing set, referencing both the gallows that hung the men, as well as the motion of swinging bodies. The seat is composed of a block of bluestone constructed at adult seat height and designed as an object the public can sit upon for reflection. Carved into the bluestone are the names of the two men the marker commemorates. Andrew and Walter's artist statement proposes that 'the children's swing seat becomes the tomb, laden with memory and history' (Andrew & Walter, 2016, cited in City of Melbourne, 2017a).

Australian architect and editor, Yiling Shen, writes that the memorial is 'unique in that it is one of the few types of architecture whose fundamental function is not shelter but rather to feel and to remember' (2020). Underlining our conversation is the following question: what happens when there is dissonance between a monument and the related, descendant community's memories and feelings? Just as monuments are part of the public archives, we position ourselves and community knowledges as archives in their own right. Over the course of our critical dialogue, we consider the potential disjuncture between what the monument conveys about history and how the observing publics experience that living history within the ongoing hyper-violence of the settler colonial nation state.

In our conversation below we draw on theorist Christina Sharpe's idea of *the wake* (2016) as a prompt for understanding the multifaceted ways settler colonialism enacts ongoing violence towards Indigenous communities by keeping the brutality of the past playing out in the present. We explore how exposure to representations of terror and horror are used by settlers to interpret, imagine and comprehend Blak pain through an overwhelming lens of white settler/invader public displays of shame and guilt, and link this affective imagining's impact on the wellbeing of Blak communities. We utilise Destiny Deacon's 'Blak' through this piece to describe Aboriginal

---

[1] Where possible in this chapter we use First Nations place names to describe the places we discuss. For example, 'Lutruwita' is the palawa kani (contemporary Tasmanian Aboriginal language) name for Tasmania, the federated island state of Australia. At the time of the hanging, Lutruwita was commonly referred to by its colonial name Van Diemen's Land, between 1803–1856, after which it became known as Tasmania. This article uses the palawa kani term 'Lutruwita' for the island, unless otherwise stated. Likewise, the City of Melbourne is becoming increasingly known by Naarm (or Narrm), a term derived from the Boon Wurrung language that refers to the river and coastline the city occupies.

# 10 Exposure Therapy: Spectacles, Monuments and the Question of Care

and Torres Strait Islander peoples while understanding how it might diverge from Sharpe's theorisations of Blackness and its context.[2] Our intention here is not to assert sameness across Blakness and Blackness, but to understand how Sharpe's wake can be instructive in our context.

Using ideas of *wake work* and *care* to signify attempts to renegotiate and reinterpret acts of racial violence whose lived effects are still circulating, we argue for a greater need to imagine ways of relating to traumatic colonial pasts that do not require a reconfiguration of violence in the present. We see wake work as involving collective, often creative engagements with notions of the past, our ancestors and present day treatments of historical violence. We discuss the broader implications of wake work as it relates to the social-temporal conditions of Australia's settler colony, identifying the need for a deeper ethical relationship between the living and those who have passed.

**Arlie Alizzi** In her book, *In the Wake: on Blackness and Being*, Christina Sharpe outlines her concept of *the wake* as a type of afterlife lived in the wake of historical trauma (2016). Alongside her discussion of this, the book recounts a period in her life where she lost three family members in quick succession. Her idea of living in the wake develops within this experience as 'the conceptual frame of and for living blackness in the diaspora in the still unfolding aftermaths of Atlantic chattel slavery' (2016, p. 2). She refers to *wake work* as work that takes place in the Black American context, in the handling of memories by living descendent communities of ancestors who suffered lynching, enslavement and other forms of what Sharpe terms 'planned terror' (2016, p. 2). She writes that Black people in the United States 'think the metaphor of the wake in the entirety of its meanings (the keeping watch with the dead, the path of a ship, a consequence of something, in the line of flight and/or sight, awakening, and consciousness)' (2016, pp. 17–18).

When I read this idea of the wake from Sharpe, who is an accomplished theorist of Black life in the United States, it feels as though it carries both a locality and an enormity which we can work with in our own context observing the operations of monuments in Naarm (Melbourne) and colonial Australia more broadly. Her loss is tied to collective loss and it is experienced physically and immediately. It's personal, bodily, and terrifying, and I think I can recognise its sentiments in some of the work of our Blak women artists here.

I know you've found this idea of the wake compelling, so maybe this is a good place for us to begin.

We have talked about the wake as a literal one, following a ship, for example. I remember you talking about a map that you created, where you plotted out sites where artworks and monuments had been made about Captain James Cook, and you marked them out alongside the trajectory of his ship (something that has always gripped me about your work is the investigative, observant eye you take to these things).

---

[2] Artist Destiny Deacon, a descendent of K'ua K'ua/Kuku and Erub/Mer people, coined the term 'Blak', first using it in the photographic triptych *Blak lik me* (1991) (Russell-Cook 2020).

I also recall when you were photographing monuments around Naarm, and the images you made of Cooks' Cottage in Fitzroy Gardens. I remember you took me to see a site at Queen Victoria Market, when we met there once near your house, and we went looking at the old Meat Market up the road. You taught me about the monument to John Batman located at the Queen Victoria Market, and the plaque commemorating him that claims he founded the settlement of Melbourne on a site that was then unoccupied, which is accompanied by a counter-plaque acknowledging the pain caused to Aboriginal people by the inaccuracies of the first.[3] During our visit, we stood and looked up at one of the internal brick walls inside the market, past the stalls of green vegetables and handbags, a spot where you'd been coming in the night, when the market was empty, to film. I can't recall whether you were planning to make a work out of that footage, or if you were just taking it for your own archival records.

**Neika Lehman** I don't know if I knew myself originally, but for the first five years of living in Naarm, the Market was a site of lots of creative reflection. It was the subject of several poems and I ended up making a short film about Queen Victoria Market being a burial site and how it related to the story of Tunnerminnerwait and Maulboyheenner, which was exhibited back home in Nipaluna (Hobart), Lutruwita.

This was happening at the same time I was composing a list of monuments, memorials and markers to frontier massacre sites across Australia. That was mainly in order to understand the extreme contrast between the small number of monuments to Aboriginal massacres and other frontier killings in Australia with the numerous monuments that memorialise Australians who died fighting in wars overseas. My friend Chelsea Hopper was working at the Australian War Memorial and mentioned an online register of monuments to offshore battles called *Places of Pride*, an initiative of former director Brendan Nelson (Australian War Memorial, 2018). The idea of the site is an online log where every war marker in Australia is in the one place. They range from smaller scale town hall plaques acknowledging fallen ANZACS, to the bigger monuments, and gathering places like memorial halls. It's a very detailed list, with over 10,000 items.

Away from the site, I've found approximately 35 publicly identified monuments dedicated to violence against Aboriginal people. Many are *home jobs*—locally produced, the product of grassroots organising or an individual initiative, and not state funded—so there is probably more out there that could be added to the list. Massacre monuments are generally place-based, on either private or public land. They are nearly always at the site of the violence. In contrast and unsurprisingly, the monuments on *Places of Pride* website only acknowledge sites of conflict that took place overseas. Sometimes Australians even like to recreate overseas battles at home: I don't know if you've heard of the beach on the South Australian Eyre Peninsula that was re-named Gallipoli Beach, due to a perceived resemblance to the ANZAC

---

[3] John Batman (1801–1839) was a colonist known for his role in leading massacres of Aboriginal people and for his contribution to the founding of the City of Melbourne via a nefarious 'treaty' agreement with local Aboriginal people at Port Philip, wherein land was exchanged for blankets, tools and rations. The treaty was soon declared void by the Commonwealth (City of Melbourne, 2017b).

# 10 Exposure Therapy: Spectacles, Monuments and the Question of Care

Cove in Turkey, where Australian and New Zealand forces landed in World War I? People gather there each year to mirror commemorative events taking place on the same date on the other side of the globe, at the Gallipoli Peninsula in Turkey, where the actual war event took place.

Regarding the Cook map you recall, I made two of them. One was a map of colonial and settler monuments to Captain James Cook. The other was a geographical map of Aboriginal artists who have responded to Cook in their creative practice; where the artists' lived, and where their Country was. I learned through doing all this that aside from some painters in the Northern Territory, the works being made about Cook were all from the east coast mobs. So following Cook's east coast voyage, I could see a direct relationship between where the practicing artist lived and where Cook had gone. You could visually track his journey through the critical creative output of First Nations artists.

To use Sharpe's term, it was like a *wake* following Cook. I'm not so interested in the national imaginary stuff surrounding Cook. It was more interesting that it was very literally tied to the land, to the places that had memory of Cook and the artistic responses that follow. The idea that geographical history still plays out emotionally and socially on the land, in the present, is crucial to me. And to my own ontology—for better and for worse.

**AA** The wake isn't metaphor for you, it's physically felt and observable.

**NL** Yes. Something immediately compelling about Sharpe's notion of the wake is the feeling that historical atrocities still unfold in the present: 'In the wake, the past that is not past reappears, always, to rupture the present' (Sharpe, 2016, p. 9). I think this follows Saidiya Hartman's idea that there is a false distinction between *then* and *now* when we talk about atrocity (2002). As Michel-Rolph Trouillot puts it: 'the past is a position' (1997, p. 15). Regarding the production of monuments to Indigenous deaths on the colonial frontier being made in a time of ongoing police killings and mass incarceration in contemporary Australia, I want to point to Hartman when she asks: 'How might we understand mourning, when the event has yet to end? When the injuries not only perdure, but are inflicted anew? Can one mourn what has yet ceased happening?' (2002, p. 758).

Sharpe's writing is specifically interested in Hartman's questions, about how historically violent events set up the conditions for a way of living that remains violent. In Sharpe's instance, she is speaking to the aftermath of Atlantic chattel slavery in contemporary Black America. But it immediately reminded me of the conditions for First Nations people in settler colonial Australia, in that there is an afterlife to the violent colonisation of this continent that is still with us today. It's in the behaviour of institutions, in culture more generally and it is processed within our bodies, our souls. Which is to say that *the wake* can be thought of as an existential mode.

For all these reasons, when I first encountered Sharpe's work on the wake, it felt like déjà vu. I have written elsewhere about how, for Tasmanian Aboriginal people, death is a heightened, hyper present, and overrepresented spectre in our experience (Lehman, 2022). The colonial myth of our extinction is like a tick deeply embedded. On the island, the rhetoric of survival dominates for that reason. But off island, the myth hides in plain sight. Living on mainland blakfella turf, in my case on Wurundjeri and Boon Wurrung Country in Naarm, you have to learn hard and fast what blakfella life is like up there, where people are versed in a pan-Aboriginal mainland expression, in addition to their tribal identity. In our close circle of First Nations friends, nearly everyone is from a different mob. Deep care grows from both shared understandings of experience and respect for the culturally specific. We all bring our ancestors to the table, knowing that our old fellas spoke their own languages while maintaining reciprocal relations.

But outside of close circles, I was surprised in Naarm to find that often in conversations with both white and Aboriginal mainlanders, people engaged with me on a cultural level that was based on past events. It seemed people couldn't help but understand my being as in proximity to the extinction mythology of Tasmanian Aboriginal people. This myth is pervasive and perverse: people's minds seem to go to it even when they know they shouldn't. The spectacle of Truganini as the *last Tasmanian*, the genocide that we remarkably survived, my blonde hair and fair skin... It is an odd experience to be on the receiving end of people's fixations on Tasmanian Aboriginal death and absence. After a while it made me feel a bit like a ghost, an aura of something that has passed.

Partly because of this experience, it's always exciting when I learn about Tasmanian Aboriginal stories on the mainland. I think Tunnerminnerwait and Maulboyheenner's was the first well-documented one I came across. I lived for many years in North and West Melbourne in adjacent suburbs that border Melbourne's CBD but still have those nineteenth century sensibilities intact, marked out by early workers' cottages and impractically wide roads. Between this out-of-time area and the city centre is the Queen Victoria Market. Shouldered by skyscrapers on one side, the bustling sprawl of low market tents and sheds are a spatial anomaly. The produce market has run continuously since the late 1870s. Despite its popularity with locals and tourists alike, there is an uneasy feeling between vendors over the future of the largest open-air market in the Southern Hemisphere. It's not hard to find out that a big reason Queen Vic is allowed to continue operating in such a cut-throat area of real estate is because the market is situated over a field of bones.

This is how I learn of Tunnerminnerwait and Maulboyheenner's story: backwards. It begins with their resting place: a very untraditional one for Palawa men, and one very far from home.[4] Before Queen Victoria Market was established, the land was first appropriated by colonists to mark Melbourne's first cemetery. Initially the graveyard and market co-existed, before the market's desirable commerce took precedence at the end of the nineteenth century. But what to do with the dead? The earth was covered with concrete, and while the market operates above, around 9000 bodies remain below. This palimpsest of urban space is not an easy turn around for redevelopers looking for quick money. While the bodies stay, so does the market, making the deceased strange emblems of anti-development and of the health of the market's small business economy.

---

[4] Palawa is the term for Tasmanian Aboriginal people.

## 10 Exposure Therapy: Spectacles, Monuments and the Question of Care

On 20th January 1842, Tunnerminnerwait and Mauboyheener were laid to rest in this first cemetery—as much as remains can rest in a foreign city centre—after being publicly executed outside Melbourne's Old Goal. They were the first in the Port Phillip colony to be publicly hanged in a state sanctioned killing. Historical accounts estimate the crowd that watched to be between 4000 and 6000 people, which was an extremely large crowd for Melbourne's population at the time. Up in the eucalypt trees closest to the gallows, Kulin folk had climbed high into the branches, escaping the rowdy crowd and with a clear view of this new form of terror and violence spectated on their soil.[5]

To respectfully speak of the *Standing by Tunnerminnerwait and Maulboyheenner* monument and the figures it commemorates, we must expand a little on the stories of the two young men from Lutruwita. We must speak beyond the moment of their killing.

Maulboyheenner had kin relations to the Plangermairener and Pairrebeenne peoples across the North East of Lutruwita, which means I am culturally tied to him as a tribe descendent of the Trawlwoolway peoples. Tunnerminnerwait belonged to the Parperloihener peoples of North West Lutruwita who, like so many original tribes and nations in Lutruwita, have no known living descendants today. Both were born into the upheaval initiated by colonial invasion and the conflict of the Frontier Wars.

While Cassandra Pybus in her recent book, *Truganini: Journey through the Apocalypse* makes mention of the uniquely powerful family Maulboyheenner grew up in, and Tunnerminnerwait's enduring love and later search for reunion with his brothers, we must leave the richness of their adolescent lives as Plangermairener, Pairrebeenne and Parperloihener children to another story (2020). While Maulboyheenner was stolen as a child from his family during a massacre carried out by John Batman (who as noted earlier, later founded the Port Phillip Colony illegally through a botched Treaty with the Wurundjeri tribe), as a teenager, Tunnerminnerwait left his home on Robbins Island and the western coastline on much more ambiguous terms. Following Methodist brick-layer and government appointed colony *conciliator*, George Augustus Robinson, on his so-called *friendly mission* to cease warfare between colonists and Aboriginal people in Lutruwita—which effectively rounded Aboriginal people up to be under Robinson's protection—Maulboyheenner and Tunnerminnerwait joined the mission and the relative safety it promised. Looking to colonial archives at least, more can be said of Maulboyheenner and Tunnerminnerwait's political lives when the two men begin to feature consistently in Robinson's journals.

In 1839, Maulboyheenner and Tunnerminnerwait were two among fourteen mostly young Tasmanian Aboriginal people who landed on Kulin Country by boat. They were brought to Port Phillip colony by Robinson, to accompany him in his new role as Chief Protector of Aborigines at Port Phillip. To the Port Phillip officials and public, the group demonstrated Robinson's *friendly* relations with the Tasmanian

---

[5] The Kulin people is an alliance of five Aboriginal groups whose Country is located in south central Victoria, Australia: the Wurundjeri, Boon Wurrung, Taungurong, Dja Dja Wurrung and Wathaurung.

Aboriginal people. As he had conciliated the Palawa in Lutruwita, so he would do so again with the Kulin.

In the preceding years, across the Tasmanian mainland, Robinson and his crews had removed nearly all Aboriginal people from their homelands to an offshore site called Wybalenna on Flinders Island. While the martial law colonial officials declared on Palawa people had officially concluded, the whole island of Tasmania had been deeply colonised by pastoralists who believed their occupation of Indigenous land as lawful. Lutruwita was no longer a safe place for its people. Many of the group who joined Robinson in Port Phillip had remaining kin at Wybalenna who had died or were dying. This group of experienced young people had all grown up in invasion and war. They understood that to survive on the Tasmanian Frontier was to keep moving. Robinson had guaranteed their safety so far, and Port Phillip was probably their safest option, even if it meant leaving vulnerable loved ones behind.

After months of friendly living with Kulin people along the polluted riverbanks of the Yarra, Tunnerminnerwait, his wife Plorenernoopner, Maulboyheenner, the infamous Truganini, and their friend Maytepueminer eventually absconded from the disease riddled metropole and walked south-east across Boon Wurrung Country. Their journey would have been partly motivated by the search for their missing friend Lacklay, who was also Maytepueminer's husband. A series of raids on settler stations to replenish their food and ammunition supplies sparked a persistent police chase that led them further and further east. Getting as far as Gunai/Kurnai Country (Gippsland, Victoria), the journey became deadly after two whalers were shot dead. Eventually a reinforced search party of twenty-three armed settlers and seven armed trackers closed in on the group and arrested them with chains. Maulboyheenner and Tunnerminnerwait were committed for trial for murder, while the women were charged as accessories before and after the fact (Pybus, 2020).

Legal scholar Kate Auty and historian Lynette Russell argue that 'even at a time when rough justice was the order of the day, Tunnerminnerwait and Maulboyheenner were abjectly treated' by the fledgling colonial justice system (2016).They conclude in their survey of the arrest, evidence and court processes, that even contemporaneously by nineteenth-century standards, the men did not receive a fair trial under the dubious and contentious character of Judge John Walpole Willis, who was described as professionally incompetent and had been previously dismissed by other jurisdictions.

As the government appointed counsel for the defence, Redmond Barry argued that the people from Lutruwita be considered not as naturalised subjects of mainland colony but as aliens, entitled by common law to be judged by a jury half consisting of the same alien people who could speak the same language as the defendants (Pybus, 2020). Judge Willis overruled Barry, denying the accused the right to give evidence because they were not Christians. When Tunnerminnerwait and Maulboyheenner were asked how they pleaded, they did not understand the notion of the question. Barry offered a plea of 'not guilty' on their behalf.

Despite being denied the right to give evidence, the jury found the men guilty, with strong recommendation for mercy 'on account of general good character and the peculiar conditions under which they are placed' (Pybus, 2020, p. 225). The

10 Exposure Therapy: Spectacles, Monuments and the Question of Care

recommendation was rejected and Willis sentenced Tunnerminnerwait and Maulboy-heenner to be hanged by the neck until dead. Willis remarked: 'The punishment that awaits you is not that of vengeance, *but of terror*, that others by the example you will afford, may be deterred from similar transgression' (1841).

This, to me, recalls Sharpe's understanding of (constitutive terror), and her assertion, citing Paul Youngquist, that the 'disaster of Black subjection was and is planned; terror is disaster and "terror has a history"' (2016, p. 5). To contemporary eyes, it is difficult not to see Tunnerminnerwait, Maulboyheenner and the other young people's act as basic retaliation, in order to simply exist on their own terms. It is also an early example of the colonial regime utilising the spectacle of terror to present the black body and being as something to be publicly terrorised and terrorising. Thus, the hanging and commentary by Judge Willis is an example of historical events that is, to quote Sharpe again: '… the ground of our everyday Black existence … living in the wake means living in and with terror in that much of what passes for public discourse *about* terror, we, Black people, become the carriers of terror, terror's embodiment' (2016, p. 15).

While I don't want to dwell on the details, in historical reportage the nature of the men's execution is described at its best as mismanaged, and otherwise an act of 'disgusting clumsiness', referring to both the inexperienced executioners and botched rigging on the flimsy structure that added further suffering to the men's passing (Finn, 1888, pp. 395–396). In the thousands strong crowd, excitement reportedly turned to disgust (Pybus, 2020, p. 228). As per the colony's code at the time, the men were left for an hour to hang. Once removed from the gallows, Tunnerminnerwait and Maulboyheenner were put in caskets and taken down-hill to the cemetery where Robinson waited for them at their grave sites, the site of today's Queen Victoria Market.

That is the story of the colony's killing of the two young men. It does not, cannot contain the spirit of themselves nor any spirit of home in Lutruwita. Not the spirit of their families and kin; the bulk of their linguistic and place-based belongings. They came from opposite sides of Lutruwita, whose differing coastlines shaped the entirety of each man's traditional lifeworld. We carry inside the weather of the places that shape us. And as comrades, they shared the medicines of windy coastal songs, stories and laughter. They had reverence for plants and animals, for law, love and marriage, and for family, who they were always trying to get back to. From birth, Tunnerminnerwait and Maulboyhenner shared the clamour and silence of surviving the apocalypse. The noose took nothing of those spirits away. They would just have to send themselves home.

In reportage of the execution, it is claimed that Tunnerminnerwait was not overly concerned by his death, because he would be going home to hunt kangaroo with his father. Tunnerminnerwait is reported as stating he had three heads: 'one for the scaffold, one for the grave, and one for V. D. Land' (Port Phillip Herald, 1842, p. 2).[6]

---

[6] V. D. Land refers to Van Diemen's Land, the colonial name for present day Lutruwita (Tasmania) between 1803–1856.

Tunnerminnerwait's three forms are various pathways, or perhaps spiritual portals. The act, the resting place, and the place the spirit travels to. For me, his statement raises many questions about the kind of traces we leave in the world, but also about Tunnerminnerwait's own beliefs and wishes for his exit. It leaves me wondering what this statement means for an artist considering how to artistically respond to his death through the monument form, particularly when his passing was unwelcome.

If the City of Melbourne proposed a call for a monument that could remember the two men, what does it mean for the successful artist to choose the only part of Tunnerminnerwait and Maulboyheenner that was given to the scaffold? Over a representation of their spirit, or their Country? I want to explore what it means for an artist and state council to prioritise the visual representation of a violent apparatus to public death.

The City of Melbourne's decision to embrace Tunnerminnerwait and Maulboyheenner's story as culturally and historically significant to the City of Melbourne was arguably due to the lobbying efforts of the Tunnerminnerwait and Maulboyheenner Commemoration Committee, an activist group convened by the settler anarchist Dr Joe Toscano since 2008.[7] The development of the monument was publicly communicated as a key outcome of the City of Melbourne's Indigenous Heritage Action Plan (2012–2015). Following an open Expression of Interest application process, three short listed artist teams presented their concepts for final consideration. Notably, the selected artist team, Brook Andrew and Trent Walter, were the only Melbourne-based, non-Tasmanian Aboriginal artist group of the final three.[8]

Dr Joe Toscano's work continues. Each year on the date of the hanging, the commemoration committee invite the public to gather at the execution site to remember the two men, often ended by a collective walk to Tunnerminnerwait and Maulboyheenner's burial site at the market nearby. This remembrance event has continued since the monument's erection in 2016, a nod to community actions that go beyond state sanctioned action plans and time constrained policies. The ceremony as embodied practice precedes and exceeds the materiality of the static monument and opens a different set of possibilities to remember the Palawa resistance fighters. On an annual basis, I imagine there is a much larger, random and less invested public that interact with the City of Melbourne's so-called *permanent marker*, particularly the large bench-like seat, which I often see people using to rest, eat and chat in a busy corner of the CBD. It reminds me of a question posed by the British critic Jonathan

---

[7] Details of Tosano's public campaign and long-standing commitment to the issue of Tunnerminnerwait and Maulboyheenner's memorialisation are given in ABC Radio National program, The forgotten war that led to Port Phillip's first public executions (Allam, 2014).

[8] The Tasmanian Aboriginal community are a small group of genocide survivors, most of whom descend from the same family groups. It is important to acknowledge the author Neika Lehman's familial relationship to both Tasmanian Aboriginal finalist groups, particularly the group consisting of Professor Greg Lehman (Neika's father), Dr Julie Gough and Tony Thorne. In consideration of this, we have decided not to discuss the potential differences a Tasmanian Aboriginal designed monument may engender. It is worth acknowledging however, the missed opportunity by the City of Melbourne for promoting self-determination that a First Nations team from Lutruwita would have enabled, particularly regarding the cultural representation of the men's story.

# 10 Exposure Therapy: Spectacles, Monuments and the Question of Care

Jones that the art historian Susan Lowish shared with me. In 2007, Jones asked the public:

> Why have war memorials been rebranded as something for everyone, no longer just for veterans or survivors, no longer the dead expressions of state patriotism, but popular, and even somehow spontaneous, contemporary, urban places to be? (Jones, 2007)

**AA** I did not attend the public unveiling of *Standing By*, or any of the memorial events you've spoken about. I've instead seen the work in that context that Jones is reflecting on; as an *urban place to be*. When I've visited the site, I mainly see tradies there eating pies and leaving cigarette butts on the gallows. I'm pretty sure they don't know it's supposed to *be* gallows. But who knows. In some ways, I think this doubled meaning— a memorial that can also be viewed as a functional object or recreational space in an urban area—is Andrews' intention.

Before the monument was conceived of, maybe before you had even arrived in Naarm at all; and before we'd met, there was a public and very critical debate on the Barak building. That building houses apartments in the city's centre and depicts on its towering facade an image of Wurundjeri leader and activist William Barak. It sits a short walk away from the memorial to Tunnerminnerwait and Maulboyheenner's execution. The debate was pretty heated. My impression was that the Wurundjeri people were heavily involved in the co-design and creation of the piece with the architecture firm, ARM, and I remember hearing Aunty Joy Murphy saying that she felt very moved by seeing Barak's face in the city. It was other critics, Aboriginal people from elsewhere living on Wurundjeri Country as visitors, who had, and still have, the intellectual issue with the symbolism of the thing. Marra critic Tristen Harwood and Lauren Burrow, a settler artist, have even called the building an example of 'Aboriginal Kitsch' (Burrow & Harwood, 2018).

I do think that there are Aboriginal artists who engage with Aboriginal kitsch very effectively. Tony Albert does it very well with his ashtray collection, Destiny Deacon with her black baby dolls. But I have a lot of discomfort with that humour and subversion being brought into the practice of public memorialisation.

**NL** That hits on something interesting about what public memorials or monument sites are for. Can you tell me why you find humour in monuments uncomfortable?

**AA** I love the humour, the irony and the satire presented in some contemporary Aboriginal art, and public art. I'm thinking about Daniel Boyd's *We Call them Pirates Out Here* (2006) and Dianne Jones' *L.H.O.O.Q. ERE!* (2000)—both great examples of work sending up Cook. There was also Jones' *The Great Heads* (2018) and her other self-portraiture done at Western Australia state parliament house in Perth, for example. I love these works. They mess with the expectations of the viewer and have the capacity to confuse and disorient. When it comes to making art about experiences of racism and violence, I value humour as a deeply felt and important coping response for Aboriginal people when trying to make sense of these things. What I think is that we have to approach the memories of the dead, though, *our* dead, with plain, straight up respect, and set aside our impulse for self-indulgent or over-intellectualised irreverence. I don't think memorialising with respect and proper care can be done with the subversive and provocative lens that has been brought to some of these events in contemporary art practice. Where in the building of monuments to Aboriginal losses is that value system of care and attention? I'm thinking about the same protocols of care which we've observed from the last five decades of work by First Nations people to return and repatriate the ancestral remains of people who were stolen from Country—work that continues today. The stories of our dead and their memories, not just their tangible physical remains, have to be treated with the same level of protocol and respect. That is a problem: how do we bring a proper decolonial mindset to the topic of monument building.

Maybe I'm being deterministic about what a memorial could or should be, and they are not my old people in *Standing By*. But in general, I think the aesthetic nature of the memorial, the arrangement of space, the invitation to engage, and the nature of the engagement which is prompted by a monument, has to be able to hold the spirit of both the people being remembered and to be able to comprehend the things which happened to them, without making that the only feature of their life and afterlives. I would not like to see my ancestors represented with a gallows or any other weapon which is associated with their death and suffering. That is not the sum of their life or their contribution to history.

**NL** That's a good point about values, particularly regarding colonial history. They were—beyond being cultural people in their own right—crucial diplomatic guides to Robinson's work across Van Diemen's Land and the Port Phillip Colony. Why should the sum of their lives be symbolically dominated by the mechanism of their death—a mechanism that is entirely impersonal and an import to these lands?

I'm curious about what it means to choose the gallows, masquerading as a children's swing set, as the main interpretive symbol for these two men. As a Tasmanian Aboriginal person and descendent of Maulboyheenner's kin, if I can speak emotionally, it is distressing and disturbing to look at. The irony of the children's swing, evoking the swinging of the two hanged bodies at the gallows, enshrined in concrete and steel suggests a very long passing of time. It gives me chills, and they are not good chills. Andrew and Walter have referred to *Standing by Tunnerminnerwait and Maulboyheenner* as 'empowering'(cited in City of Melbourne, 2017a). My initial reaction and long-standing response is not of emotional or intellectual empowerment. This withstands great critical dialogues I have had with Elders from both Lutruwita and Naarm, interested academics, and with student groups I have taken to the site for interpretation. Of course, the monument is sensational and controversial enough a design that it compelled us to write this conversation, but uninteresting in the sense that controversy is a basic financial PR tactic. The feeling the monument leaves me with is a kind of intellectual deflation, a de-generation in imaginative thinking. The sad and lingering question: where are Tunnerminnerwait and Maulboyheenner in this artistic representation, beyond bodies swinging from nooses?

Sharpe muses, 'one is oriented to one's work from the location of the body and all that that may mean' (Sharpe, 2018, pp. 173–174). Perhaps because I am Trawlwoolway, the symbolism of the gallows is extra difficult to witness because of the extinction myth that is always haunting us. As a person in the twenty-first century, I am associated with a nineteenth century extinction myth, a myth that claims I stopped living as a human and started living as a ghost in 1876. For all these reasons, I can't

# 10 Exposure Therapy: Spectacles, Monuments and the Question of Care

help but experience the aesthetic choices made by Andrew and Walter as strangely macabre, blunt, and tone deaf to the experience of contemporary Tasmanian Aboriginal people. Extinction, as an infinite death, a cessation of being is still something we fight against. Artists understand the power of symbols and images, it's what they trade in. So, I come back to my question, why this direct re-presentation of the act of historical violence?

Violence against First Nations peoples and Black folk is, as Hartman argues, already hyper visible, and in fact, the nature of its performative 'staging' indicates how the 'exercise of power' is 'inseparable from its display' (Hartman, 1997, p. 7). We are from communities constantly dodging the harm of police and the so-called justice system. They were doing it then and they are doing it now, and perhaps that is a part of Andrew and Walter's premise, but I am not sure why Aboriginal observers of the monument would want to be reminded of one device in the long history of our on-going state sanctioned killing.

The gallows, by design, was made to create a spectacle of terror. Michel Foucault addresses this in *Discipline and Punish* (1995), demonstrating how public torture and execution devices were made, by design, to evoke fear and terror in a society's people. And while he goes on to demonstrate the Western prison system's general move towards concealing state inflicted pain and punishment, history shows us this has not been the case for black and Indigenous people. Instead, the public institutional torture, punishment and often times public death of the bla(c)k body is still ritualistic and hyper visible. Hartman argues that despite, and because of, the consistent spectacular character of representations of black suffering in the public world, the hypervisibility of black punishment and pain becomes subject to a 'casualness', a 'benumbing' familiarity, rather than becoming the 'opportunity for self-reflection' (1997, pp. 3–4).

So what, I want to ask, is the point of making a spectacle of bla(c)k killing, out of what historically was already an intentional and disciplinary spectacle of bla(c)k killing? Why construct an affective spectacle that represents our state-imposed deaths? The monument tells the story of the most literal death of Tunnerminnerwait's head: the one that went to the scaffold. What could have been told of his other two?

**AA** I want to talk through the difference you name; between caring for the memory of a person through public memorial, and this idea of memorial as a contemporary colonial public spectacle. In a lecture I saw you give in 2019, you compared the Andrew and Walter's *Standing By* work to the 2017 Minneapolis iteration of Sam Durant's public artwork, *Scaffold*. A bit more context: the City of Melbourne called out for a public art proposal to memorialise Tunnerminnerwait and Maulboyheenner in May 2015. It was erected in 2016. Durant's work was erected in Minneapolis in 2017. *Scaffold* was larger in scale to *Standing By*, comprising of a two-story wooden installation in the public sculpture garden of the Walker Art Centre in Minneapolis. It intended to represent a composite in physical terms of gallows used in seven significant executions by hanging in the United States, including reference to one of the most infamous mass hangings of Indigenous people in the United States in 1862 where 38 Dakota men were executed. *Scaffold* at the time was compared to the painter Dana Schutz's representation of the open casket of murdered African American boy,

Emmett Till, featured in the Whitney Biennial also in 2017. The two artists, both white, were accused of making spectacles of Black and Indigenous death, against claims by the artists that their intention had been to educate and discomfit the white audiences.[9]

I raised the Sam Durant piece in conversation with a friend, J, at dinner the other night, and they said they'd seen it in person in Germany in 2012 at documenta, not in Minneapolis, meaning the installation comprised of a representation of the gallows that killed Dakota men in 1862 toured internationally beyond the original site of the hanging that it reproduces. This is back in 2012, four years before the installation of *Standing By*, so it's possible that Andrew was aware of, and took notes from, Sam Durant's work. J, a writer and, at the time, a practicing artist, was present at the documenta *Scaffold* for a performance night. They mentioned that they'd performed some (their description) 'dreadful spoken word' in English in the garden where it was installed. They said that some German women approached them after and said, 'we didn't understand what you were saying, but we understood the feeling'. J said to me when we first had this conversation that they were really impacted by the work. They said, 'I couldn't help but be astounded, moved by its scale, the enormity of work matching the enormity of the violence. As an artist, I'm so drawn to the materiality of it'.

A few days later, however, we saw each other again. They told me they'd rewatched the video footage they'd taken of the event and they were shocked to see a detail they'd forgotten: that people were allowed to climb the gallows, to touch them, to walk all the way up to the top. They said it made the work turn in their memory from powerful to grotesque.

I was interested in both their description of the spectator-participants climbing the gallows, which were quite high, to look down, as well as the function of their memory: that re-remembering that took place between conversations, the different meanings attached to that artwork in both recountings, from the same person.

I'm fascinated too by *Scaffold*'s alienation from place. Prior to being shown in Minneapolis, the place of its removal and eventual destruction after protest from the Dakota community there, it was shown at documenta in Germany and also Scotland and the Hague, where, as Erika Doss explains, it 'hosted concerts and lectures, and children played on its jungle gym-like framework' (2022, p. 22). It was exhibited in Europe before ever being located in the place whose history it was telling.

There are grotesque elements to the viewing of *Standing By*, as well as to what I imagine to be the experience of climbing *Scaffold*, which I find unbearable. There is a sense that the reproduction and physical reference to violent acts against Indigenous people, as Hartman describes, are inseparable from the original power relationship that produced those acts in the first place. But here, they are fashioned into something

---

[9] Schutz is on record explaining the work drew on her empathy for Till's mother: 'The thought of anything happening to your child is beyond comprehension … their pain is your pain. My engagement with this image was through empathy with his mother' (Schutz, 2017, cited in Drew, 2022). Durant explained in a statement at the time of the Walker Art Centre controversy: 'I made Scaffold as a learning space for people like me, white people who have not suffered the effects of a white supremacist society and who may not consciously know that it exists' (Durant, 2017).

# 10 Exposure Therapy: Spectacles, Monuments and the Question of Care

that attempts abstraction and maybe even satire. I don't think that experience is productive for me as an Aboriginal viewer. Another work Andrew made in 2010, *Jumping Castle War Memorial*, intended to pay homage to Aboriginal people who were made to perform in human zoos. Bundjalung and Kullili man Daniel Browning has written about the experience of seeing that work and observing the audience's engagement with it. He notes the contradiction between the claim to criticality in the send up of the jumping castle and the effect of the object in space:

> the jumping castle … seemed to exploitatively draw a line between actual human suffering and hollow spectacle, reinscribing trauma in the process. I seriously doubt that a non-Indigenous viewer would engage with the traumatic histories that the work apparently invoked as they decided whether to jump or not to jump. (Browning, 2021, n.p.)

Daniel has recognised the importance of asking questions of the works we encounter as part of this critical 'monuments' movement. The procurement and construction of these monuments—whether they can be easily classified as public artworks or they exist in other terms—seems to happen in a few different ways. Some monuments are constructed in response to community needs and desires to engage with the past and to honour and care for the ancestors, and some seem more responsive to a market demand, driven by a settler audience who are the primary consumers of Aboriginal art (and the benefactors of what Hartman helpfully points out as the spectacle of subjection). As Doss has pointed out, Durant's idea with *Scaffold* was to make the work 'a platform for raising White consciousness about "the collateral damage of the imperial project,"' (Durant cited in Doss, 2022, p. 22). This may be radicalising or enlightening for white audiences, but it doesn't do the work we are invested in in First Nations contexts. It is not what we'd recognise as 'wake work' in Sharpe's terms, but belongs more in the category of the performance of power. It does not do that wake work of talking to the ancestors, connecting with them and honouring their lives.

**NL** And honouring their lives by treating our own with care. Care they were so frankly denied. That's a great description of a potential movement. Complex, with many different communities invested with differing desires.

**AA** I'm not anti-monument, nor am I against the idea presented by Jones above that the monument become *a place to be* in urban spaces. We live in urban space. As you've shown me, our dead are buried in urban space. We are surrounded by death, bones, and bodies, *and* living the wake as an existential mode; a way of experiencing things. We carry that around. Maybe what is needed is a strong moral code, a values-driven process through which a monument can be built and maintained.

**NL** I can just see the *devil's advocate* types in the art scene getting agitated by the idea of a moral code as being adjacent to censorship. But I agree with you, and there has to be different considerations of care in public monuments compared with the freedom of a contemporary art exhibition. If the 'monument' is publicly accessible, then it has a responsibility to a diversity of publics. If it is a monument to a traumatic issue or event, a code that ensures the monument does not elicit more trauma, particularly for the group who have historically suffered, seems reasonable to me. It's about wellbeing, and dare I say it, healing. And genuine relations between all the actors involved in the monument's creation and maintenance, beyond the initial briefing period.

**AA** I hear what you're saying. When I said moral code, I should make clear that I don't mean another disciplinary structure intended to regulate self-expression or what artists are *allowed* to talk about, but maybe a stronger sense of a *values of relation* that is triggered by the encounter with a monument. This recalls to mind a few significant experiences of memorialisation that have helped me to conceptualise the encounter with a memorial as a relational experience, rather than as an act of spectatorship:

I visited the CRAB Park Memorial to missing and murdered Indigenous Women a few times in 2017. That memorial is placed in the Downtown Eastside of Vancouver, Canada in an area where those murders and disappearances still occur. I visited during a time that a national inquiry and campaign was underway to investigate that epidemic of women disappearing. The memorial is a small plaque placed on a boulder, positioned in such a way that when you read it you're looking north into Vancouver Harbour, and candles that are placed there are sheltered from the wind coming off the water. The plaque reads: *THE HEART HAS ITS OWN MEMORY. In honour of the spirit of the people murdered in the Downtown Eastside. Many were women and many were native Aboriginal women. Many of the cases remain unsolved. All my relations. Dedicated July 29, 1997.*

My experience in Vancouver, seeing this boulder and its dedication and knowing the continuing grief and rage experienced by Indigenous communities in relation to the Missing and Murdered Indigenous Women (MMIW) inquiry, taught me that the memorial and the history are coinciding. The social conditions around the park, it appears, have not altered; the disappearances continue and are not adequately addressed by the local non-Indigenous community. Still, the memory of those women is held very dear. Candles are lit there, dedications are written on stones and placed at the site daily. People come to touch that boulder and remember them and talk to them. The site is always active and available to the living who are mourning their daughters, sisters, mothers and cousins.

Another instructive experience was hearing Dianne Jones and Genevieve Grieves speak about the work they made about the two Noongar men in York, Western Australia who were hanged for the murder of settler, Sarah Cook. Dianne's MFA research culminated in an exhibition in 2015. When I heard Dianne explain how she used her own body in the work, I remember being impacted by hearing from her how important it was that the violence itself was not represented directly, because it didn't need to be. Genevieve also spoke very clearly to the importance of not forcing the audience through the violence. It recalls to mind how Bundjalung writer Melissa Lucashenko has put this approach a different way, in relation to writing; 'You don't take the audience down a dark path, and leave them there. I feel really strongly about that' (cited in Arlie 2022).

I could see how present the violence of the story felt for Dianne and Genevieve as they followed and bore witness to it, as Aboriginal women putting themselves in the frame of the story. They visited the site of the hanging on Noongar Country and collected objects, chains, pieces of glass and other things, and brought them to

# 10 Exposure Therapy: Spectacles, Monuments and the Question of Care

exhibit in galleries on the east coast, back to Footscray Community Arts Centre and the Linden Centre for Contemporary Art in St Kilda.

There's also this other component of memorial building that often starts with a competition for funding. This ties into my earlier point about the consumer demand for art works exploring these violent histories; cities, states and other public bodies want to use public art as a form of 'post' colonial commemoration, and this generates a certain response. The public call out to artist teams to apply for the Tunnerminnerwait and Maulboyheenner's memorial effectively made it a design competition. These elements—the competition and the spectacle—problematise and negatively frame public monuments to Aboriginal people, particularly when the spectacle is taken as a good in itself, presented solely for the benefit of the (white) settler audience and their awakening.

**NL** The idea of it being an open *competition*, rather than as an *invitation* for the men's descendants and contemporary community (the Tasmanian Aboriginal community) to work with the Melbourne City Council, is odd in itself. It's a very European model for doing business: *may the best and learned win!* I wonder how different things would have been if the two parties, Melbourne City Council and the men's descendants, went on a design journey together. But I want to go back to your reference to Lucashenko, about not leaving audiences somewhere 'bad'.

When I hear this, I wonder if she's not simply saying Blak narratives deserve a happy ending sometimes, or even that there needs to be intelligent care given when considering the wellbeing of the Blak audience. I hear Lucashenko's words as a call to expand the narratives we tell and are told about us. To move beyond *condemned* narratives: those narrative types imposed by the state.

If we consider, as James and Costa Vargas argue in the US, that Black death is a constitutive aspect of democracy, and that the ongoing state-sanctioned imprisonment and murder of Aboriginal people is not only normative, but a necessary part of a settler democracy, how do First Nations people live in relation to this death—a death partially a 'requirement' of the colony (2014, p. 193)? How do we think imaginatively and act creatively from such a position?

Similarly, there's a reference to Sylvia Wynter in Sharpe's essay about the idea of a doomed narrative of blackness. Wynter considers the black position in society as one of a 'narratively condemned status' (1994, p. 70), which reminds me of Fanon's concept of the 'zone of non-being'. In *Black Skin, White Masks*, Fanon claims the anti-black world cannot sustain or contain the affirmation of black being, hence the black subject occupies what he calls the 'zone of non-being', 'the result of a series of aberrations of affect, rooted at the core of a universe from which he must be extricated' (2008, p. 2).

The question of how to live in the anti-black world, is arguably the foundation stone of both *Black Skin, White Masks* and Sharpe's essays in *The Wake*. To have a claim to life in its own terms, a life that is not simply determined by the incessant effort to survive, the 'insistent unhumaning' of the West towards black people, but to choose to live despite this (Sharpe, 2018, p. 172). To constitute a '*yes* that vibrates to cosmic harmonies' (Fanon, 2008, p. 2).

I am interested in whether Fanon would consider this affirmation of life, to insist on experience that is not determined by black death, as the nucleus for revolutionarily acts. In reading these Black scholars, I had the strong feeling that the same question applies to Indigenous populations. I think storytelling, as Lucashenko seems to be pointing to, is a crucial tool to imagine ways out of this existential condemnation, and that this imagining is crucial to our health and well-being.

Poka Laenui suggests five distinct phases of decolonisation, beginning with (1) rediscovery and recovery, (2) mourning, (3) dreaming, (4) commitment and (5) action (2000). While Laenui doesn't believe there is a strict demarcation from one phase to the next, meaning they may co-exist in time, if one phase is made impossible, it hinders the entire process. I think about this in the Australian context regarding mourning, where particular forms of mourning are encouraged—like the whole obsession with ANZAC day and commemorating soldiers who died in wars fought overseas—but not others. It also makes it very hard to move beyond mourning when the event you are grieving is being denied. That's how it seems regarding the ongoing reluctance of governments to accept the reality of attempted genocide in Tasmania. Or that most massacres that happened across the continent on the frontier were initiated by colonial officials. This denial is something First Nations artists have been working to change for a long time. Perhaps there have been small progresses over time, but to accept the weight and volume of these historical events would be to accept the momentous volume of invasion's wake in the present, something that is not in the best interests of maintaining state power.

So, what if we switch to the phase of *dreaming*, what Laenui called the most important phase of decolonisation (2000). What if we dream up very different narratives than the condemned ones designated for us and not by us? If this expands the way we imagine the possibilities of the present, it can also shift the possibilities in the way we treat those who have already passed.

Do we always look at ourselves as vessels of knowledge, as living archives of ancestral experience? What happens if we understand ourselves as conduits to the past, that it is alive and robust within us? Can we then begin to live less in relation to internalised colonial mythology? Look to state-sanctioned places where knowledge is held: we always encounter gaps in the colonial records room. There are no gaps in our imagination; no gaps in the history that's sitting in the room with *you*. We will find gaps in the public archive, the public monument, but there are no such gaps in our community histories, in our collective knowledge. You know how when you find out a new family story over dinner that stirs you, and you are reminded that all you ever need to do is think to ask the question? Perhaps we are too focused on speaking back to what we find in those colonial archives. And it's not just the stories themselves that distract and allure, it's in the *way* they are told too.

So I wonder, if we know all these things, why do we need the public monument at all? I am wondering who all this monument business is for?

**AA** I think this is a really important question to ask. What are the things that are known in the community, that are not part of that public archive, that the public monument fails to discuss? Should that knowledge be made public, and why?

# 10 Exposure Therapy: Spectacles, Monuments and the Question of Care

When you screened the film *Black Man's Houses* in Hobart in 2017 for what I think was its approaching 25th anniversary, I was in the audience. The film documents the community re-occupation of Wybalenna, Flinders Island, and reestablishment of the graveyard of over 100 Aboriginal people, who died at the site of the concentration camp established by George Augustus Robinson for survivors of the *Black War*, the period of violent conflict between Lutruwita's Aboriginal people and colonisers carried out in the 1820s and 1830s. The film also documents the political gathering and monument made by community activists for the ancestors who suffered at that site. During the panel and discussion session afterwards, I remember researcher and historian Lyndall Ryan speaking to the community present in the theatre about the concept of *dark tourism*. Specifically, Ryan spoke about Wybalenna as a vital site for the public imaginary which needed to be cultivated as a site of dark tourism much like other heritage sites that commemorate the suffering incurred by genocide such as Auschwitz in Germany and the Killing Fields of Cambodia. She said every Australian needed to go to Wybalenna. I do wonder though, the presence of that viewing public, coupled with the mass appeal of an international dark tourist economy, would dramatically change things on Flinders Island, right?

**NL** Yes. As it stands, Wybalenna is quite a highly visited, but quiet place. The tourist economy isn't visible.

**AA** From my memory of the film, and hearing you talk about the monument at Wybalenna, it seemed like there were a few important functions it was serving that evaded the practice of dark tourism and its effects. Rather than educating strangers, it is a site that allows the nearby descendants and affected community to collectively process their rage at what had happened on the island because of Robinson's actions. It is a site of collective identity formation for the Tasmanian Aboriginal community, and it is also an opportunity to re-engage with those ancestors and their experiences of the Black War and its aftermath. Although, as you've written, not all Aboriginal people connected to the island agree on the way to best care for those ancestors, their remains and how to honour their memories and experiences (Lehman, 2020).

**NL** Our old people had, still have, significant places. Structural and pictorial figurations to signify messages from the profane to the sacred. While *the monument* might be a western term with a particular set of ideas attached to it, we shouldn't forget that we also have a history of memorialising events and places beyond a simple oral tradition. In the contemporary context, what that looks like differs a lot between communities.

**AA** When you talked about Tunnerminnerwait, Maulboyheenner, and their companions, you spoke about these things; their spirit, their comradeship, their reverence, their kin. I wonder whether those things can be articulated aesthetically in the public, visual language of monuments?

**NL** It raises the issue that memory is encoded differently for different people. But if those more intangible qualities are considered an aesthetic priority to be developed between a group; a shared and well-dialogued vision, I think they can be. Particularly with attention to the material composition and its resonances into visual language. Once something is up, from my own perspective I believe in custodian commitments to ongoing care for the site, whether through physical care or ceremony. But if we are talking about government commissions, state sanctioning brings a whole world of bureaucracy that limits the capacity to envisage and dream freely what appropriate form a memorial can take. Australia is a nation state obsessed with rules and occupational health and safety, which impacts and limits material design choices. For example, in the case of *Standing by Tunnerminnerwait and Maulboyheenner*, the City of Melbourne stipulated that the design and material composition should have an anticipated lifespan of 25 years and be 'relatively maintenance free' (City of Melbourne, 2016).

Beyond the bureaucracy, I think it's about being intentional and accountable to the process between your own visions and that of the community you are visually representing. I believe in the deep power materials and objects have in the way they impact storytelling—the direct access they have to spirit, to our souls. To paraphrase something Metis scholar David Garneau once said in visit to Naarm in 2018: *art is a kind of social medicine*. Medicine is powerful and should not be underestimated. Materials and visual language are art medicine's active ingredients, and they can heal or harm depending on the context.

Who is the memorial for? It seems crucial to me, that artists creating public works, particularly about sensitive or traumatic issues, consider how the visual and material language will communicate with the community the artwork purports to represent, rather than merely try 'educating strangers', as you describe it, through shock value or affects akin to dark tourism. What messages do materials send, and to who? What is the cultural history of a particular object or material for a particular group of people? How does that play out in the present moment? How does a swing set masquerading as a gallows rendered in bluestone and steel, that mimics the colonial building materials of the nearby Old Melbourne Goal, do justice to the community memory and spirit of these Palawa ancestors, who resisted colonialism until death? I'm not anti-modern materials by any means, but I'm also thinking of Audre Lorde when she makes her famous claim: 'the masters tools will never dismantle the masters house' (2018). In the Imperial regulation of life and the imagination, the gallows are surely an ultimate master's tool.

**AA** I thought about you when I read the way Christina Sharpe described care as a practice of making 'a small path through the wake' (2018, p. 174). She writes about care as world-making, and about her mother's care which took place inside the home as a means of addressing harm done outside the home space. When I read the way she described that care that takes place in the home, and spoke about that work as *wake work*—as a way to make a small path through the wake by creating beauty, joy, and liveable moments—it got me thinking about the distance between acts of care in the home space, the non-performative acts of care which are not meant to be viewed by the public, and the tension between this care and the theatre of monuments. There is a theatre to the erection of a monument, to the planning, design, and discussion of them. There's a theatre to the building and to the destruction of them at certain moments too.

In our conversations over the last few years, we've discussed together the distinction between what Sharpe calls *wake work*, and these interventions which involve the recreation of spectacles of violence, post-colonial confession, and blood and gore.

# 10 Exposure Therapy: Spectacles, Monuments and the Question of Care

We've observed many forms of settler engagement with memorialisation since this conversation began, to the point where we've started calling them (first as a joke, then a bit more seriously) *exposure therapy*.

What we've been privately calling *exposure therapy*—if I could articulate it outside of our in-joke—occurs across public art, performance, and monument building, but it extends further into writing, memoir, speech-making, and the social media confessional. It is a certain theatre of violence, confession, regret and shame which public monument-making and writing about historical racialised trauma draw upon to sustain itself.

To a degree, it's art and writing provoked by social movements for treaty, truth-telling, reconciliation, and contemporary conversations about racial justice and historical reckoning. It draws upon the languages and confessional (exposure-based) modes of critical whiteness studies, local engagements with the Black Lives Matter movement, and the consequent revisiting of the relationships between colonial statues and the people who are alive and walking around them on the streets.

**NL** Exposure therapy is the belief in and desire for the affective qualities of exposure to bla(c)k trauma. It's the belief that this exposure produces a moral good in the spectator. And in the case of monuments, exposure therapy desires the uninhibition of public shame, and perhaps the more this expression of shame is witnessed, the better the *therapy* is.

**AA** As is the case with *Scaffold* and *Standing By Tunnerminnerwait & Maulboyheenner*, exposure therapy utilises representations of horror, terror and violence to help settlers interpret, imagine and comprehend Black and Indigenous pain. I should qualify that Aboriginal people are not exempt from producing this kind of work; but it is framed by a certain mode of settler consumption.

In practice, from what we've observed, exposure therapy involves declarations and re-enactments as its primary form of expression. It's conducted through confessions and apologies along with the recreation, re-enacting, and the re-staging of violent acts suffered by Aboriginal people, in order to symbolically demonstrate a *processing* of the trauma and violence which has been perpetuated. Often the victims, or their stories, are the ones on display, and their descendants are the ones likely to be most negatively impacted by the staging, but they are not, as with Durant's work, the target audience. Visually, it is expressed in the signifiers of killing: bullets, bodies, gravestones and gallows.

To draw again on a question from Sharpe: 'What is produced by the continued circulation of brutality? For whom? To what end? What is the call to look and look again at that violence in the form of the brutalised body?' (Sharpe, 2018, p. 179).

**NL** Sharpe's words conjure recent criticism by First Nations researchers Dr Lilly Brown, Natalie Ironfield and Latoya Aroha Rule (2021) regarding *Incarceration Nation* (2021), a documentary directed by Guugu Yimithirr man Dean Gibson. While commending the film's clear and evidenced demonstration of the Australian carceral system's genocidal intent towards Fist Nations peoples, the researchers questioned whether the film had potential to produce further harm for Aboriginal and Torres Strait Islander viewers. Brown, Ironfield and Rule called for further ethical considerations of how we speak about violence without reproducing it, and how to honour lived experiences of brutality without reproducing the settler desire for what Unangax̂ scholar Eve Tuck calls damage-centered research (Tuck, 2009).

**NL** Over the time of writing this chapter, I accepted a fellowship position to complete my PhD at RMIT University. It wasn't until after unpacking and looking for a break spot out the back of my building, did I register my office runs parallel with the old procession line, where government officials would have walked Tunnerminnerwait and Maulboyheenner's bodies down to Melbourne's old cemetery in 1842. If I dared, I could have my mid-morning coffee on the monument bench.

**AA** I hope we have been able to leave our readers with some prompts for understanding not only those memorialising and pedagogical objects we have discussed, but also the processes through which they are built and conceptualised. I hope we have underlined the importance of thinking about how to build such objects with care, without replicating the harms carried by the colonial disciplinary spectacle of Bla(c)k death, without reinscribing and reinforcing images of debased and violated Bla(c)k bodies we have been visually saturated by. I am confident that the demand for memorial objects by cities, and by their non-Indigenous viewing publics will continue, with or without encouragement from the Aboriginal communities with which those cities live. Some of those memorial objects might be developed with the capacity to heal the wounds endured by communities living with ongoing colonial violence and power structures. I hope we can develop ways to live with those objects and their afterlives productively and care-fully. You have given me a lot to think about.

# References

Allam, L. (2014). The forgotten war that led to Port Phillip's first public executions. *ABC Radio National.* https://www.abc.net.au/radionational/programs/archived/hindsight/a-for gotten-war/5926302. Accessed 18 January 2023.

Alizzi, A. (2022, March 19). The influence. *The Saturday Paper.* https://www.thesaturdaypaper.com. au/the-influence/2022/03/19/melissa-lucashenko/164760840013537. Accessed 14 June 2023.

Australian War Memorial. (2018). *Places of pride.* https://placesofpride.awm.gov.au/. Accessed 7 June 2023.

Auty, K., & Russell, L. (2016). *Hunt them, hang them: The 'Tasmanian' in Port Phillip 1841–1842.* Legal Service Bulletin Cooperative.

Browning, D. (2021). Nothing if not uncritical: Revisiting re-visions and Indigenous art criticism. *Artlink, 41*(3), 16–23.

Burrow, L., & Harwood, T. (2018). Forgetting architecture and the new aboriginal kitsch. *Un Magazine, 12*(1).

City of Melbourne. (2016). *Executed in Franklin Street.* https://www.melbourne.vic.gov.au/arts-and-culture/city-gallery/exhibition-archive/Pages/executed-in-franklin-street.aspx. Accessed 16 January 2023.

City of Melbourne. (2017a). Standing by Tunnerminerwait and Maulboyheenner. *City Collection.* https://citycollection.melbourne.vic.gov.au/standing-by-tunnerminnerwait-and-maulboyhe enner/. Accessed 17 January 2023.

City of Melbourne. (2017b). John Batman memorial. *City Collection.* https://citycollection.melbou rne.vic.gov.au/john-batman-memorial/. Accessed 17 January 2023.

## 10 Exposure Therapy: Spectacles, Monuments and the Question of Care

Costa Vargas, J., & James, J. A. (2014). Refusing blackness-as-victimisation: Trayvon Martin and the Black Cyborgs. In G. Yancy & J. Jones (Eds.), *Pursuing Trayvon Martin: Historical contexts and contemporary manifestations of racial dynamics* (pp. 193–205). Lexington Books.

Drew, K. (2022). The misguided empathy of Dana Schutz's open casket. *Vulture.* https://www.vulture.com/2022/01/dana-schutz-open-casket-emmett-till-painting.html. Accessed 14 June 2023.

Durant, S. (2017). A statement from Sam Durant. *Walker News.* https://walkerart.org/magazine/a-statement-from-sam-durant-05-29-17. Accessed 14 June 2023.

Doss, E. (2022). Failure as success: Sam Durant's scaffold, Angela two stars' Okciyapi, and the conundrum of critique. In C. Cartiere & T. Schrag (Eds.), *The failures of public art and participation* (pp. 22–42). London: Routledge.

Fanon, F. (1952). *Peau noire, masques blancs.* Éditions du Seuil. English edition.

Fanon, F. (2008). *Black skin, White masks* (R. Philcox, Trans.). Grove Books.

Finn, E. (1888). *The Chronicles of early Melbourne, 1835 to 1852, anecdotal and personal.* Fergusson and Mitchell.

Foucault, M. (1975). *Surveiller et punir: naissance de la prison.* Gallimard (English Edition).

Foucault, M. (1995). *Discipline & punish: The birth of the prison* (A. Sheridan, Trans.). Vintage.

Gibson, D. (Director). (2021). *Incarceration Nation* [Film]. Bacon Factory Films Pty Ltd & Bent 3 Land Productions. NITV.

Hartman, S. (1997). *Scenes of subjection: Terror, slavery, and self-making in nineteenth century America.* Oxford University Press.

Hartman, S. (2002). The time of slavery. *The South Atlantic Quarterly, 101*(4), 757–776.

Jones, D. (2015). What lies buried will rise: Exploring a story of violent crime, retribution, and colonial memory. Masters thesis. *University of Melbourne.* https://rest.neptune-prod.its.unimelb.edu.au/server/api/core/bitstreams/029dc07b-aa49-56ba-b5cf-c4ad89a6ba92/content. Accessed 6 June 2023.

Jones, J. (2007, January 26). Too many memories? *The Guardian.* https://www.theguardian.com/artanddesign/2007/jan/26/architecture. Accessed 15 January 2023.

Laenui, P. (2000). Processes of decolonization. In M. Battiste (Ed.), *Reclaiming indigenous voice and vision* (pp. 150–160). UBC Press.

Lehman, N. (2020). Those who stay: Caring for memory at Wybalenna. *Art and Australia.* https://www.artandaustralia.com/online/online/image-not-nothing-concrete-archives/those-who-stay-caring-memory-wybalenna.html. Accessed 6 June 2023.

Lehman, N. (2022). Disobedient time. In J. Gough (Ed.), *Tense past* (pp. 173–193). Tebrikunna Press.

Lorde, A. (2018). *The master's tools will never dismantle the master's house.* Penguin.

Pybus, C. (2020). *Truganini: Journey through the Apocalypse.* Allen and Unwin.

Port Phillip Herald. (1842, January 21). https://news.google.com/newspapers?nid=EVKlETVVbN8C&dat=18420121&printsec=frontpage&hl=en. Accessed 14 June 2023.

Russell-Cook, M. (2020). DESTINY: The art of Destiny Deacon. *DESTINY.* NGV. https://www.ngv.vic.gov.au/essay/destiny-the-art-of-destiny-deacon/. Accessed 7 June 2023.

Russell, L. (2016, July 18). Maulboyheenner and Tunnerminnerwait. *Australian Feminist History Network Blog.* http://www.auswhn.org.au/blog/maulboyheenner-tunnerminnerwait/. Accessed 16 January 2023.

Rule, L. A., Brown, L., & Ironfield, N. (2021, August 30). Incarceration Nation exposes the racist foundations of policing and imprisonment in Australia, but at what cost? *The Conversation.* https://theconversation.com/incarceration-nation-exposes-the-racist-foundations-of-policing-and-imprisonment-in-australia-but-at-what-cost-165951. Accessed 6 June 2023.

Sharpe, C. (2016). *In the wake: On blackness and being.* Duke University Press.

Sharpe, C. (2018). And to survive. *Small Axe, 22*(3), 171–180.

Shen, Y. (2020, January 1). How will future generations respond to modern-day memorial architecture? *Arch Daily.* https://www.archdaily.com/898654/how-will-future-generations-respond-to-modern-day-memorial-architecture?kth. Accessed 15 January 2023.

Trouillot, M.-R. (1997). *Silencing the past: Power and the production of history.* Beacon.

Thomas, S. (Director). (1992). *Black Man's Houses* [Film]. Ronin Films.

Tuck, E. (2009). Suspending damage: A letter to communities. *Harvard Educational Review, 7*(3), 409–427.

Willis, J. W. (1841). 11. Robert Timmy Jimmy Smallboy & Ors. The Judge Willis Casebooks Box 55. *Royal Historical Society.* https://www.historyvictoria.org.au/the-judge-willis-casebooks/transc ripts-of-the-judge-willis-casebooks/box-55-documents/#11. Accessed 16 January 2023.

Wynter, S. (1994). 'No humans involved': An open letter to my colleagues. *Forum N.H.I.: Knowledge for the 21st Century, 1*(1), 42–73.

**Arlie Alizzi** is a Yugambeh writer, editor and researcher. He lives and works on Yawuru Country, in Rubibi (Broome). Arlie's writing, mainly focussed on First Nations arts, literature and culture, has been published in outlets such as ABC, Sydney Morning Herald, SBS, The Saturday Paper, Artlink, and Liminal Magazine.

Arlie Alizzi and Neika Lehman first met in 2015, and have since collaborated on a number of projects in writing, teaching, curatorship, and editing. They remain close friends, and their mutual critical interest in (de)colonial monuments, memorialisation, and art as a form of nationalist rhetoric has been informed and inspired by their relationships with many activist people in so-called Australia, particularly First Nations women.

**Neika Lehman** is a writer, researcher and PhD candidate. Their poetry, essays and criticism appear in un Mag, Art + Australia, The Saturday Paper, Cordite, Overland, Australian Poetry Journal, Best Australian Poems among others. Neika descends from the Trawlwoolway Peoples of Tebrakunna Country, lutruwita (Tasmania) and currently resides in Narrm (Melbourne).